OF LIBERTY

>Lettered by: **Tom B. Long & Robbie Robbins**

>Design by: **Robbie Robbins & Michael Heisler**

>Original Series Edited by: **Kris Oprisko**

>Collection Edited by: **Aaron Myers**

IDW Publishing is:
Ted Adams, Co-President
Robbie Robbins, Co-President
Chris Ryall, Publisher/Editor-in-Chief
Kris Oprisko, Vice President
Neil Uyetake, Art Director
Dan Taylor, Editor
Aaron Myers, Editorial Assistant
Chance Boren, Editorial Assistant
Matthew Ruzicka, CPA, Controller
Alex Garner, Creative Director
Yumiko Miyano, Business Development
Rick Privman, Business Development

KONAMI

ISBN 10: 1-933239-78-6
ISBN 13: 978-1-93323-978-1
09 08 07 06 1 2 3 4 5

www.idwpublishing.com

Special thanks to Hideo Kojima, Ryan Payton, and the entire Metal Gear Solid team at Konami.

TACTICAL ESPIONAGE ACTION

METAL GEAR SOLID®

SONS OF LIBERTY

VOLUME ONE

>Written by: **Alex Garner**

>Art by: **Ashley Wood**

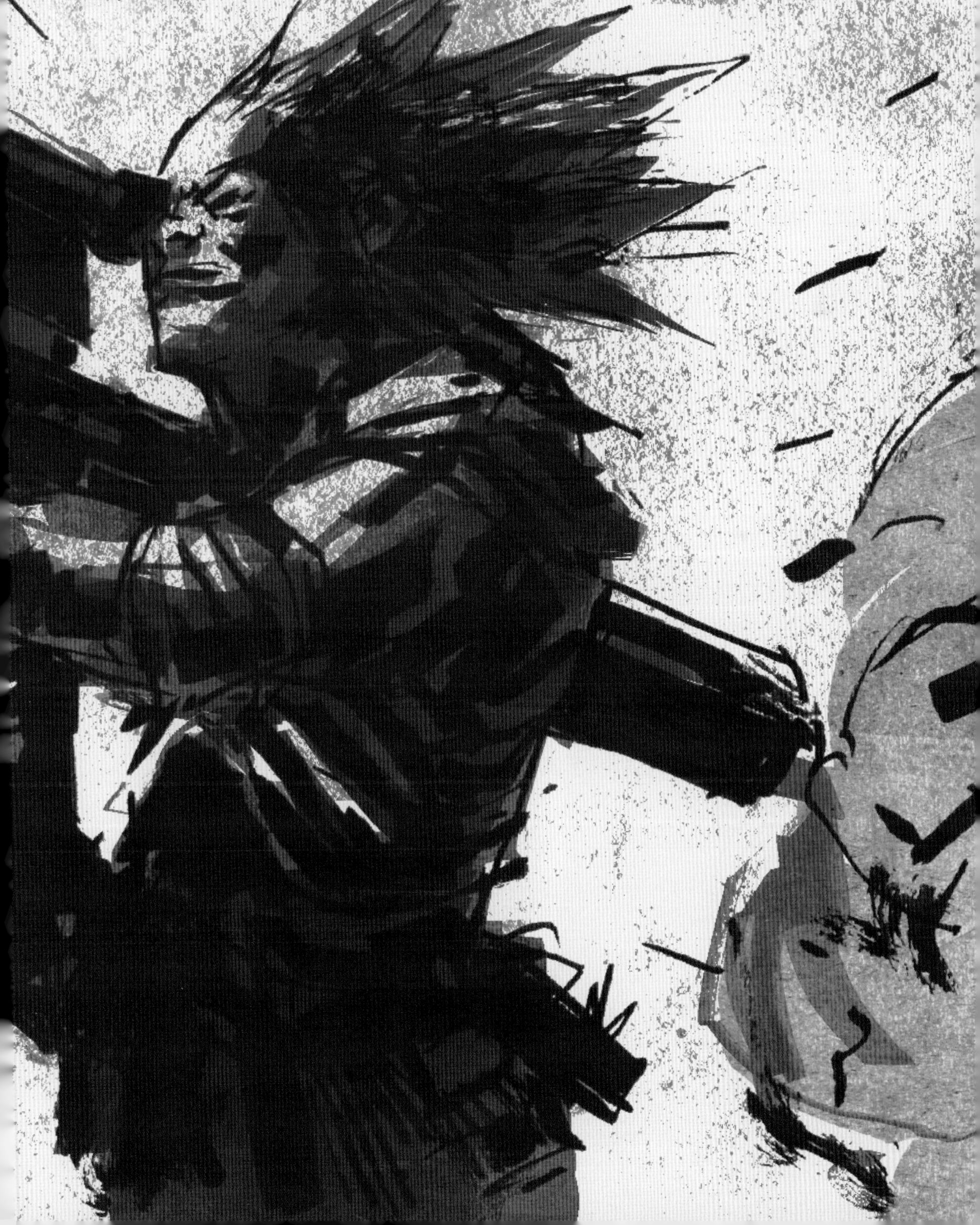

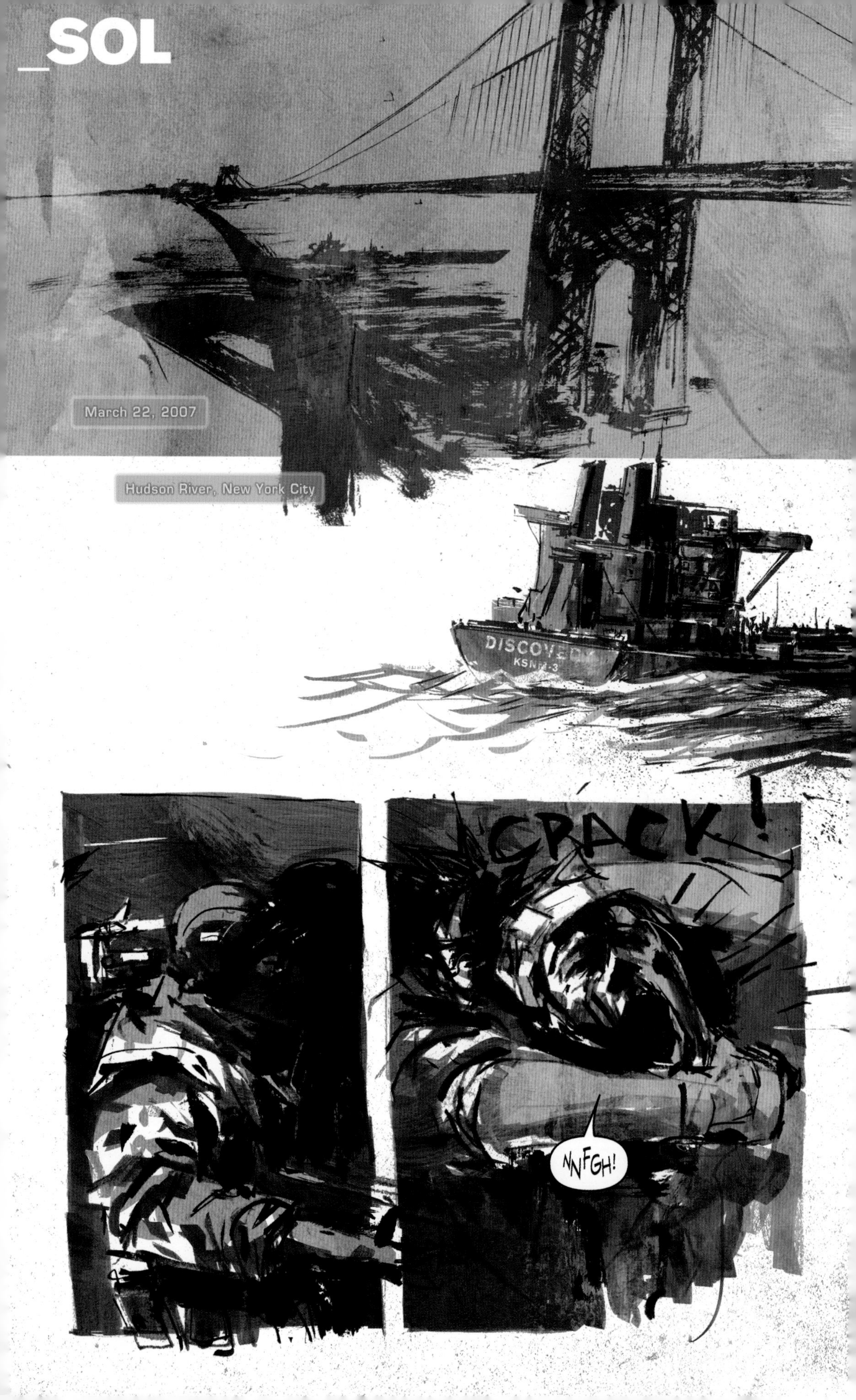
_SOL
March 22, 2007
Hudson River, New York City
DISCOVERY
CRACK!
NNFGH!

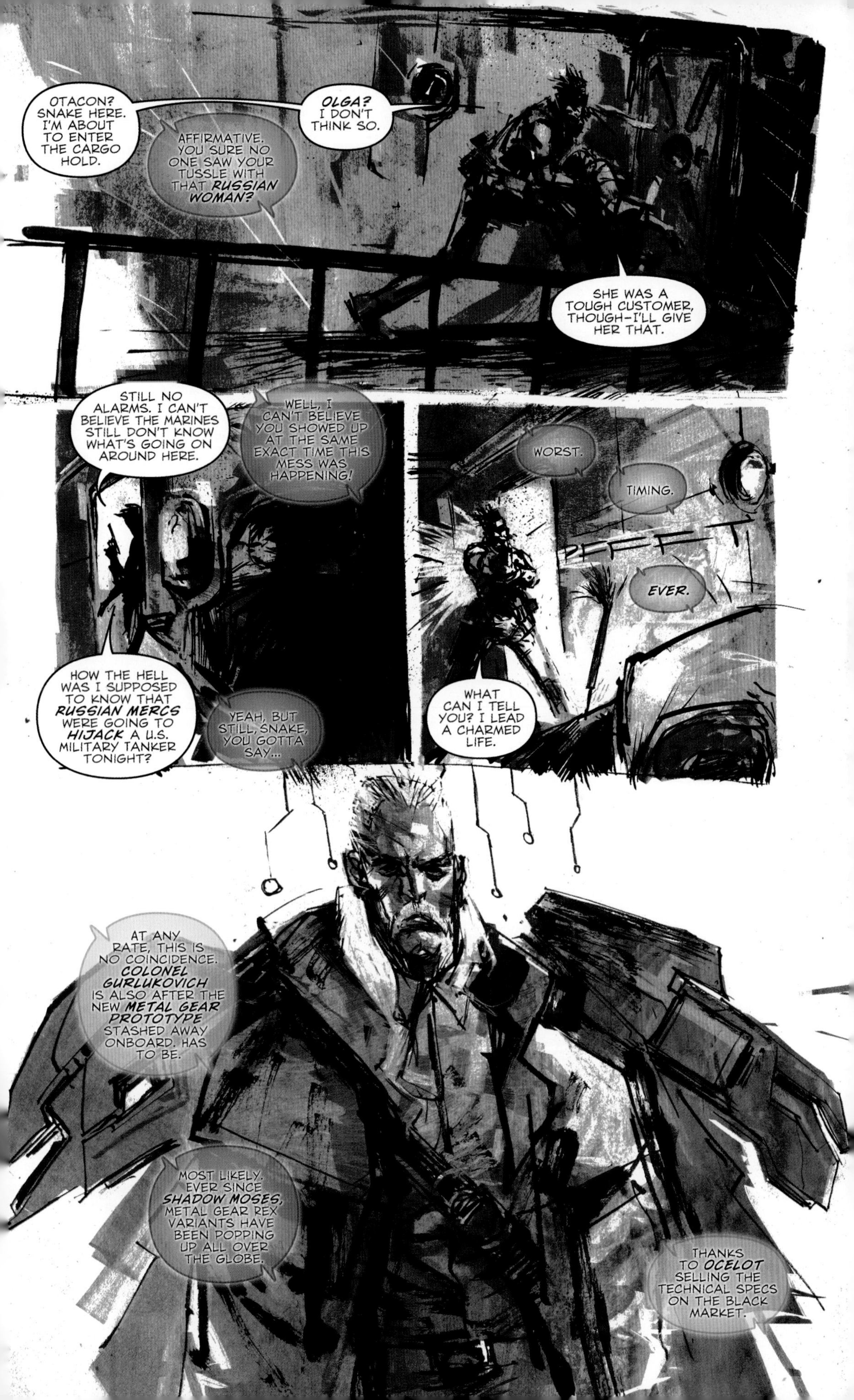
OTACON? SNAKE HERE. I'M ABOUT TO ENTER THE CARGO HOLD.
AFFIRMATIVE. YOU SURE NO ONE SAW YOUR TUSSLE WITH THAT RUSSIAN WOMAN?
OLGA? I DON'T THINK SO.
SHE WAS A TOUGH CUSTOMER, THOUGH--I'LL GIVE HER THAT.
STILL NO ALARMS. I CAN'T BELIEVE THE MARINES STILL DON'T KNOW WHAT'S GOING ON AROUND HERE.
WELL, I CAN'T BELIEVE YOU SHOWED UP AT THE SAME EXACT TIME THIS MESS WAS HAPPENING!
HOW THE HELL WAS I SUPPOSED TO KNOW THAT RUSSIAN MERCS WERE GOING TO HIJACK A U.S. MILITARY TANKER TONIGHT?
YEAH, BUT STILL, SNAKE, YOU GOTTA SAY...
WORST.
TIMING.
PFFFT
EVER.
WHAT CAN I TELL YOU? I LEAD A CHARMED LIFE.
AT ANY RATE, THIS IS NO COINCIDENCE. COLONEL GURLUKOVICH IS ALSO AFTER THE NEW METAL GEAR PROTOTYPE STASHED AWAY ONBOARD. HAS TO BE.
MOST LIKELY. EVER SINCE SHADOW MOSES, METAL GEAR REX VARIANTS HAVE BEEN POPPING UP ALL OVER THE GLOBE.
THANKS TO OCELOT SELLING THE TECHNICAL SPECS ON THE BLACK MARKET.

BUT THIS NEW AMPHIBIOUS VERSION IS MUCH FASTER AND MORE POWERFUL THAN ANYTHING WE'VE EVER SEEN BEFORE! SHE'S PRETTY MUCH DESIGNED TO MOP THE FLOOR WITH ALL THE OTHER MODELS.
AN ANTI-METAL GEAR METAL GEAR...
ALL WE NEED IS EVIDENCE OF ITS EXISTENCE. WHICH MEANS...
I KNOW, I KNOW. JUST TAKE PHOTOS. NO KILLING OR BLOWING STUFF UP.
YOU'RE NO FUN.
SERIOUSLY, SNAKE. YOU AND I FORMED PHILANTHROPY TO EXPOSE AND GET RID OF ALL METAL GEAR WEAPONS GLOBALLY. WE HAVE A VITAL RESPONSIBILITY TO THE PUBLIC TRUST!
KID, WE MAY BE OFFICIALLY RECOGNIZED BY THE U.N., BUT PUBLIC PERCEPTION IS THAT WE'RE STILL VERY FRINGE.
HANG ON A SEC...
NNN!
JEEZ, SNAKE, EASE UP ON THAT POOR MARINE. HE'S NO TERRORIST.
HE'LL BE ALL RIGHT. A LITTLE BEAUTY SLEEP NEVER HURT ANYONE.
WHOA.

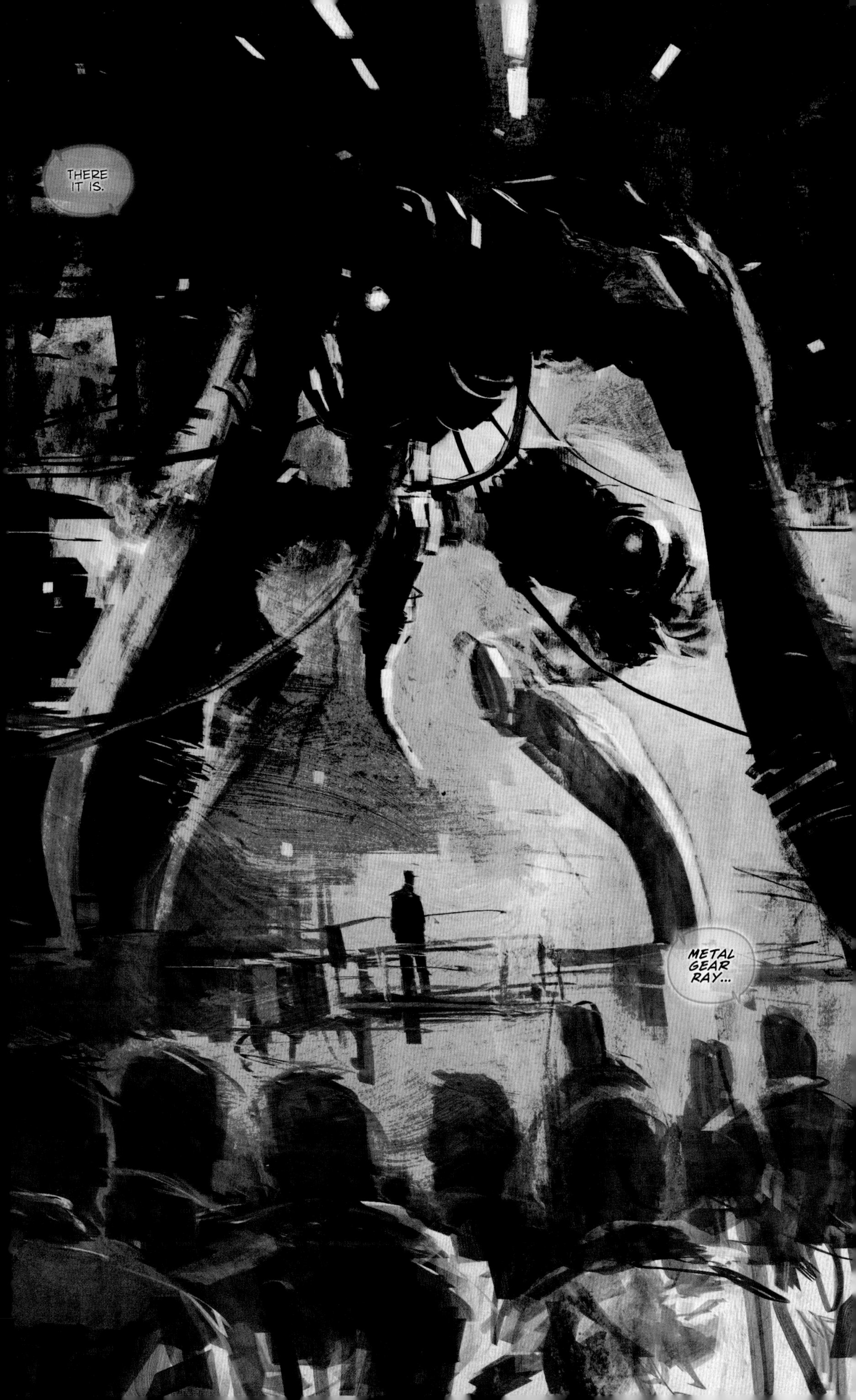
THERE IT IS.
METAL GEAR RAY...

IMPRESSIVE.
YOU SHOULD SEE HOW SLEEK THIS METAL GEAR IS, OTACON. IT MAKES OL' REXXY LOOK LIKE A DUMPSTER WITH LEGS.
YEAH, YEAH... JUST MAKE SURE YOU REMOVE THE LENS CAP BEFORE SHOOTING, OKAY?
HEH. OUR BOY IS RIGHT ON SCHEDULE.
SMILE FOR YOUR ADORING PUBLIC, HERO.
KLICK
KLICK
KLICK
AFTER I'M DONE WITH YOU, THEY'LL ALL THINK YOU'RE PUBLIC ENEMY NUMBER ONE.

2 YEARS LATER

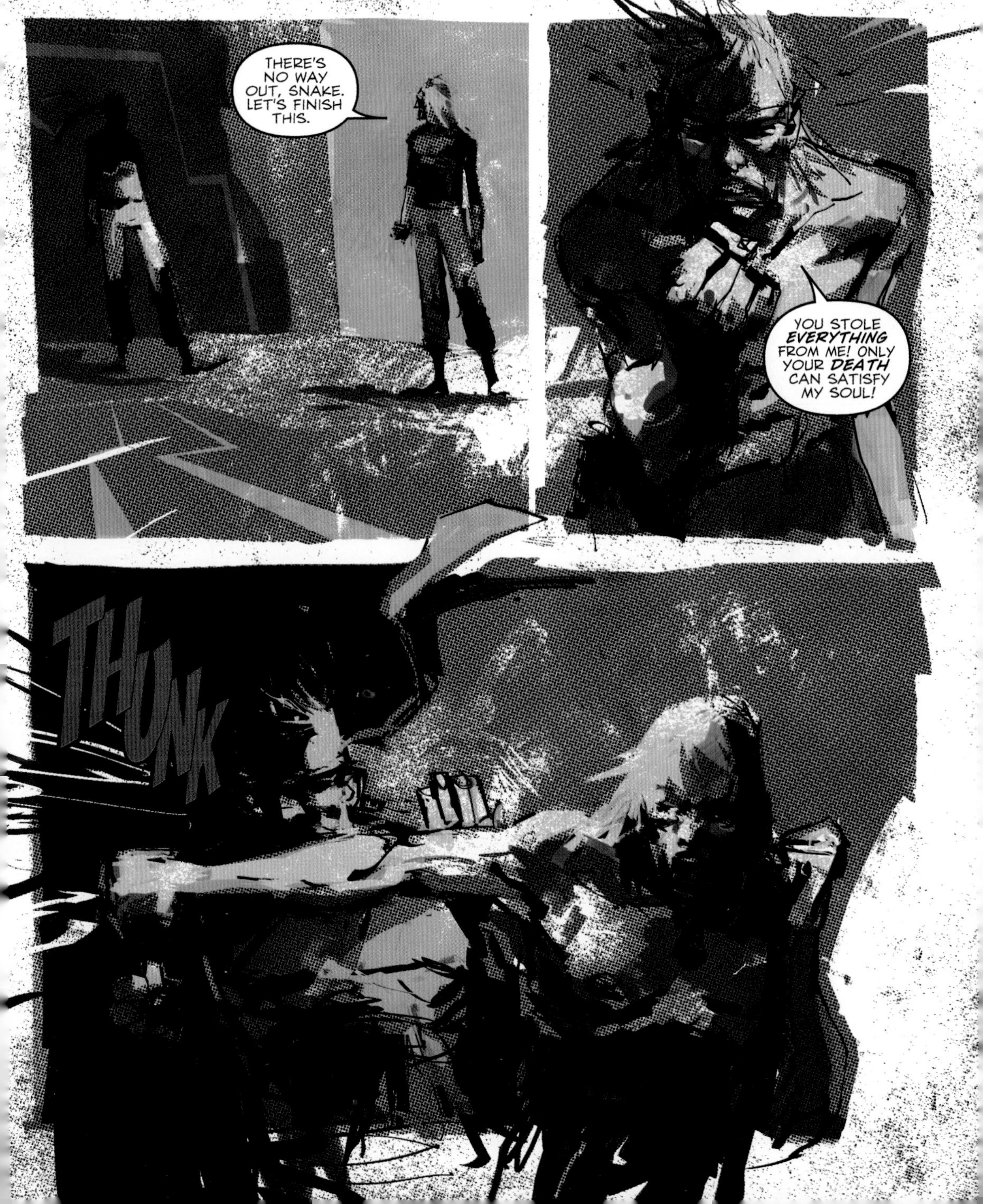
THERE'S NO WAY OUT, SNAKE. LET'S FINISH THIS.
YOU STOLE EVERYTHING FROM ME! ONLY YOUR DEATH CAN SATISFY MY SOUL!
THUNK

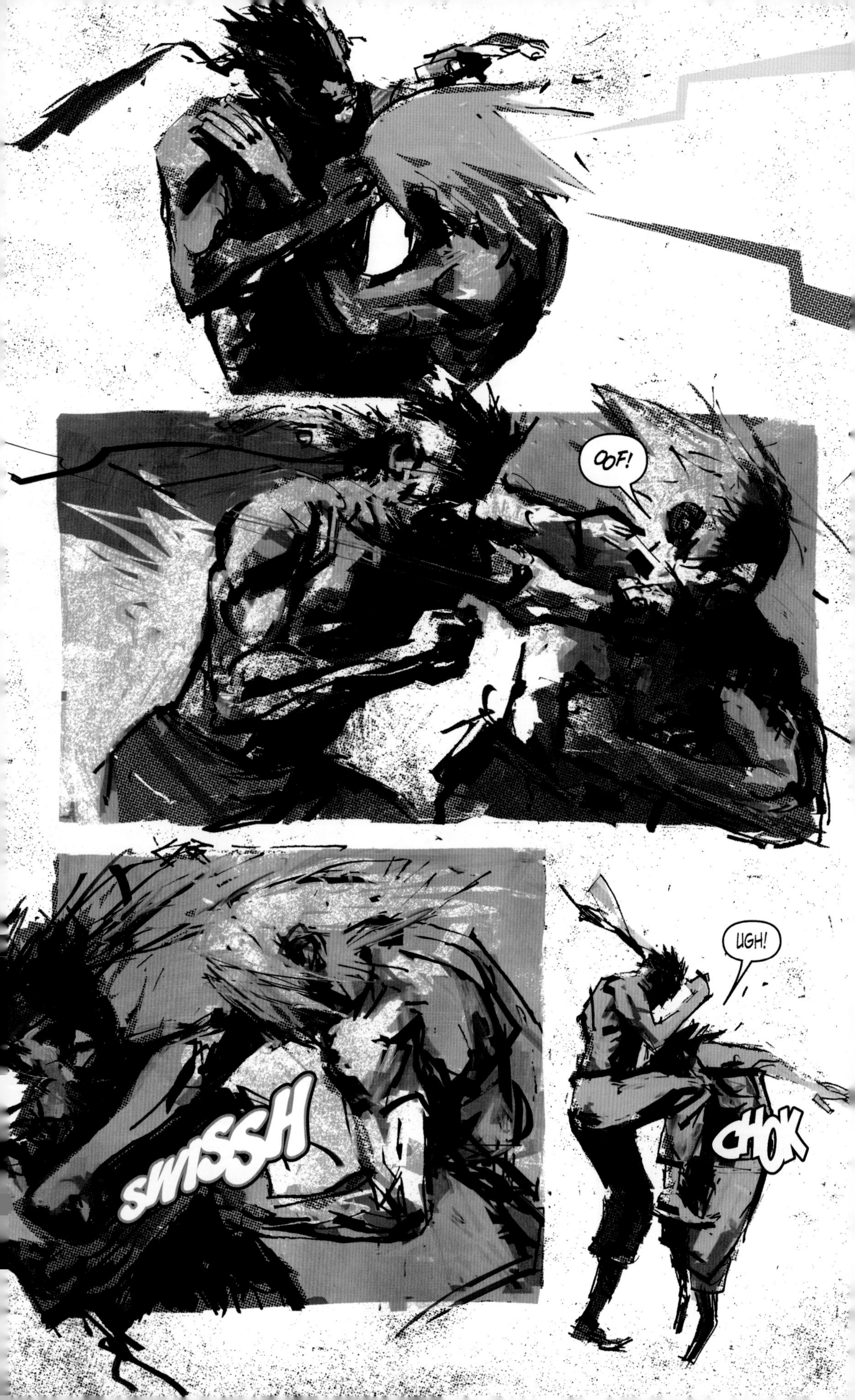
OOF!
SWISSH
UGH!
CHOK

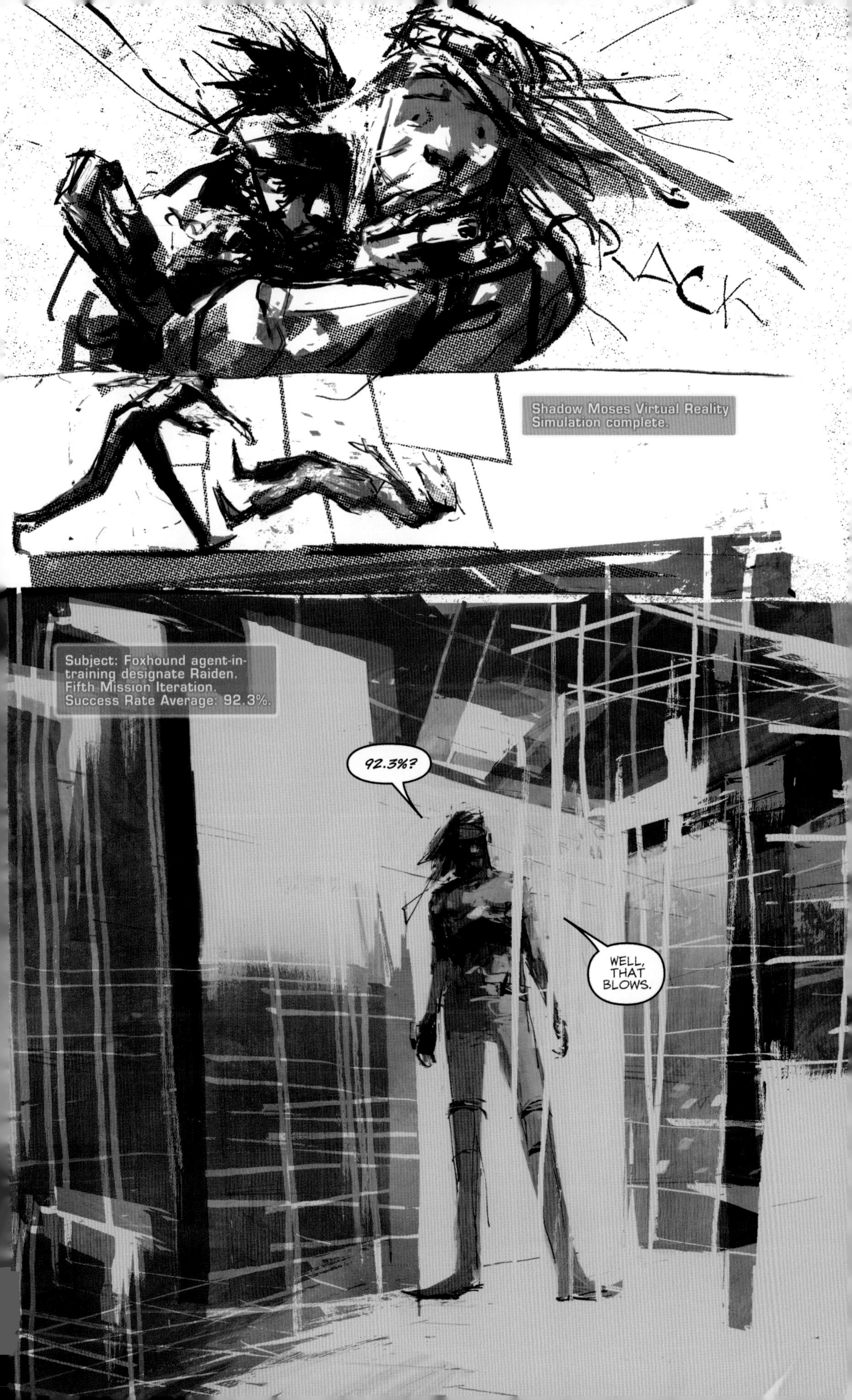
Shadow Moses Virtual Reality Simulation complete.
Subject: Foxhound agent-in-training designate Raiden. Fifth Mission Iteration. Success Rate Average: 92.3%.
92.3%?
WELL, THAT BLOWS.

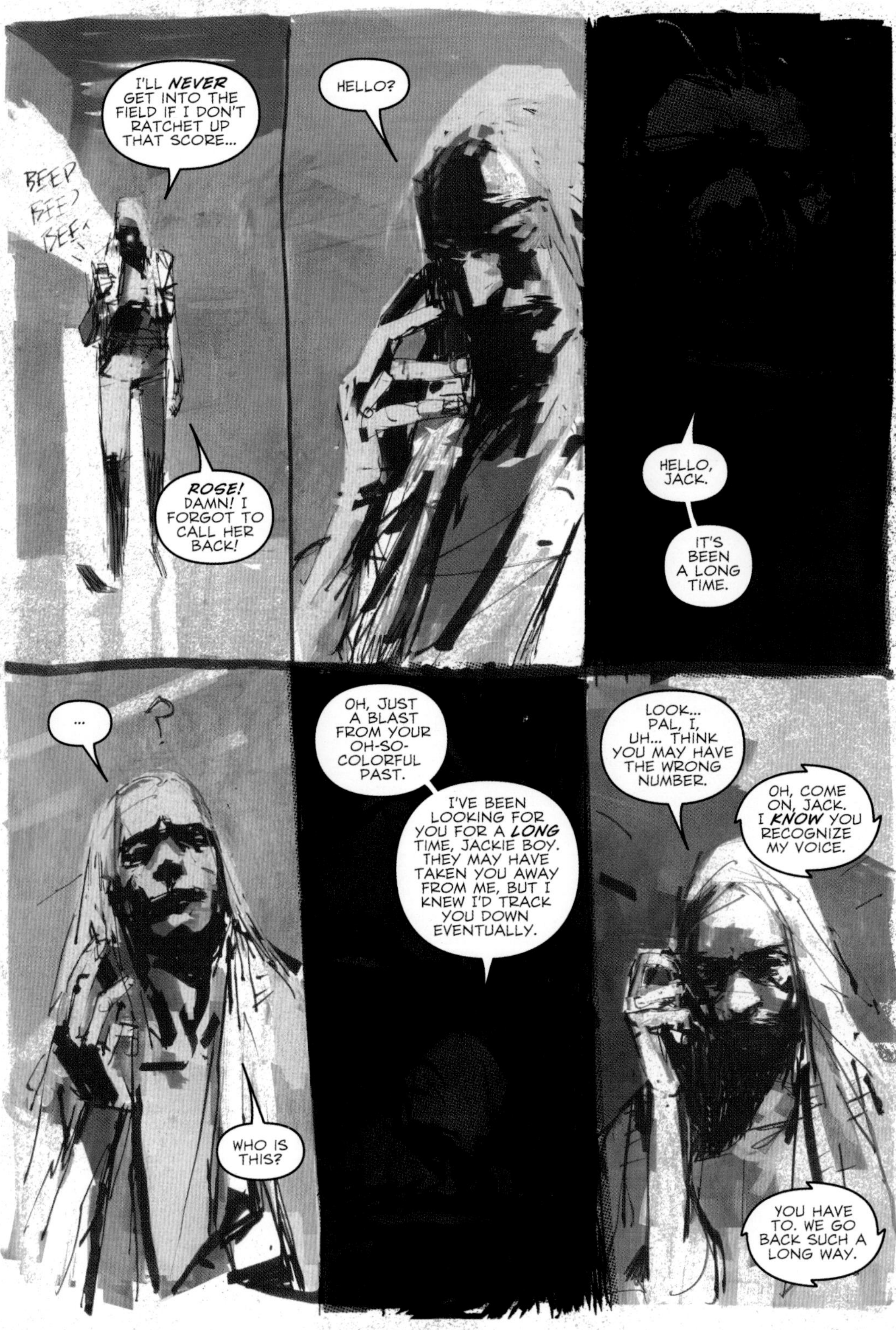

I'LL NEVER GET INTO THE FIELD IF I DON'T RATCHET UP THAT SCORE...
BEEP
ROSE! DAMN! I FORGOT TO CALL HER BACK!
HELLO?
HELLO, JACK.
IT'S BEEN A LONG TIME.
...
?
WHO IS THIS?
OH, JUST A BLAST FROM YOUR OH-SO-COLORFUL PAST.
I'VE BEEN LOOKING FOR YOU FOR A LONG TIME, JACKIE BOY. THEY MAY HAVE TAKEN YOU AWAY FROM ME, BUT I KNEW I'D TRACK YOU DOWN EVENTUALLY.
LOOK... PAL, I, UH... THINK YOU MAY HAVE THE WRONG NUMBER.
OH, COME ON, JACK. I KNOW YOU RECOGNIZE MY VOICE.
YOU HAVE TO. WE GO BACK SUCH A LONG WAY.

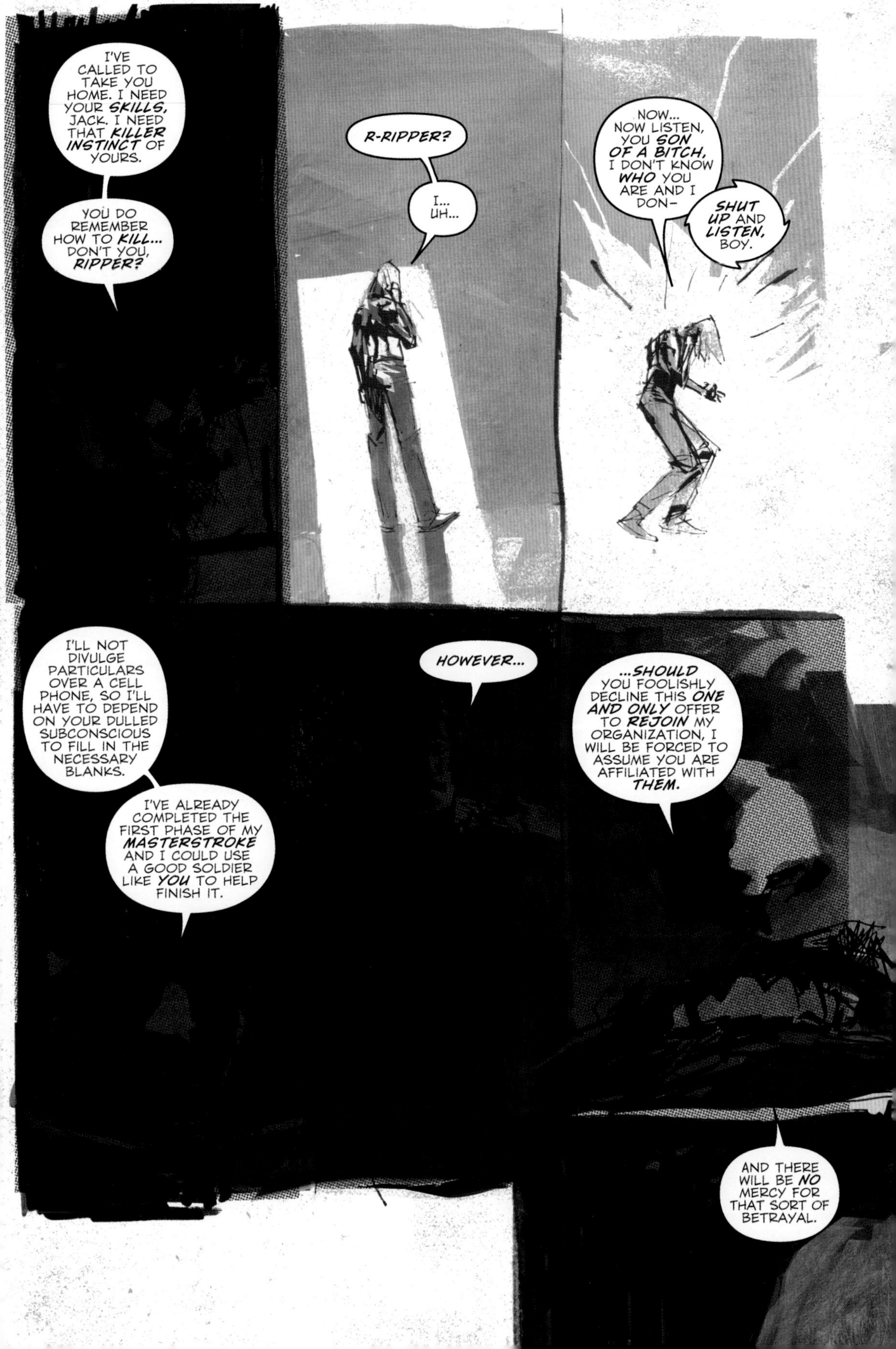
I'VE CALLED TO TAKE YOU HOME. I NEED YOUR SKILLS, JACK. I NEED THAT KILLER INSTINCT OF YOURS.
YOU DO REMEMBER HOW TO KILL... DON'T YOU, RIPPER?
R-RIPPER?
I... UH...
NOW... NOW LISTEN, YOU SON OF A BITCH, I DON'T KNOW WHO YOU ARE AND I DON-
SHUT UP AND LISTEN, BOY.
I'LL NOT DIVULGE PARTICULARS OVER A CELL PHONE, SO I'LL HAVE TO DEPEND ON YOUR DULLED SUBCONSCIOUS TO FILL IN THE NECESSARY BLANKS.
I'VE ALREADY COMPLETED THE FIRST PHASE OF MY MASTERSTROKE AND I COULD USE A GOOD SOLDIER LIKE YOU TO HELP FINISH IT.
HOWEVER...
...SHOULD YOU FOOLISHLY DECLINE THIS ONE AND ONLY OFFER TO REJOIN MY ORGANIZATION, I WILL BE FORCED TO ASSUME YOU ARE AFFILIATED WITH THEM.
AND THERE WILL BE NO MERCY FOR THAT SORT OF BETRAYAL.

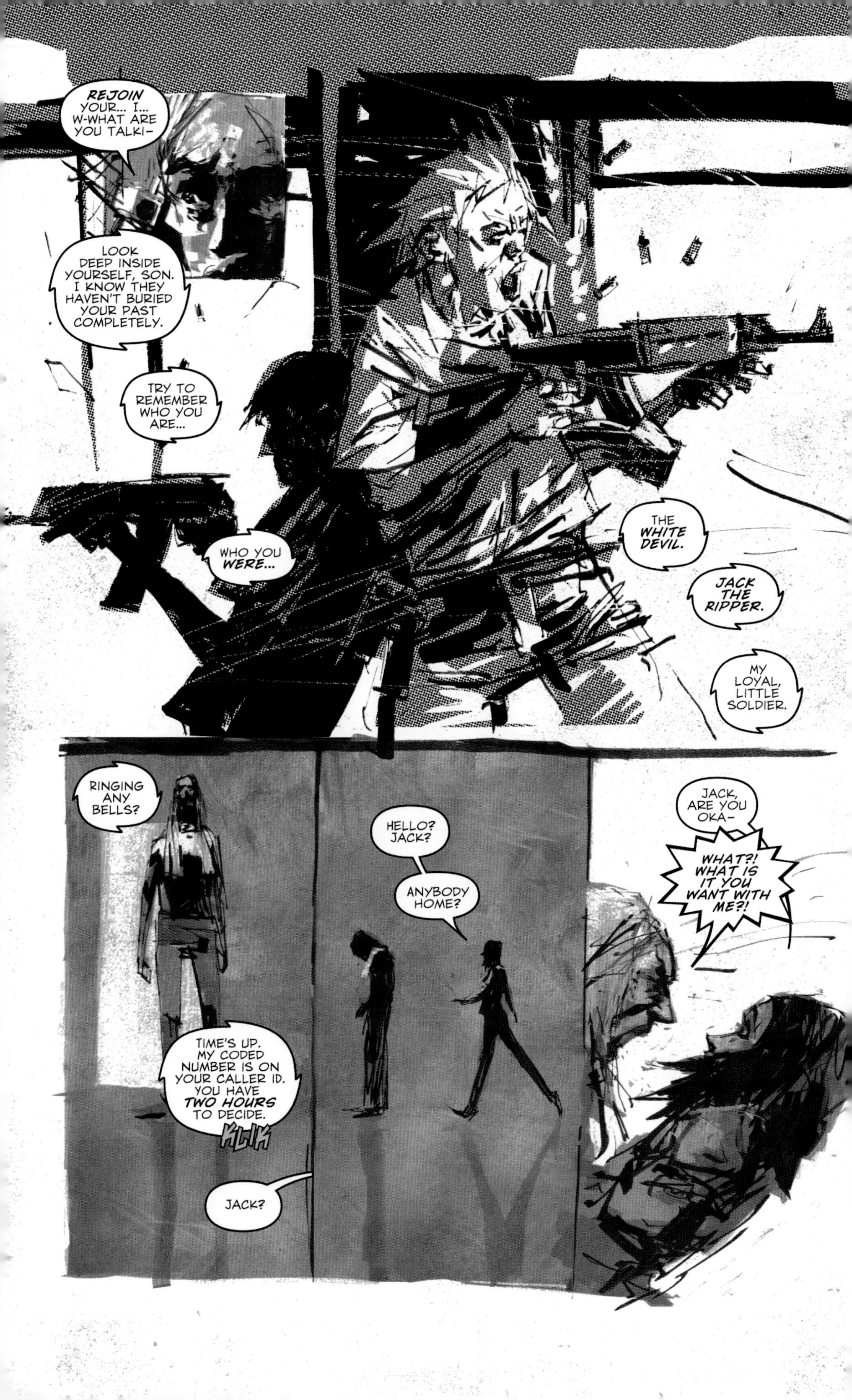
REJOIN YOUR... I... W-WHAT ARE YOU TALKI-
LOOK DEEP INSIDE YOURSELF, SON. I KNOW THEY HAVEN'T BURIED YOUR PAST COMPLETELY.
TRY TO REMEMBER WHO YOU ARE...
WHO YOU WERE...
THE WHITE DEVIL.
JACK THE RIPPER.
MY LOYAL, LITTLE SOLDIER.
RINGING ANY BELLS?
TIME'S UP. MY CODED NUMBER IS ON YOUR CALLER ID. YOU HAVE TWO HOURS TO DECIDE.
KLIK
JACK?
HELLO? JACK?
ANYBODY HOME?
JACK, ARE YOU OKA-
WHAT?! WHAT IS IT YOU WANT WITH ME?!

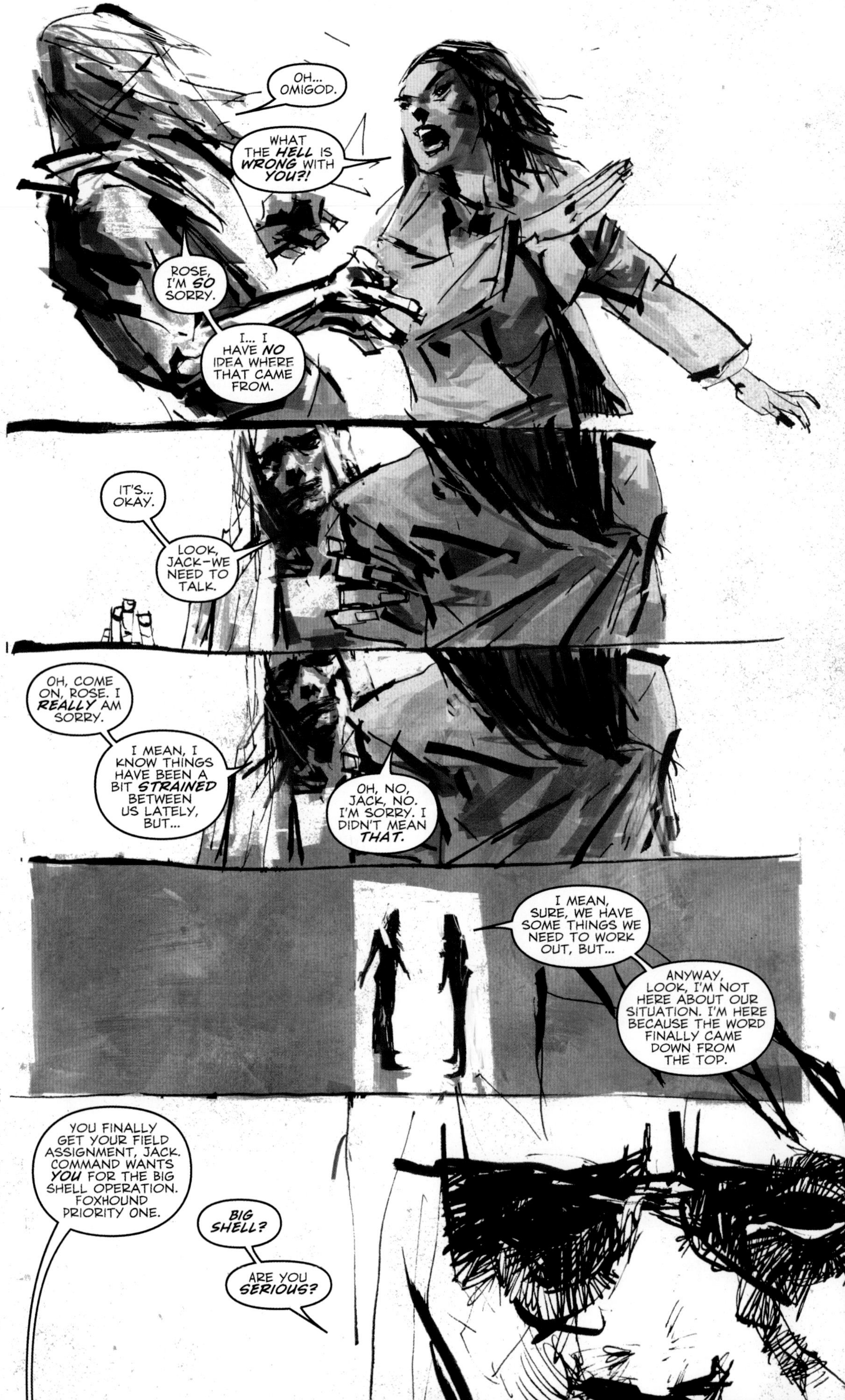
OH... OMIGOD.
WHAT THE HELL IS WRONG WITH YOU?!
ROSE, I'M SO SORRY.
I... I HAVE NO IDEA WHERE THAT CAME FROM.
IT'S... OKAY.
LOOK, JACK—WE NEED TO TALK.
OH, COME ON, ROSE. I REALLY AM SORRY.
I MEAN, I KNOW THINGS HAVE BEEN A BIT STRAINED BETWEEN US LATELY, BUT...
OH, NO, JACK, NO. I'M SORRY. I DIDN'T MEAN THAT.
I MEAN, SURE, WE HAVE SOME THINGS WE NEED TO WORK OUT, BUT...
ANYWAY, LOOK, I'M NOT HERE ABOUT OUR SITUATION. I'M HERE BECAUSE THE WORD FINALLY CAME DOWN FROM THE TOP.
YOU FINALLY GET YOUR FIELD ASSIGNMENT, JACK. COMMAND WANTS YOU FOR THE BIG SHELL OPERATION. FOXHOUND PRIORITY ONE.
BIG SHELL?
ARE YOU SERIOUS?

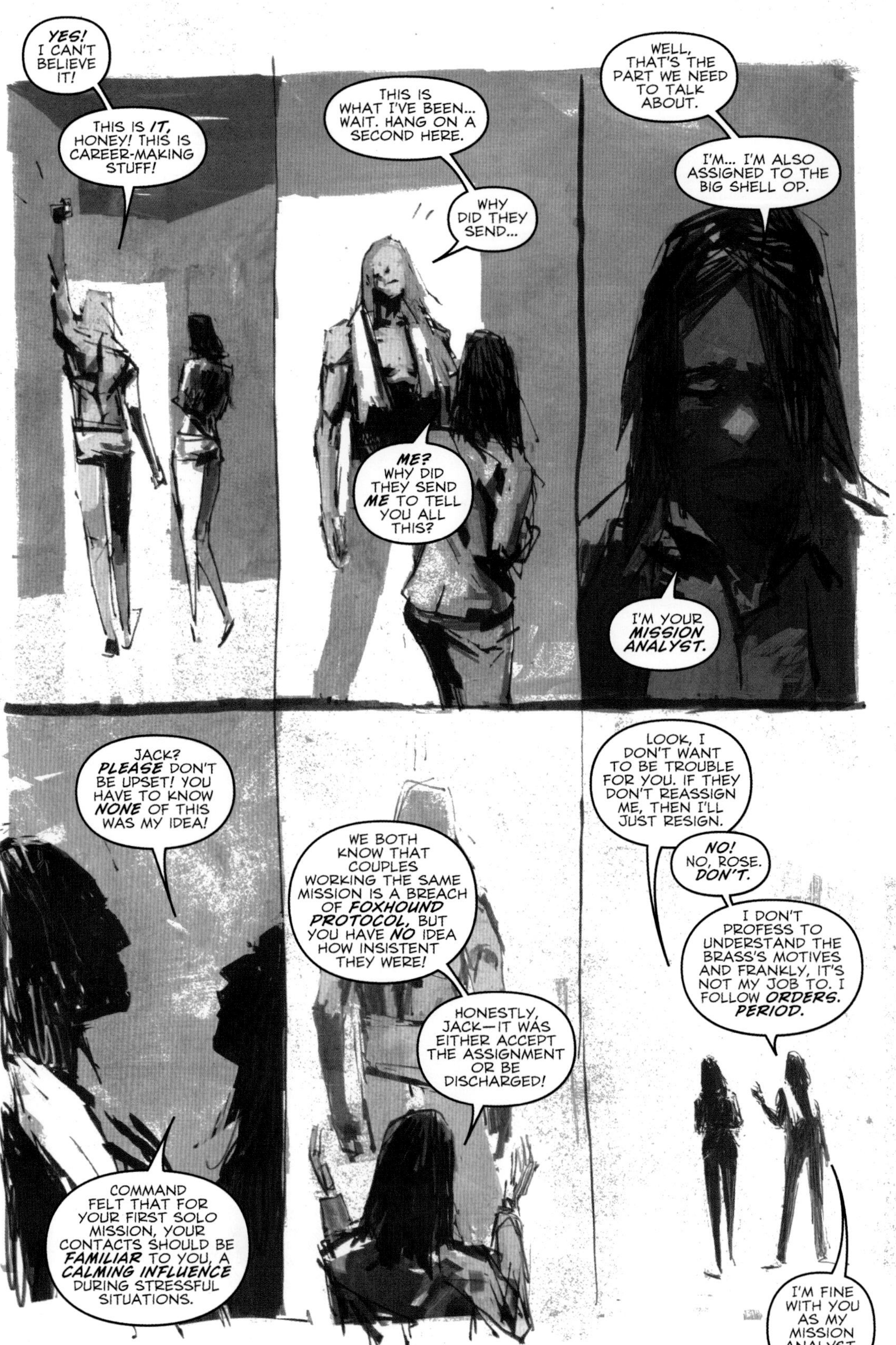
YES! I CAN'T BELIEVE IT!
THIS IS IT, HONEY! THIS IS CAREER-MAKING STUFF!
THIS IS WHAT I'VE BEEN... WAIT. HANG ON A SECOND HERE.
WHY DID THEY SEND...
ME? WHY DID THEY SEND ME TO TELL YOU ALL THIS?
WELL, THAT'S THE PART WE NEED TO TALK ABOUT.
I'M... I'M ALSO ASSIGNED TO THE BIG SHELL OP.
I'M YOUR MISSION ANALYST.
JACK? PLEASE DON'T BE UPSET! YOU HAVE TO KNOW NONE OF THIS WAS MY IDEA!
COMMAND FELT THAT FOR YOUR FIRST SOLO MISSION, YOUR CONTACTS SHOULD BE FAMILIAR TO YOU, A CALMING INFLUENCE DURING STRESSFUL SITUATIONS.
WE BOTH KNOW THAT COUPLES WORKING THE SAME MISSION IS A BREACH OF FOXHOUND PROTOCOL, BUT YOU HAVE NO IDEA HOW INSISTENT THEY WERE!
HONESTLY, JACK—IT WAS EITHER ACCEPT THE ASSIGNMENT OR BE DISCHARGED!
LOOK, I DON'T WANT TO BE TROUBLE FOR YOU. IF THEY DON'T REASSIGN ME, THEN I'LL JUST RESIGN.
NO! NO, ROSE. DON'T.
I DON'T PROFESS TO UNDERSTAND THE BRASS'S MOTIVES AND FRANKLY, IT'S NOT MY JOB TO. I FOLLOW ORDERS. PERIOD.
I'M FINE WITH YOU AS MY MISSION ANALYST. REALLY.

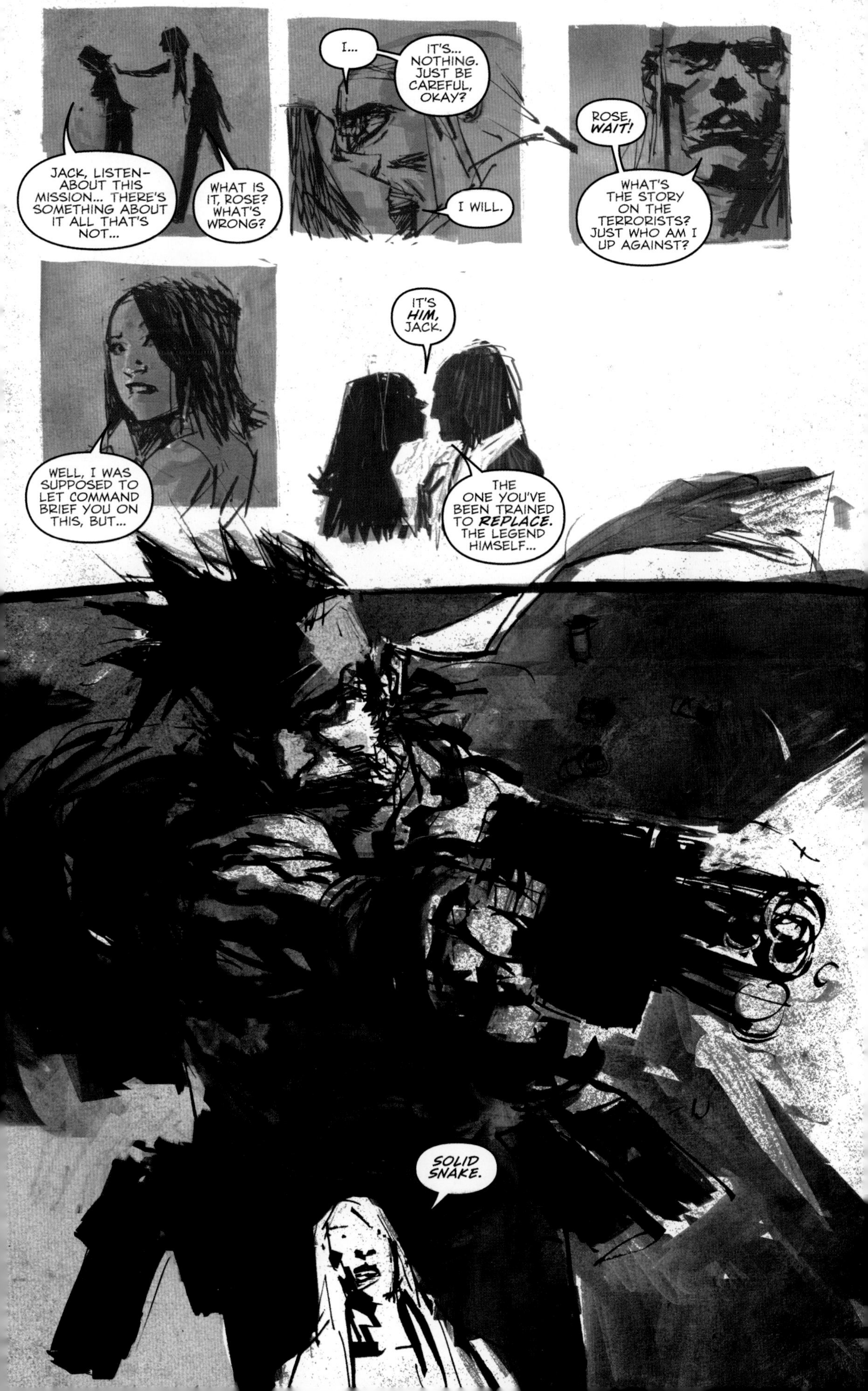
JACK, LISTEN—ABOUT THIS MISSION... THERE'S SOMETHING ABOUT IT ALL THAT'S NOT...
WHAT IS IT, ROSE? WHAT'S WRONG?
I...
IT'S... NOTHING. JUST BE CAREFUL, OKAY?
I WILL.
ROSE, WAIT!
WHAT'S THE STORY ON THE TERRORISTS? JUST WHO AM I UP AGAINST?
WELL, I WAS SUPPOSED TO LET COMMAND BRIEF YOU ON THIS, BUT...
IT'S HIM, JACK.
THE ONE YOU'VE BEEN TRAINED TO REPLACE. THE LEGEND HIMSELF...
SOLID SNAKE.

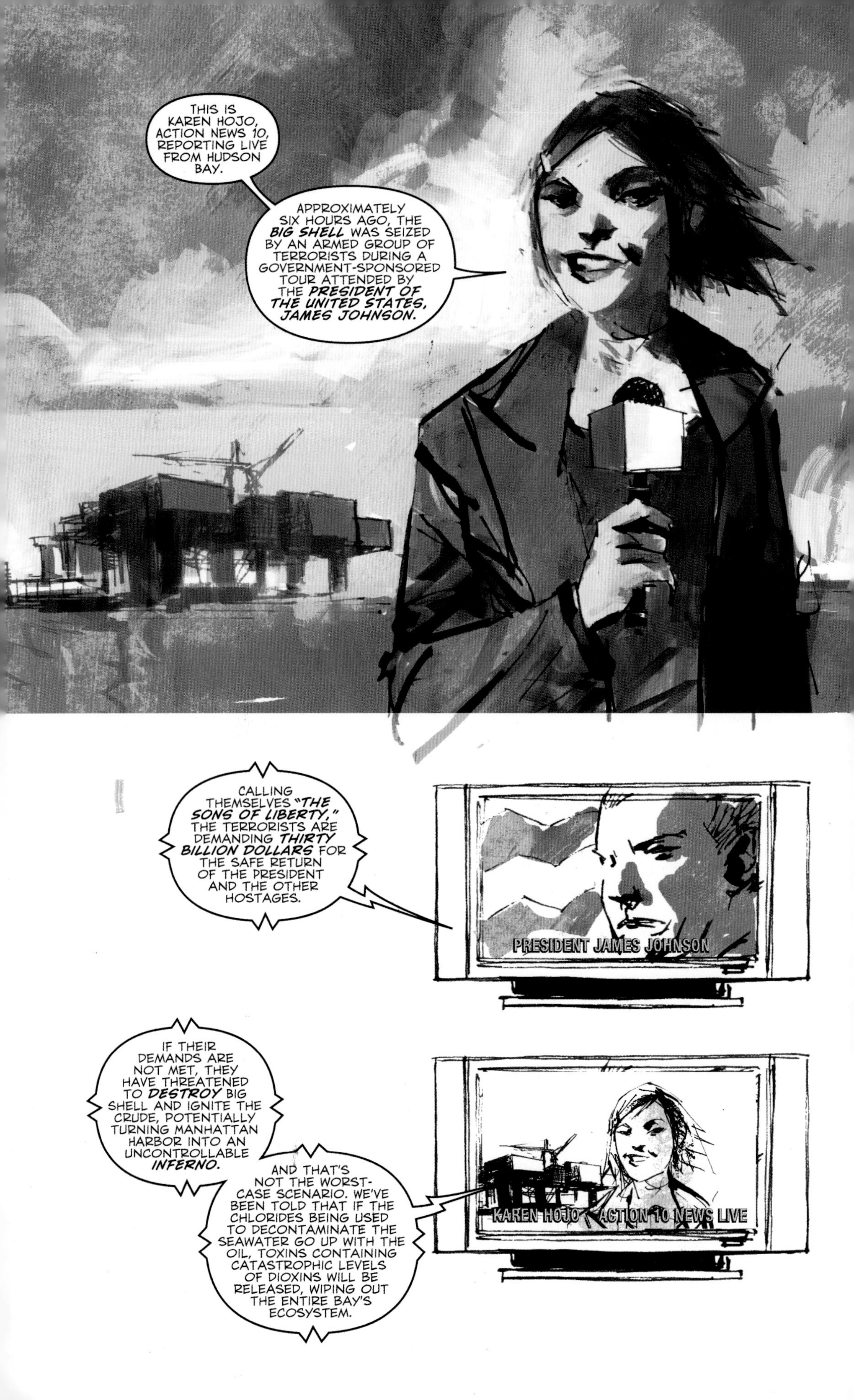
THIS IS KAREN HOJO, ACTION NEWS 10, REPORTING LIVE FROM HUDSON BAY.
APPROXIMATELY SIX HOURS AGO, THE BIG SHELL WAS SEIZED BY AN ARMED GROUP OF TERRORISTS DURING A GOVERNMENT-SPONSORED TOUR ATTENDED BY THE PRESIDENT OF THE UNITED STATES, JAMES JOHNSON.
CALLING THEMSELVES "THE SONS OF LIBERTY," THE TERRORISTS ARE DEMANDING THIRTY BILLION DOLLARS FOR THE SAFE RETURN OF THE PRESIDENT AND THE OTHER HOSTAGES.
PRESIDENT JAMES JOHNSON
IF THEIR DEMANDS ARE NOT MET, THEY HAVE THREATENED TO DESTROY BIG SHELL AND IGNITE THE CRUDE, POTENTIALLY TURNING MANHATTAN HARBOR INTO AN UNCONTROLLABLE INFERNO.
AND THAT'S NOT THE WORST-CASE SCENARIO. WE'VE BEEN TOLD THAT IF THE CHLORIDES BEING USED TO DECONTAMINATE THE SEAWATER GO UP WITH THE OIL, TOXINS CONTAINING CATASTROPHIC LEVELS OF DIOXINS WILL BE RELEASED, WIPING OUT THE ENTIRE BAY'S ECOSYSTEM.
KAREN HOJO ACTION 10 NEWS LIVE

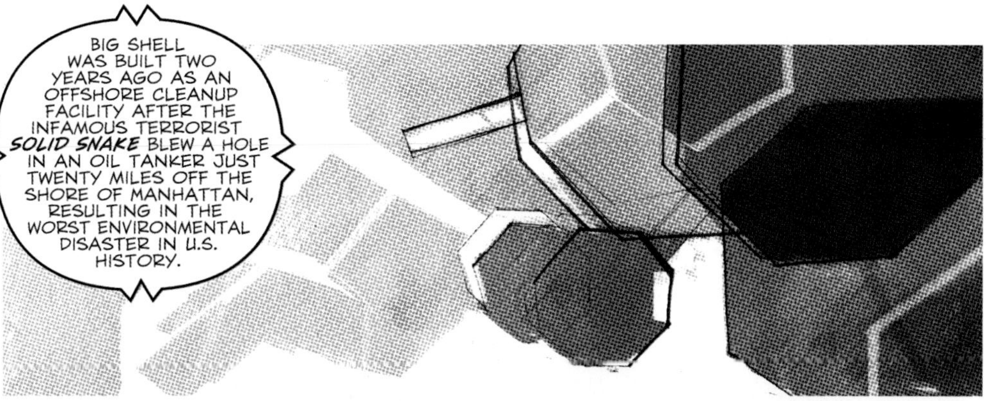
BIG SHELL WAS BUILT TWO YEARS AGO AS AN OFFSHORE CLEANUP FACILITY AFTER THE INFAMOUS TERRORIST **SOLID SNAKE** BLEW A HOLE IN AN OIL TANKER JUST TWENTY MILES OFF THE SHORE OF MANHATTAN, RESULTING IN THE WORST ENVIRONMENTAL DISASTER IN U.S. HISTORY.

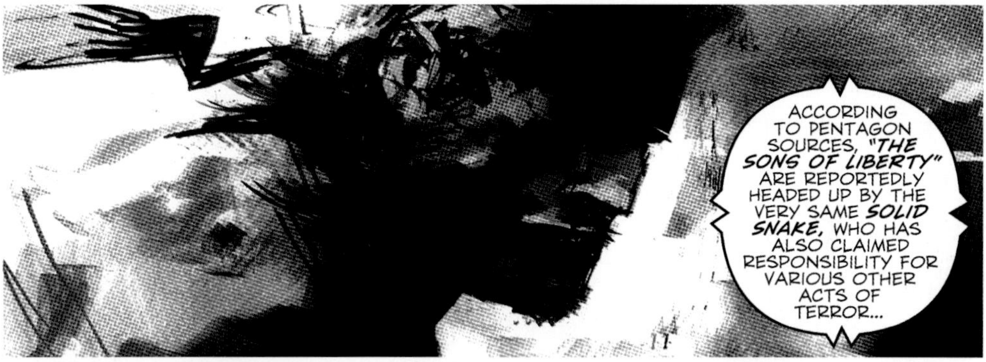
ACCORDING TO PENTAGON SOURCES, **"THE SONS OF LIBERTY"** ARE REPORTEDLY HEADED UP BY THE VERY SAME **SOLID SNAKE,** WHO HAS ALSO CLAIMED RESPONSIBILITY FOR VARIOUS OTHER ACTS OF TERROR...

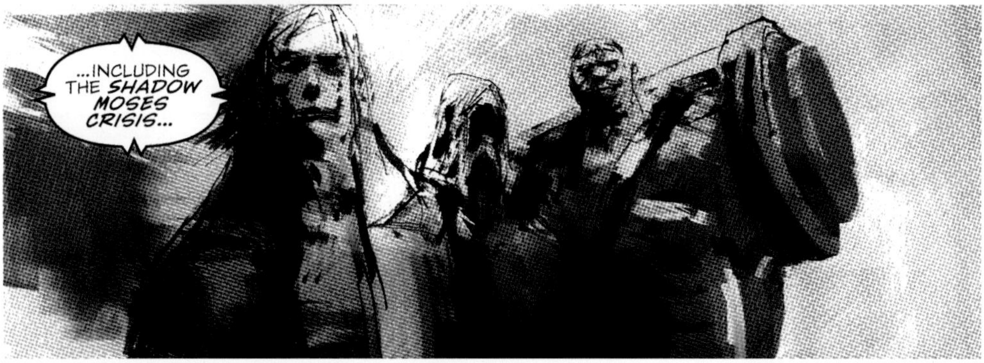
...INCLUDING THE **SHADOW MOSES CRISIS...**

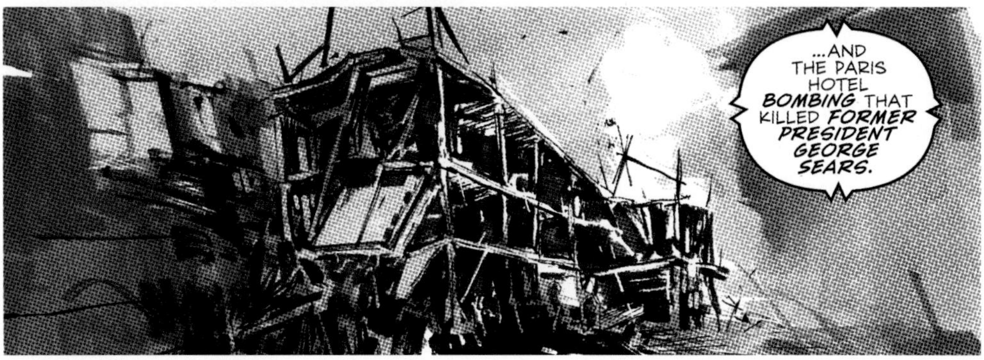
...AND THE PARIS HOTEL **BOMBING** THAT KILLED **FORMER PRESIDENT GEORGE SEARS.**

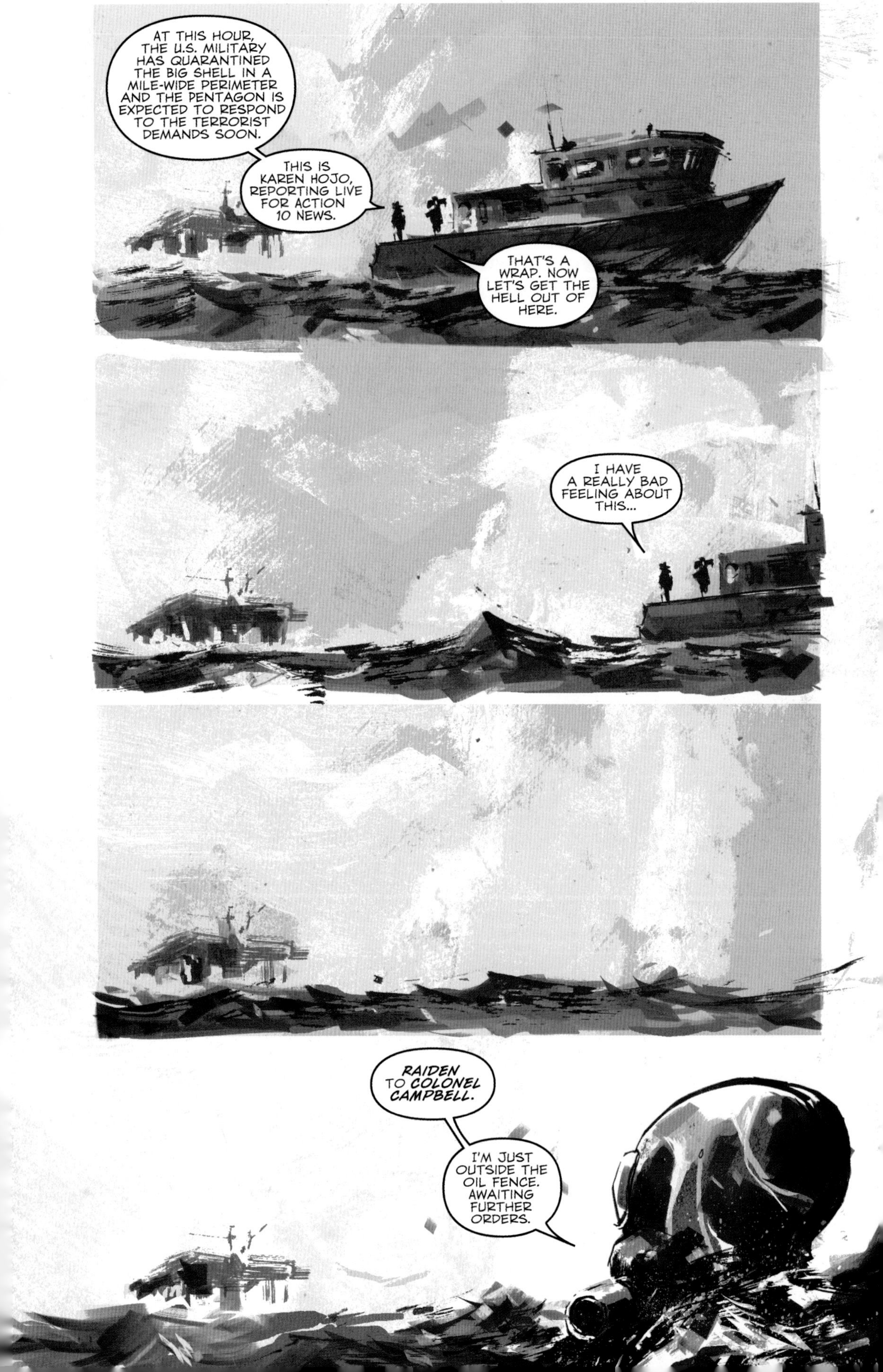
AT THIS HOUR, THE U.S. MILITARY HAS QUARANTINED THE BIG SHELL IN A MILE-WIDE PERIMETER AND THE PENTAGON IS EXPECTED TO RESPOND TO THE TERRORIST DEMANDS SOON.
THIS IS KAREN HOJO, REPORTING LIVE FOR ACTION 10 NEWS.
THAT'S A WRAP. NOW LET'S GET THE HELL OUT OF HERE.
I HAVE A REALLY BAD FEELING ABOUT THIS...
RAIDEN TO COLONEL CAMPBELL.
I'M JUST OUTSIDE THE OIL FENCE. AWAITING FURTHER ORDERS.

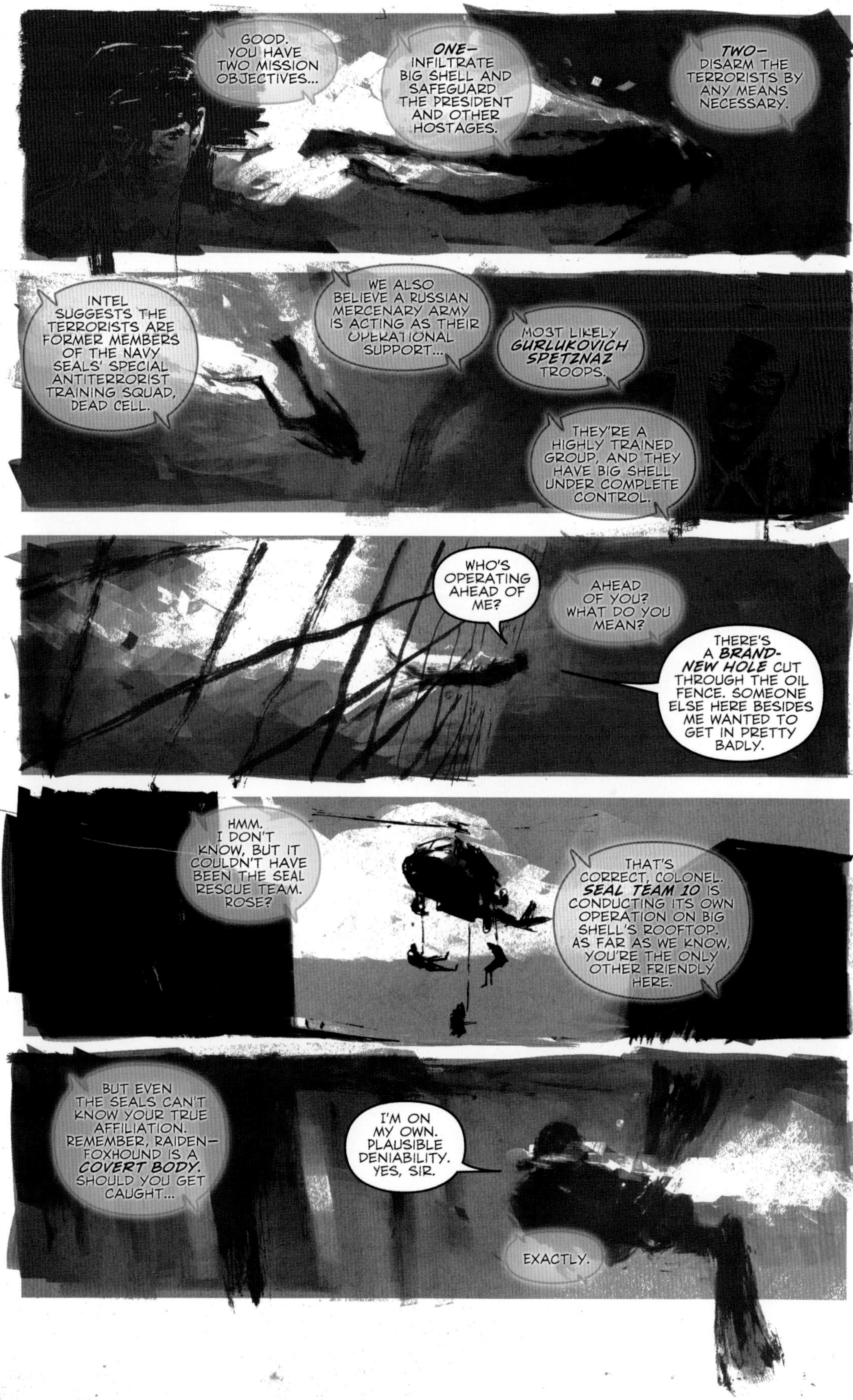
GOOD. YOU HAVE TWO MISSION OBJECTIVES...
ONE— INFILTRATE BIG SHELL AND SAFEGUARD THE PRESIDENT AND OTHER HOSTAGES.
TWO— DISARM THE TERRORISTS BY ANY MEANS NECESSARY.
INTEL SUGGESTS THE TERRORISTS ARE FORMER MEMBERS OF THE NAVY SEALS' SPECIAL ANTITERRORIST TRAINING SQUAD, DEAD CELL.
WE ALSO BELIEVE A RUSSIAN MERCENARY ARMY IS ACTING AS THEIR OPERATIONAL SUPPORT...
MOST LIKELY GURLUKOVICH SPETZNAZ TROOPS.
THEY'RE A HIGHLY TRAINED GROUP, AND THEY HAVE BIG SHELL UNDER COMPLETE CONTROL.
WHO'S OPERATING AHEAD OF ME?
AHEAD OF YOU? WHAT DO YOU MEAN?
THERE'S A BRAND-NEW HOLE CUT THROUGH THE OIL FENCE. SOMEONE ELSE HERE BESIDES ME WANTED TO GET IN PRETTY BADLY.
HMM. I DON'T KNOW, BUT IT COULDN'T HAVE BEEN THE SEAL RESCUE TEAM. ROSE?
THAT'S CORRECT, COLONEL. SEAL TEAM 10 IS CONDUCTING ITS OWN OPERATION ON BIG SHELL'S ROOFTOP. AS FAR AS WE KNOW, YOU'RE THE ONLY OTHER FRIENDLY HERE.
BUT EVEN THE SEALS CAN'T KNOW YOUR TRUE AFFILIATION. REMEMBER, RAIDEN— FOXHOUND IS A COVERT BODY. SHOULD YOU GET CAUGHT...
I'M ON MY OWN. PLAUSIBLE DENIABILITY. YES, SIR.
EXACTLY.

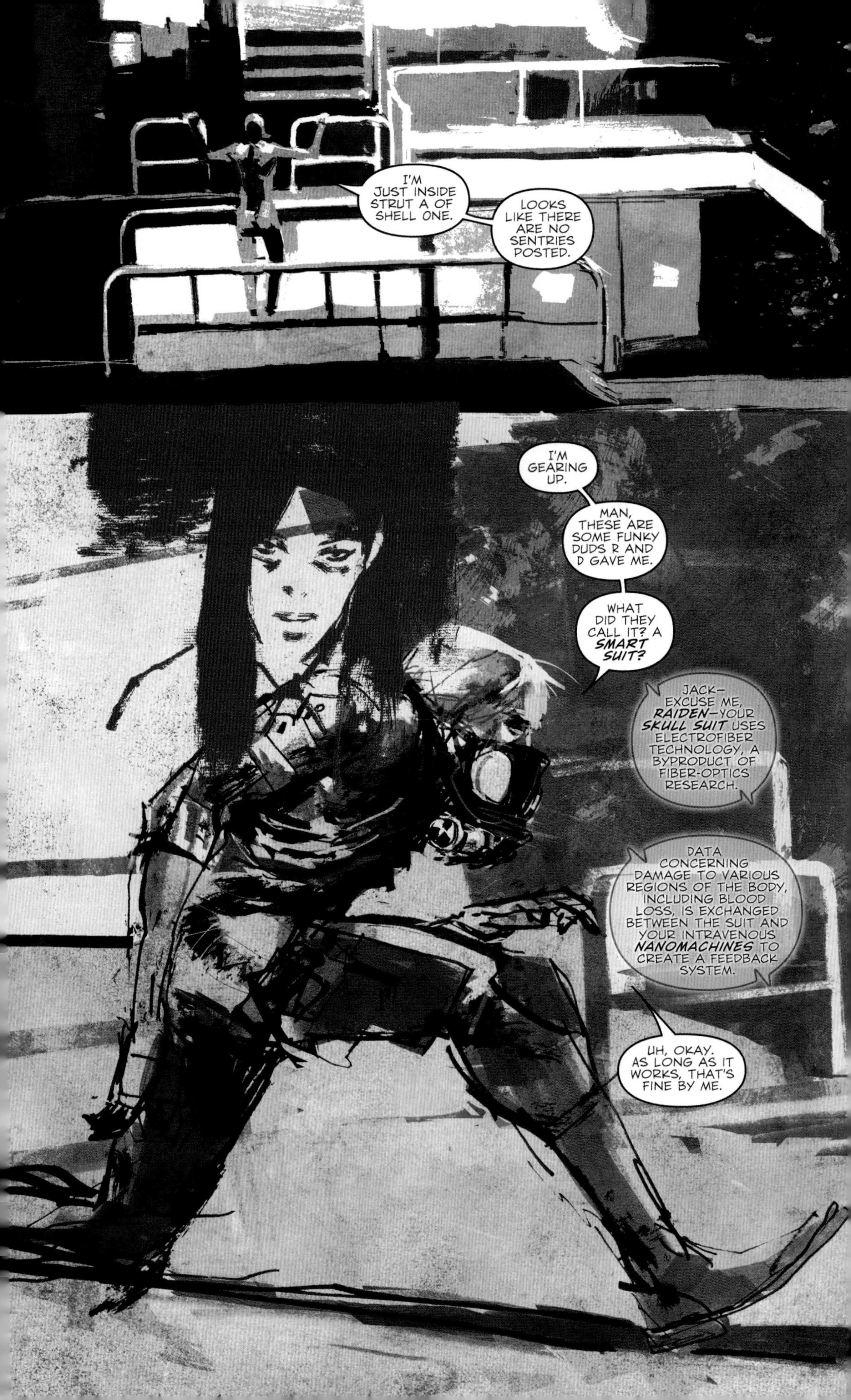

I'M JUST INSIDE STRUT A OF SHELL ONE.
LOOKS LIKE THERE ARE NO SENTRIES POSTED.
I'M GEARING UP.
MAN, THESE ARE SOME FUNKY DUDS R AND D GAVE ME.
WHAT DID THEY CALL IT? A SMART SUIT?
JACK—EXCUSE ME, RAIDEN—YOUR SKULL SUIT USES ELECTROFIBER TECHNOLOGY, A BYPRODUCT OF FIBER-OPTICS RESEARCH.
DATA CONCERNING DAMAGE TO VARIOUS REGIONS OF THE BODY, INCLUDING BLOOD LOSS, IS EXCHANGED BETWEEN THE SUIT AND YOUR INTRAVENOUS NANOMACHINES TO CREATE A FEEDBACK SYSTEM.
UH, OKAY. AS LONG AS IT WORKS, THAT'S FINE BY ME.

IT'S QUIET.
TOO QUIET.
I'VE SIGHTED AN ENEMY SENTRY. LOOKS LIKE SOMEONE ALREADY TOOK HIM OUT.
NO SHOTS FIRED. MINIMAL STRUGGLE. A VERY CLEAN TAKEDOWN OF RUSSIA'S FINEST.
COLONEL, THERE'S OBVIOUSLY SOMEONE ELSE OPERATING HERE BESIDES ME. SOMEONE WITH A LOT OF TALENT.
COLONEL?
I... DON'T HAVE A RESPONSE TO THAT. YOU JUST NEED TO STAY FOCUSED ON YOUR ROLE IN THIS MISSION, RAIDEN. NOW, I WANT YOU TO...
EXCUSE ME, COLONEL. I'VE JUST INTERCEPTED A SEAL TEAM ALPHA TRANSMISSION...

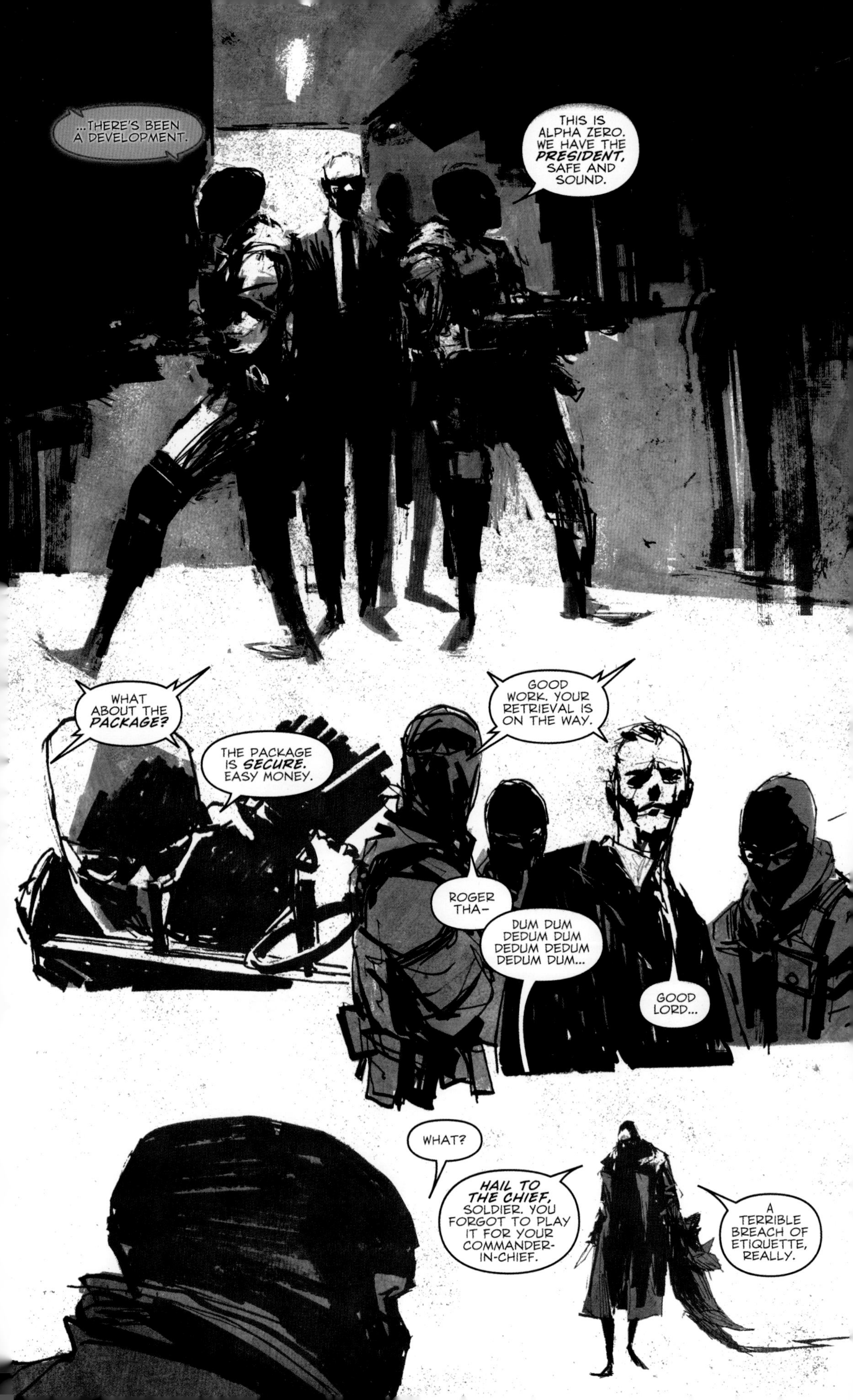
...THERE'S BEEN A DEVELOPMENT.
THIS IS ALPHA ZERO. WE HAVE THE PRESIDENT, SAFE AND SOUND.
WHAT ABOUT THE PACKAGE?
THE PACKAGE IS SECURE. EASY MONEY.
GOOD WORK. YOUR RETRIEVAL IS ON THE WAY.
ROGER THA-
DUM DUM DEDUM DUM DEDUM DEDUM DEDUM DUM...
GOOD LORD...
WHAT?
HAIL TO THE CHIEF, SOLDIER. YOU FORGOT TO PLAY IT FOR YOUR COMMANDER-IN-CHIEF.
A TERRIBLE BREACH OF ETIQUETTE, REALLY.

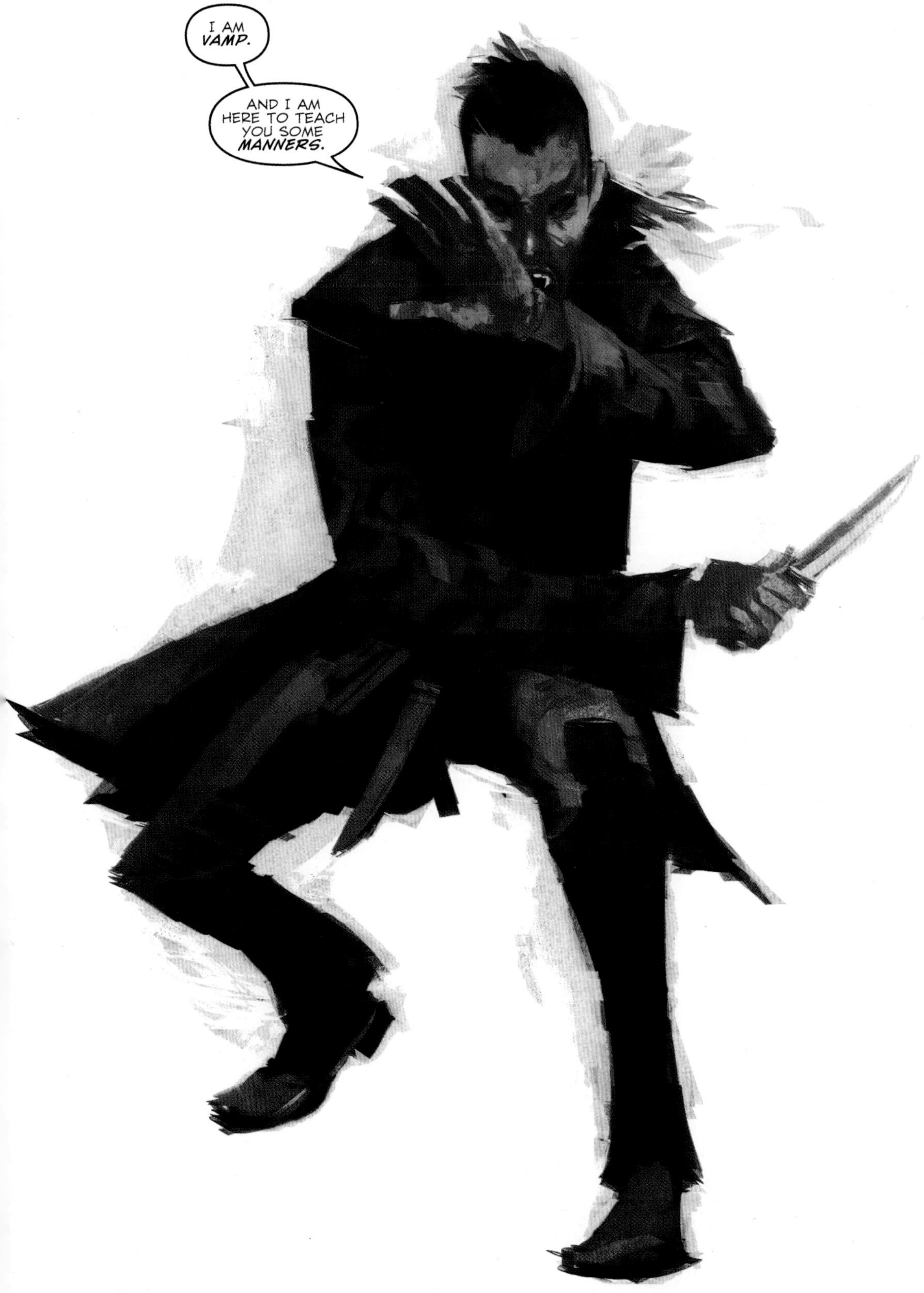
I AM VAMP.
AND I AM HERE TO TEACH YOU SOME MANNERS.

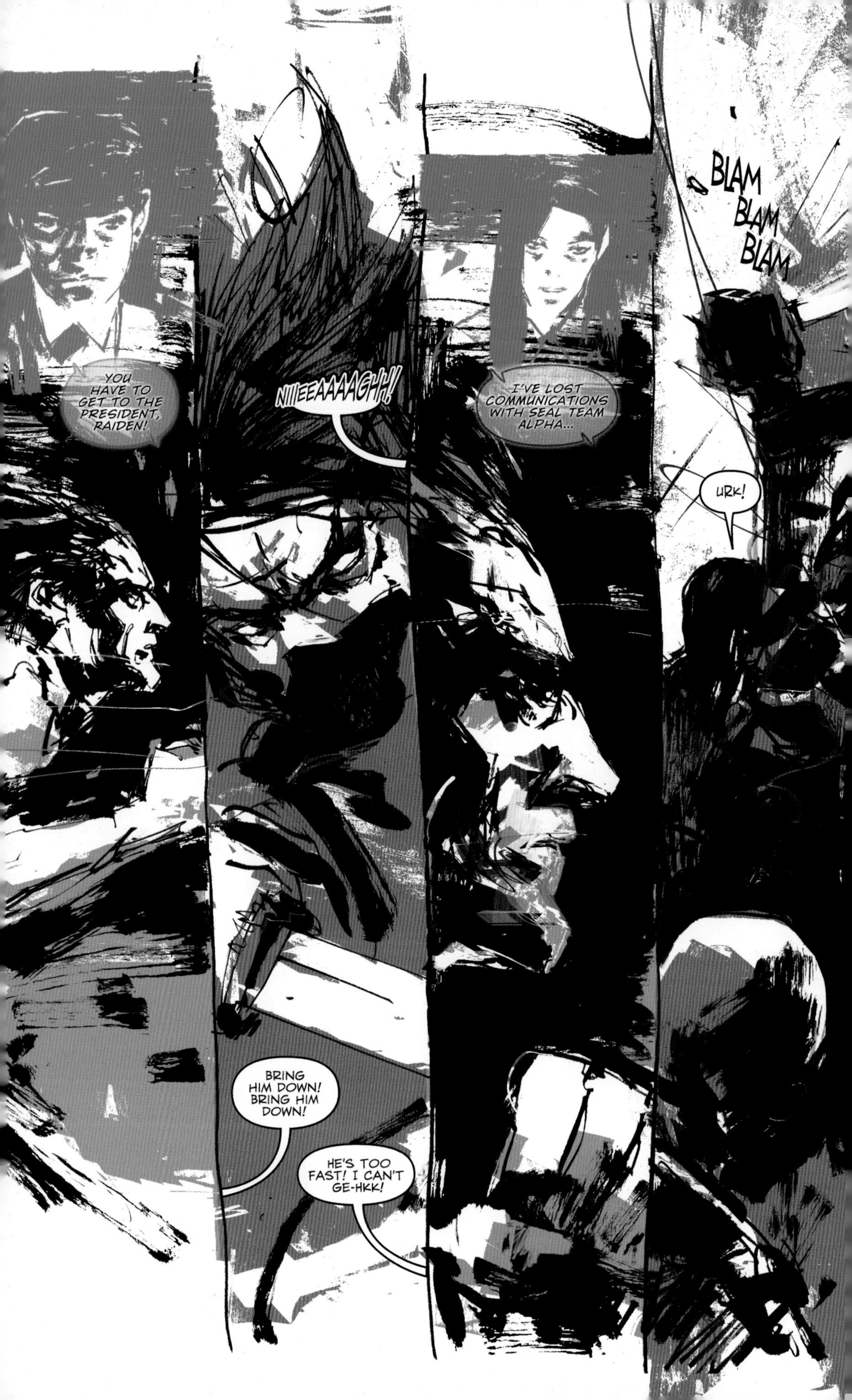
YOU HAVE TO GET TO THE PRESIDENT, RAIDEN!
NIIIEEAAAAGH!
I'VE LOST COMMUNICATIONS WITH SEAL TEAM ALPHA...
BLAM BLAM BLAM
URK!
BRING HIM DOWN! BRING HIM DOWN!
HE'S TOO FAST! I CAN'T GE-HKK!

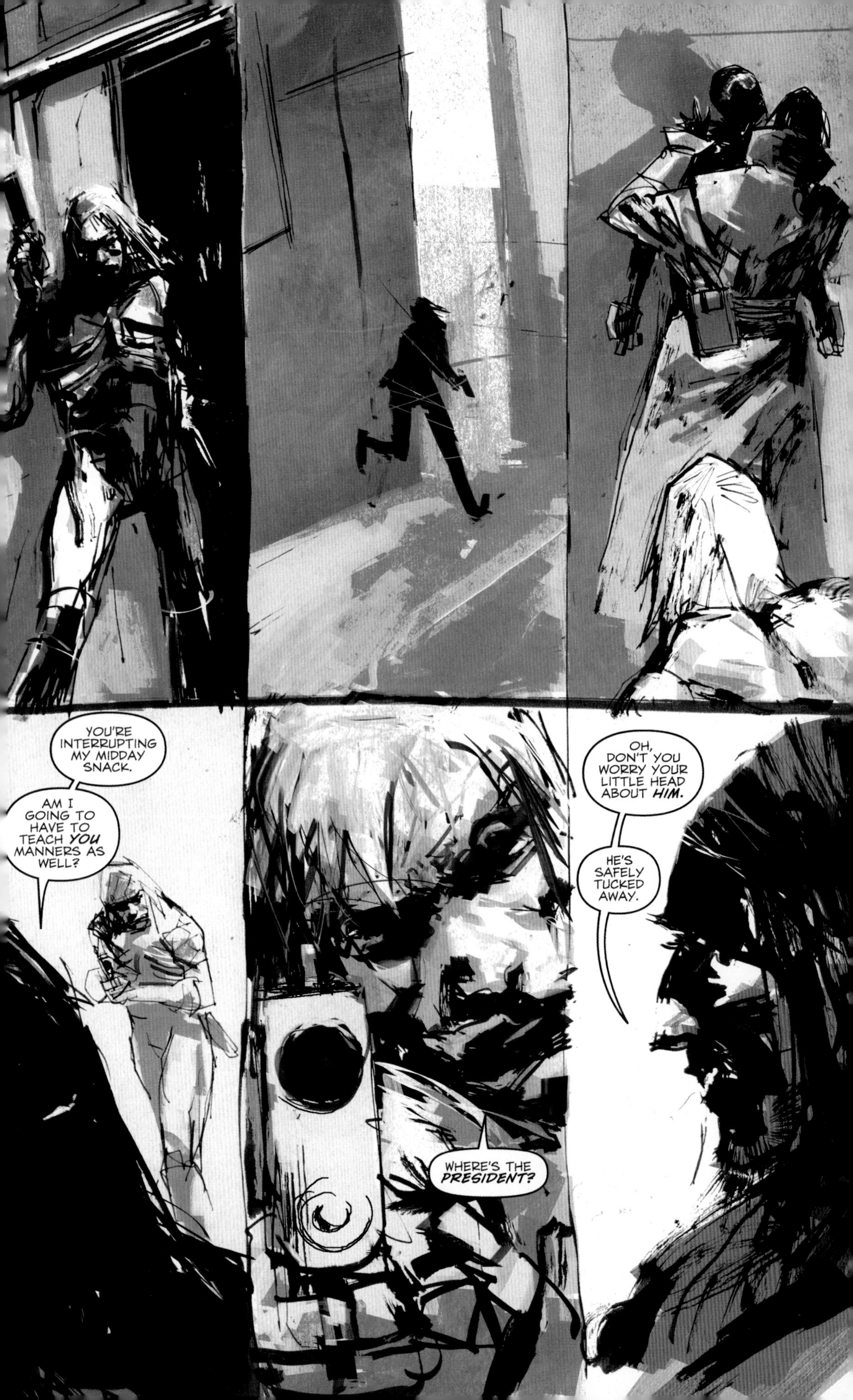
YOU'RE INTERRUPTING MY MIDDAY SNACK.
AM I GOING TO HAVE TO TEACH *YOU* MANNERS AS WELL?
WHERE'S THE *PRESIDENT?*
OH, DON'T YOU WORRY YOUR LITTLE HEAD ABOUT *HIM*.
HE'S SAFELY TUCKED AWAY.

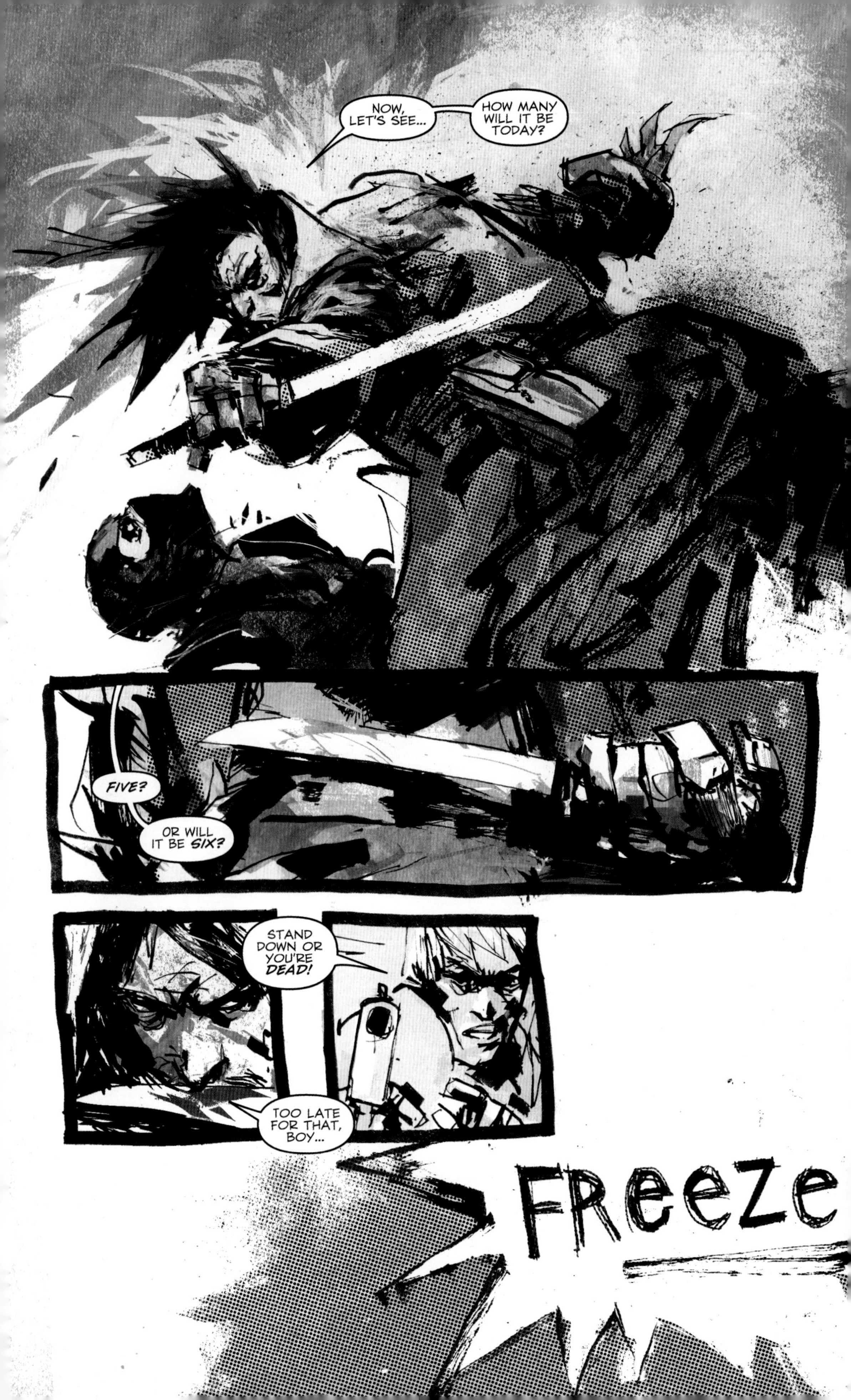
NOW, LET'S SEE...
HOW MANY WILL IT BE TODAY?
FIVE?
OR WILL IT BE SIX?
STAND DOWN OR YOU'RE DEAD!
TOO LATE FOR THAT, BOY...
FREEZE

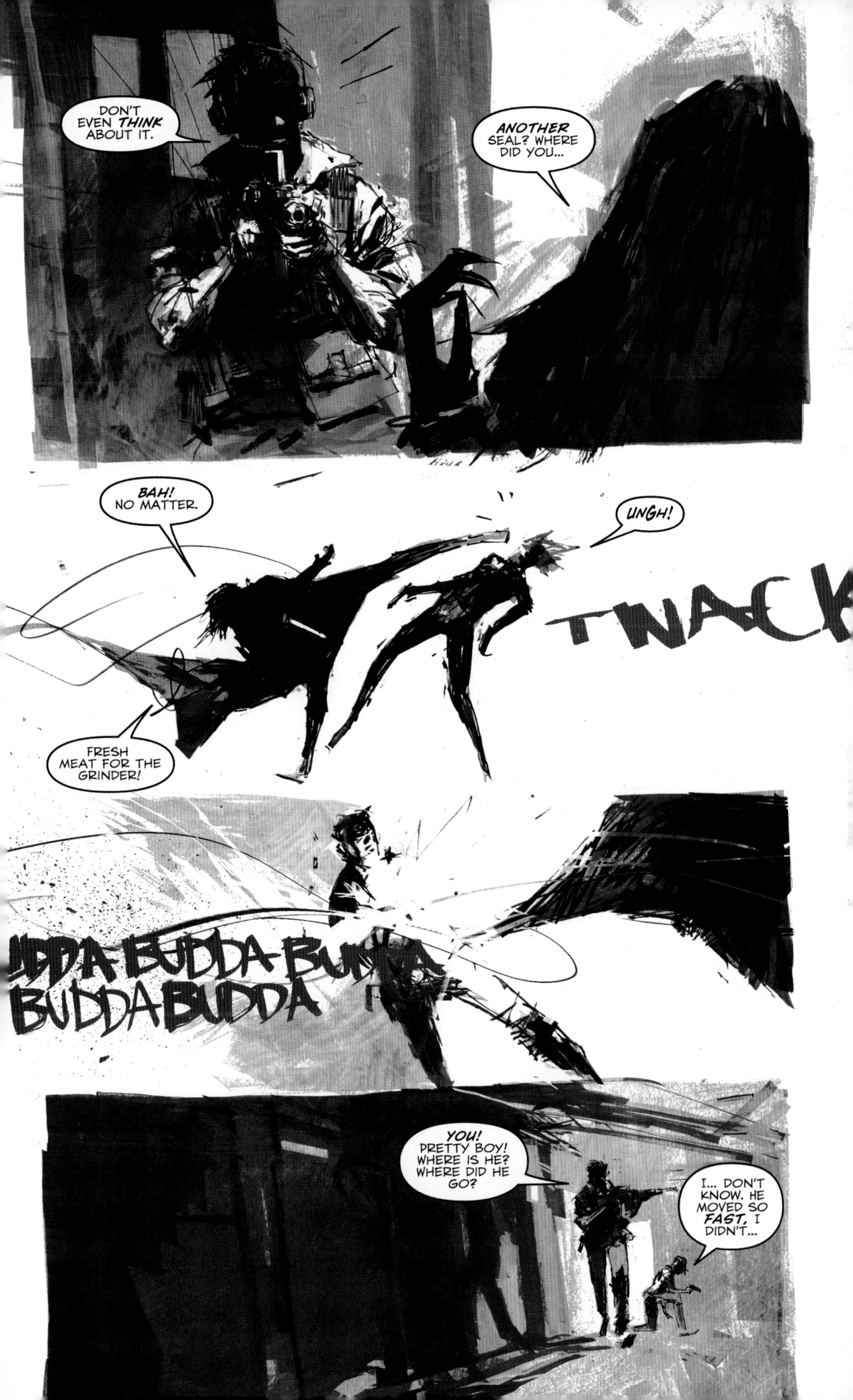
DON'T EVEN *THINK* ABOUT IT.
ANOTHER SEAL? WHERE DID YOU...
BAH! NO MATTER.
UNGH!
TNACK
FRESH MEAT FOR THE GRINDER!
UDDA BUDDA
BUDDA BUDDA
YOU! PRETTY BOY! WHERE IS HE? WHERE DID HE GO?
I... DON'T KNOW. HE MOVED SO *FAST*, I DIDN'T...

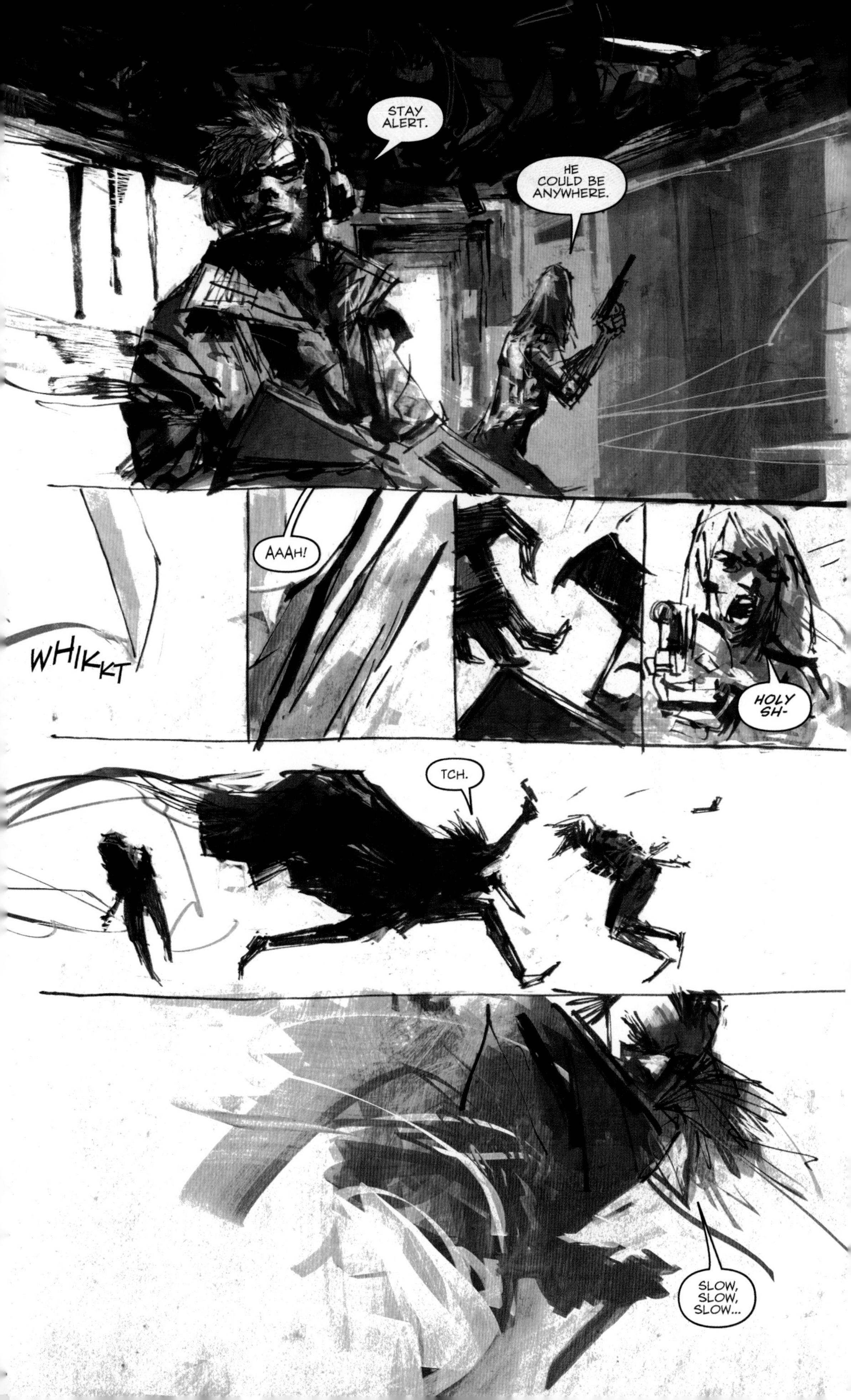
STAY ALERT.
HE COULD BE ANYWHERE.
WHIKKT
AAAH!
HOLY SH-
TCH.
SLOW, SLOW, SLOW...

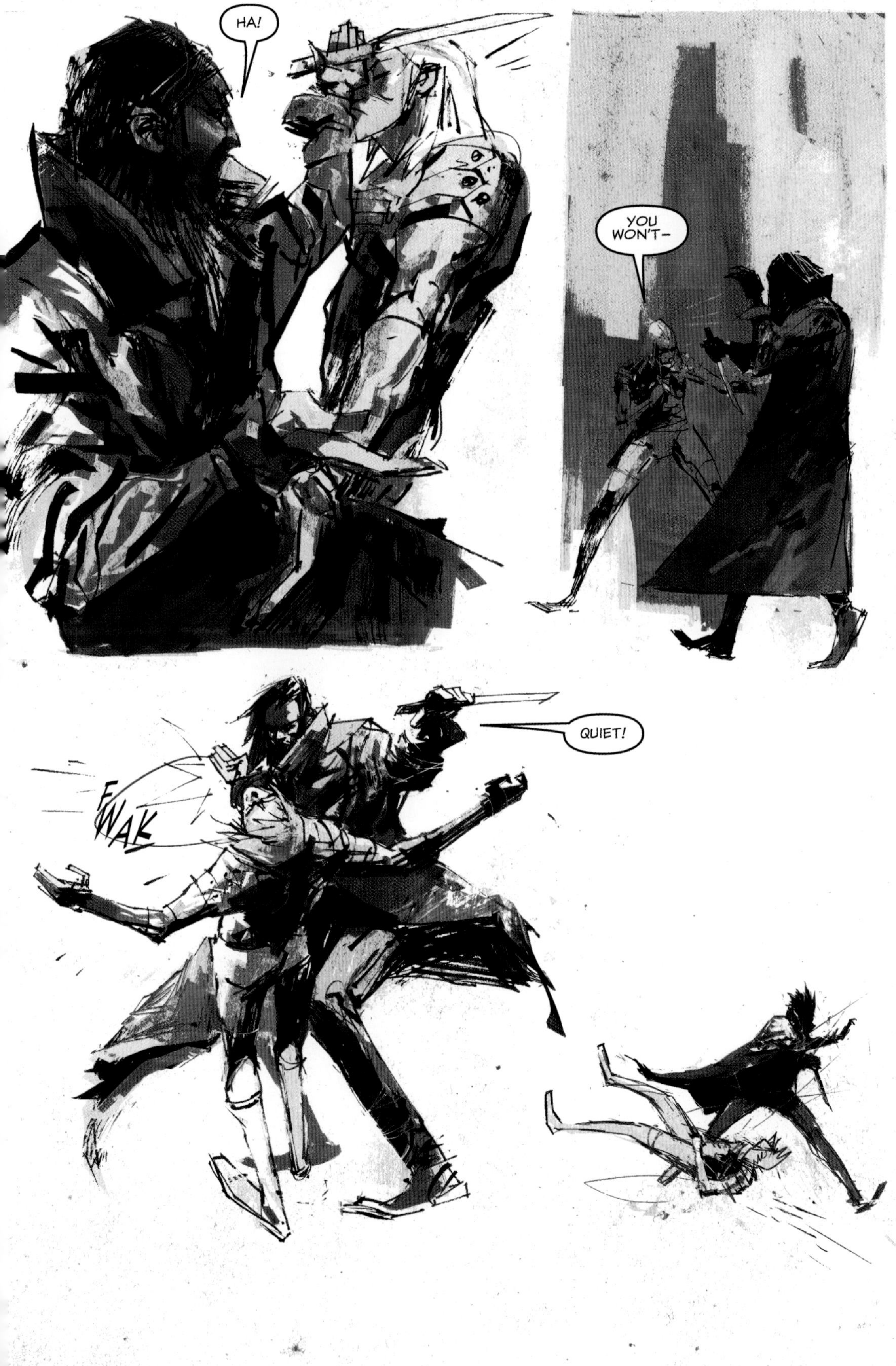
HA!
YOU WON'T–
QUIET!
FWAK

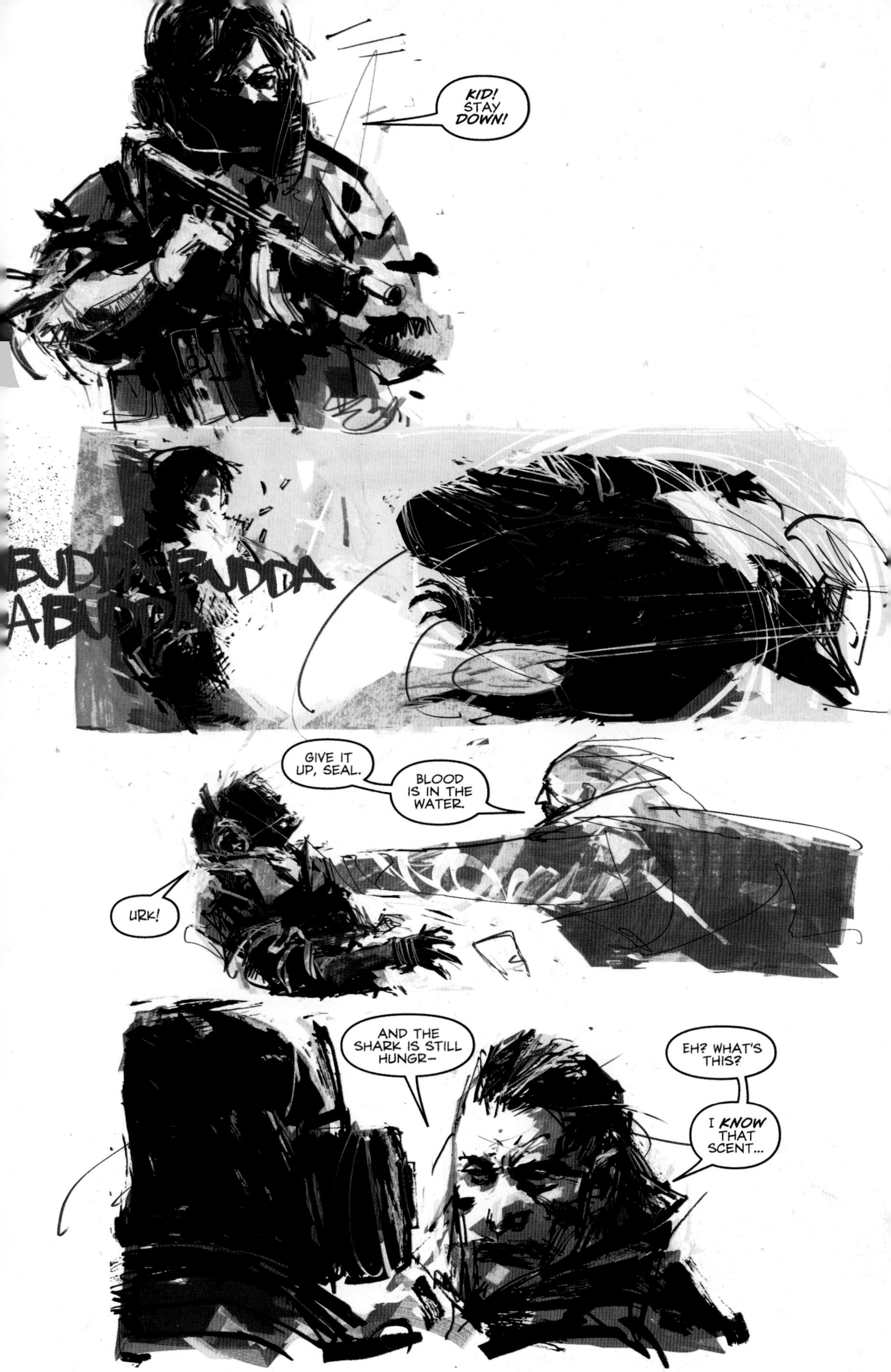
KID! STAY DOWN!
BUDDA
GIVE IT UP, SEAL.
BLOOD IS IN THE WATER.
URK!
AND THE SHARK IS STILL HUNGR-
EH? WHAT'S THIS?
I KNOW THAT SCENT...

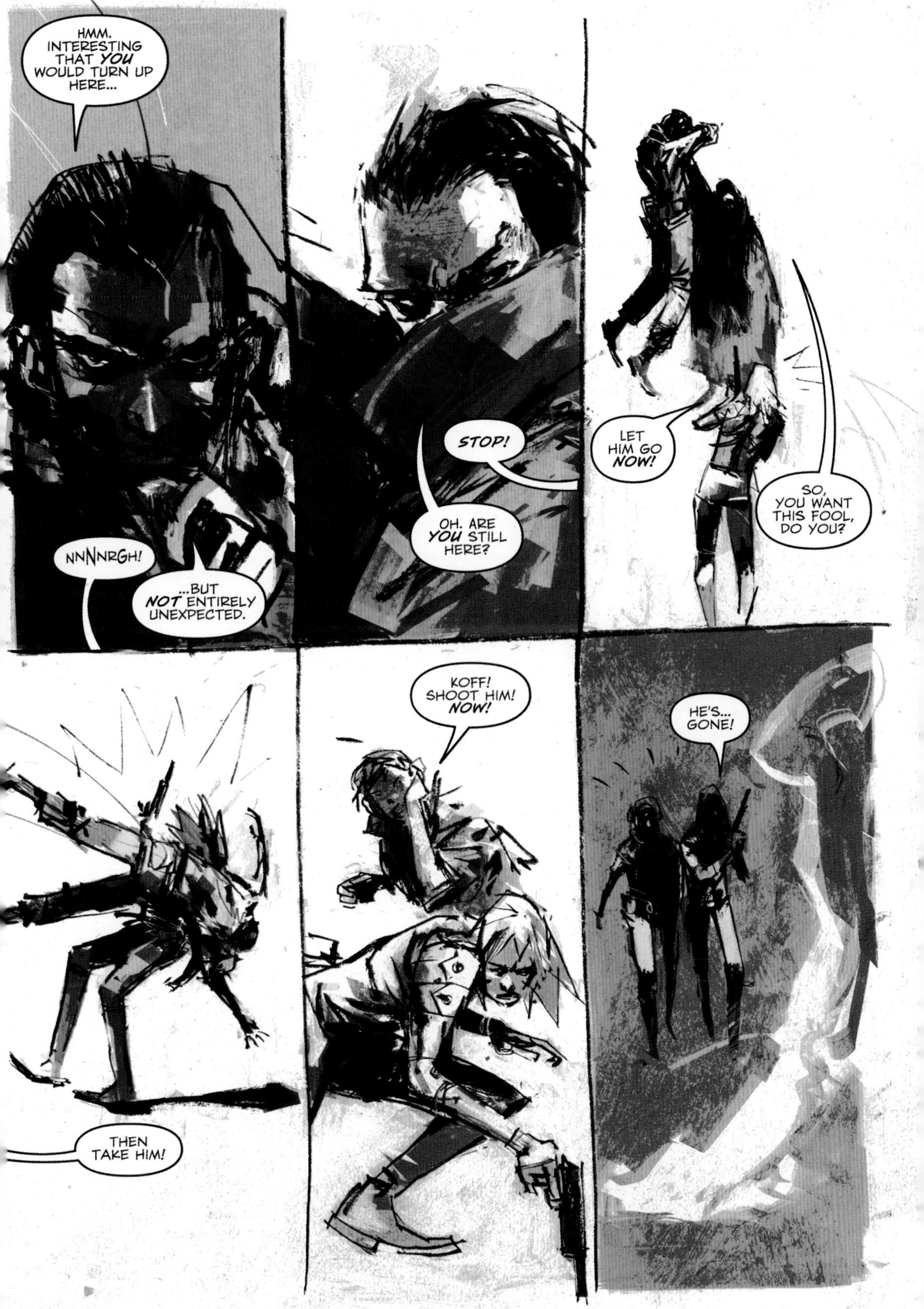
HMM. INTERESTING THAT YOU WOULD TURN UP HERE...
NNNNRGH!
...BUT NOT ENTIRELY UNEXPECTED.
STOP!
OH. ARE YOU STILL HERE?
LET HIM GO NOW!
SO, YOU WANT THIS FOOL, DO YOU?
THEN TAKE HIM!
KOFF! SHOOT HIM! NOW!
HE'S... GONE!

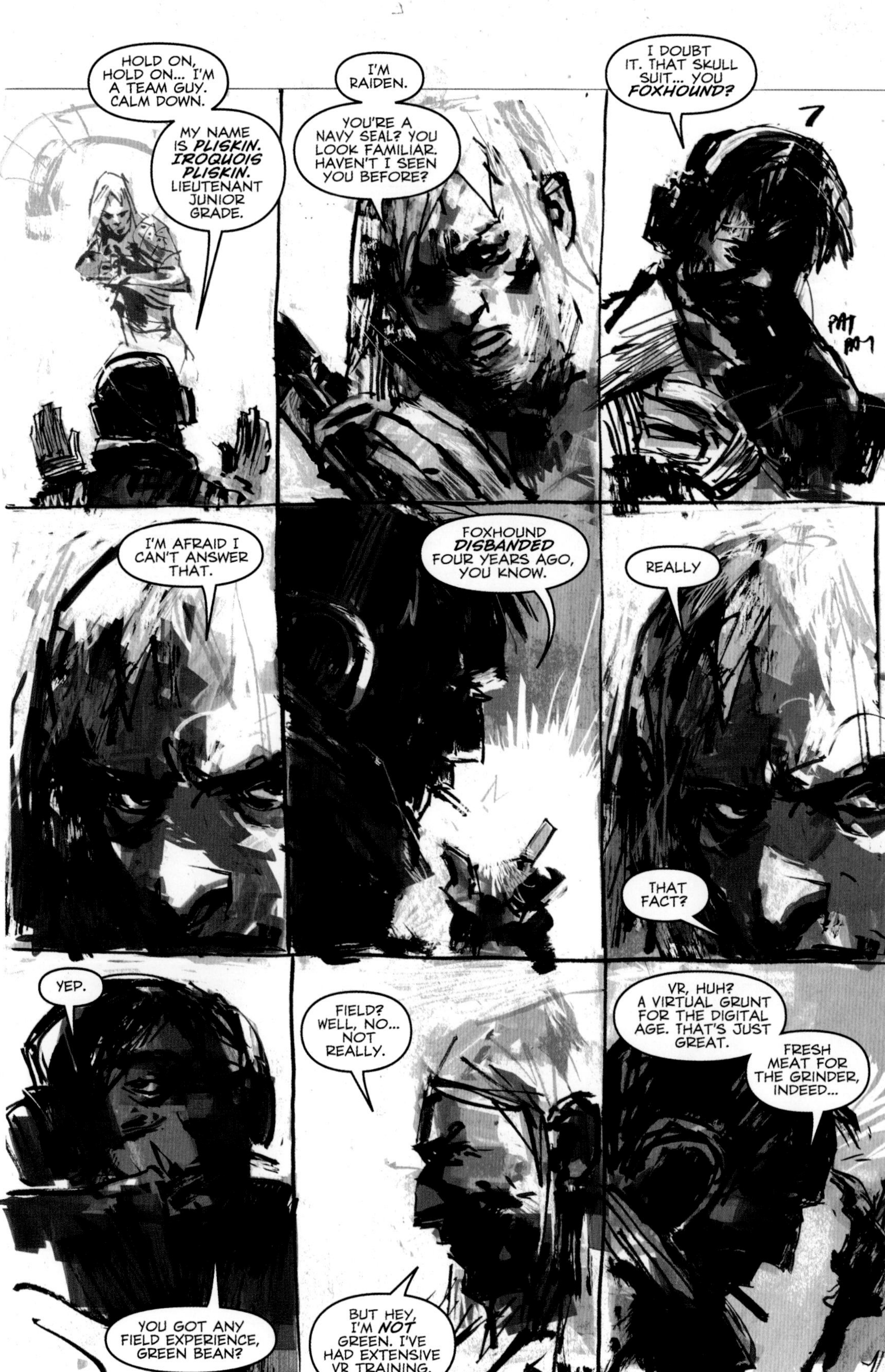
HOLD ON, HOLD ON... I'M A TEAM GUY. CALM DOWN.
MY NAME IS PLISKIN. IROQUOIS PLISKIN. LIEUTENANT JUNIOR GRADE.
I'M RAIDEN.
YOU'RE A NAVY SEAL? YOU LOOK FAMILIAR. HAVEN'T I SEEN YOU BEFORE?
I DOUBT IT. THAT SKULL SUIT... YOU FOXHOUND?
I'M AFRAID I CAN'T ANSWER THAT.
FOXHOUND DISBANDED FOUR YEARS AGO, YOU KNOW.
REALLY
THAT FACT?
YEP.
YOU GOT ANY FIELD EXPERIENCE, GREEN BEAN?
FIELD? WELL, NO... NOT REALLY.
BUT HEY, I'M NOT GREEN. I'VE HAD EXTENSIVE VR TRAINING.
VR, HUH? A VIRTUAL GRUNT FOR THE DIGITAL AGE. THAT'S JUST GREAT.
FRESH MEAT FOR THE GRINDER, INDEED...

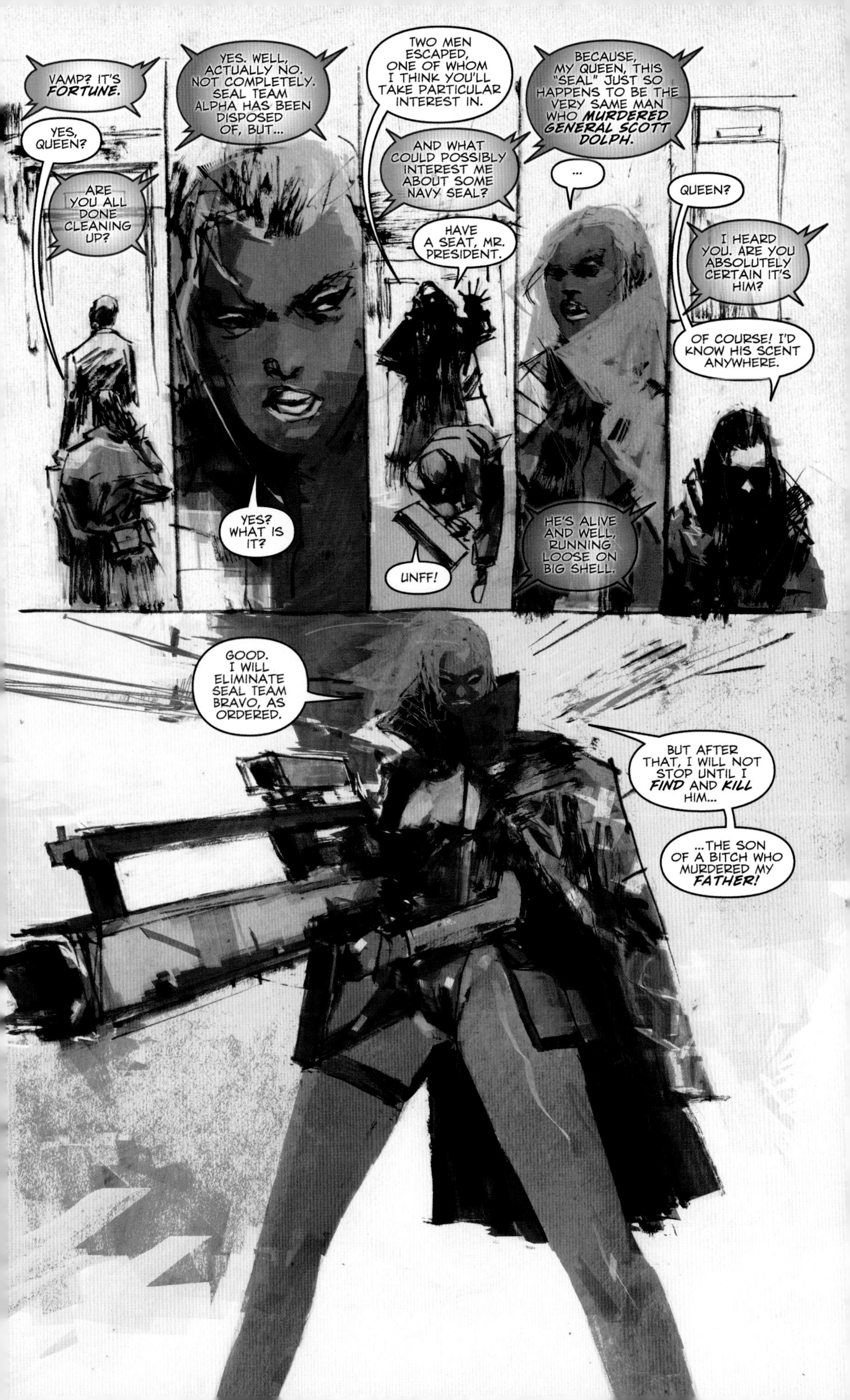
VAMP? IT'S FORTUNE.
YES, QUEEN?
ARE YOU ALL DONE CLEANING UP?
YES. WELL, ACTUALLY NO. NOT COMPLETELY. SEAL TEAM ALPHA HAS BEEN DISPOSED OF, BUT...
YES? WHAT IS IT?
TWO MEN ESCAPED, ONE OF WHOM I THINK YOU'LL TAKE PARTICULAR INTEREST IN.
AND WHAT COULD POSSIBLY INTEREST ME ABOUT SOME NAVY SEAL?
HAVE A SEAT, MR. PRESIDENT.
UNFF!
BECAUSE, MY QUEEN, THIS "SEAL" JUST SO HAPPENS TO BE THE VERY SAME MAN WHO MURDERED GENERAL SCOTT DOLPH.
...
HE'S ALIVE AND WELL, RUNNING LOOSE ON BIG SHELL.
QUEEN?
I HEARD YOU. ARE YOU ABSOLUTELY CERTAIN IT'S HIM?
OF COURSE! I'D KNOW HIS SCENT ANYWHERE.
GOOD. I WILL ELIMINATE SEAL TEAM BRAVO, AS ORDERED.
BUT AFTER THAT, I WILL NOT STOP UNTIL I FIND AND KILL HIM...
...THE SON OF A BITCH WHO MURDERED MY FATHER!

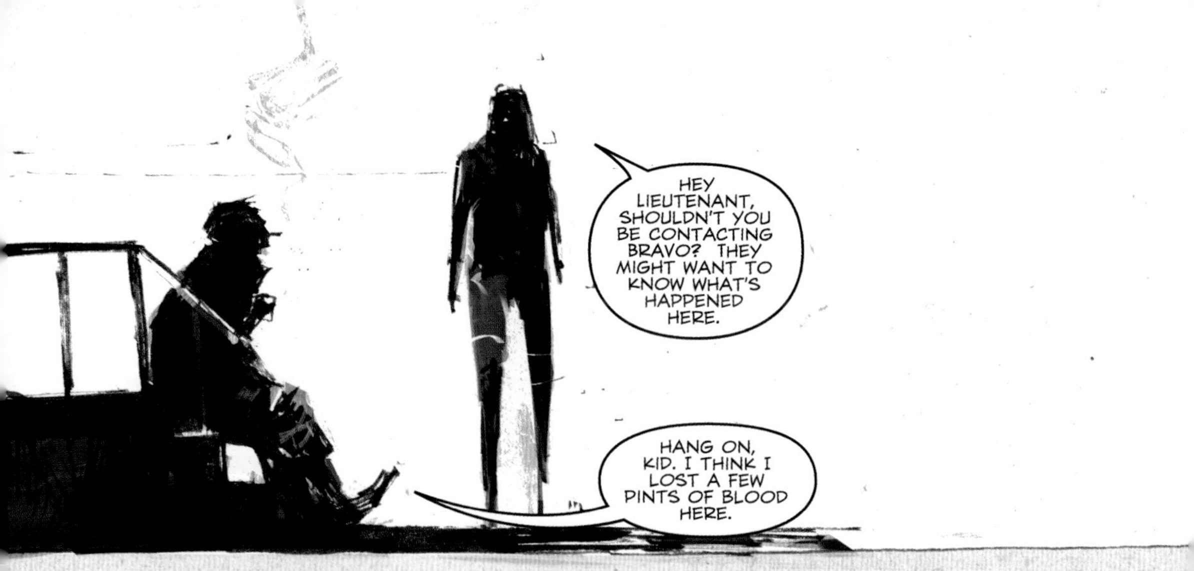
HEY LIEUTENANT, SHOULDN'T YOU BE CONTACTING BRAVO? THEY MIGHT WANT TO KNOW WHAT'S HAPPENED HERE.
HANG ON, KID. I THINK I LOST A FEW PINTS OF BLOOD HERE.

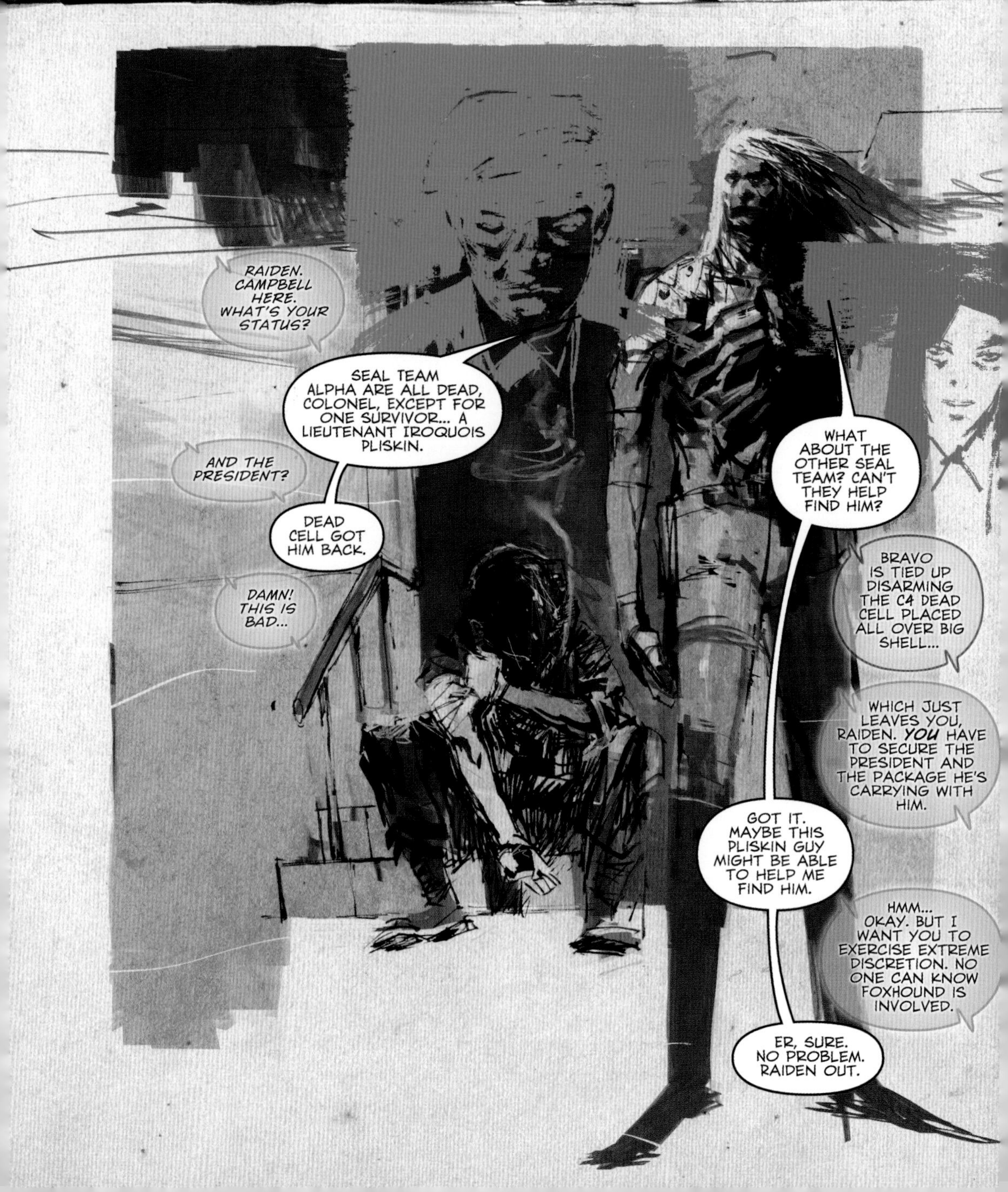
RAIDEN. CAMPBELL HERE. WHAT'S YOUR STATUS?
SEAL TEAM ALPHA ARE ALL DEAD, COLONEL, EXCEPT FOR ONE SURVIVOR... A LIEUTENANT IROQUOIS PLISKIN.
AND THE PRESIDENT?
DEAD CELL GOT HIM BACK.
DAMN! THIS IS BAD...
WHAT ABOUT THE OTHER SEAL TEAM? CAN'T THEY HELP FIND HIM?
BRAVO IS TIED UP DISARMING THE C4 DEAD CELL PLACED ALL OVER BIG SHELL...
WHICH JUST LEAVES YOU, RAIDEN. *YOU* HAVE TO SECURE THE PRESIDENT AND THE PACKAGE HE'S CARRYING WITH HIM.
GOT IT. MAYBE THIS PLISKIN GUY MIGHT BE ABLE TO HELP ME FIND HIM.
HMM... OKAY. BUT I WANT YOU TO EXERCISE EXTREME DISCRETION. NO ONE CAN KNOW FOXHOUND IS INVOLVED.
ER, SURE. NO PROBLEM. RAIDEN OUT.

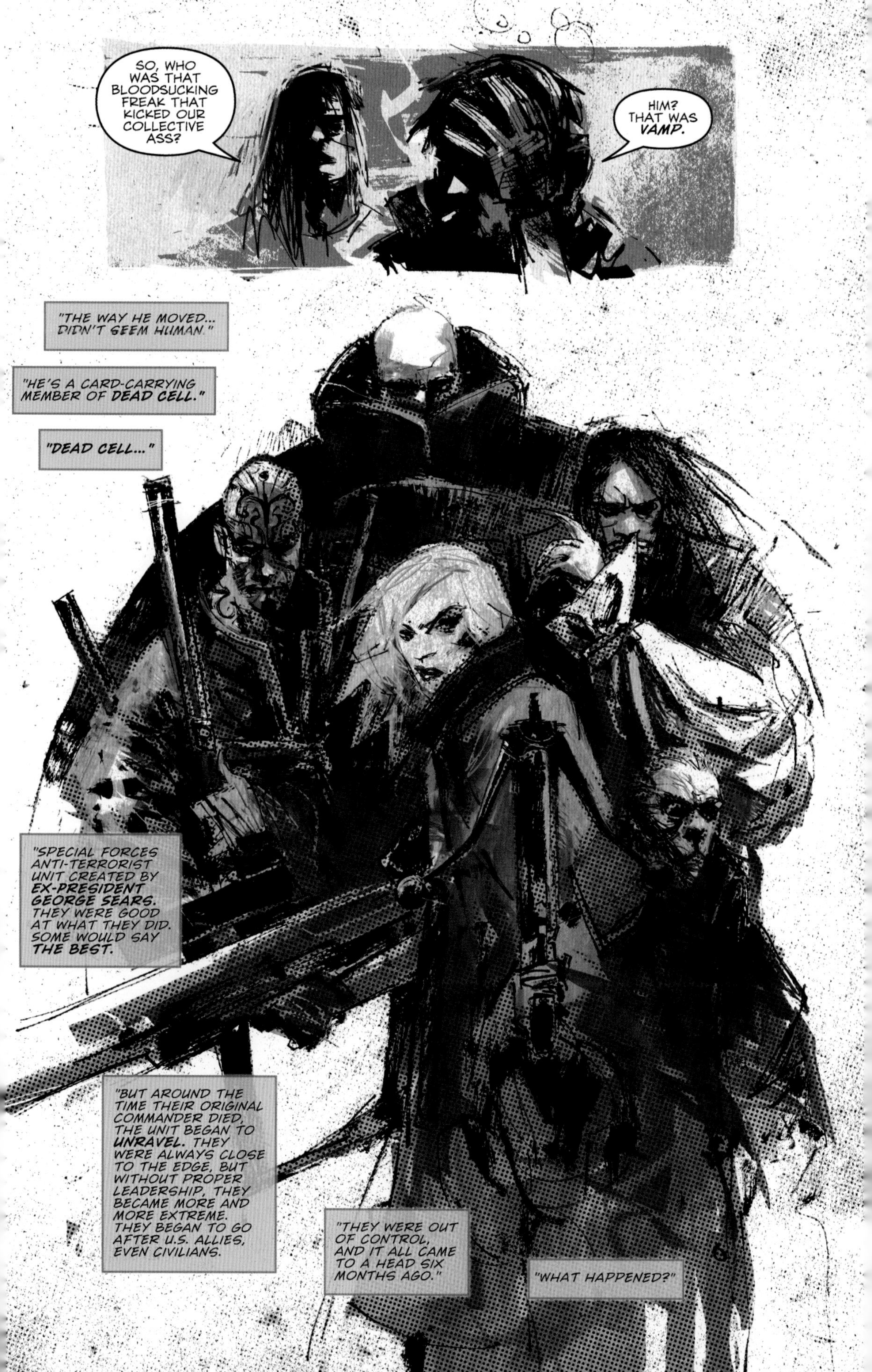
SO, WHO WAS THAT BLOODSUCKING FREAK THAT KICKED OUR COLLECTIVE ASS?
HIM? THAT WAS VAMP.
"THE WAY HE MOVED... DIDN'T SEEM HUMAN."
"HE'S A CARD-CARRYING MEMBER OF DEAD CELL."
"DEAD CELL..."
"SPECIAL FORCES ANTI-TERRORIST UNIT CREATED BY EX-PRESIDENT GEORGE SEARS. THEY WERE GOOD AT WHAT THEY DID. SOME WOULD SAY THE BEST.
"BUT AROUND THE TIME THEIR ORIGINAL COMMANDER DIED, THE UNIT BEGAN TO UNRAVEL. THEY WERE ALWAYS CLOSE TO THE EDGE, BUT WITHOUT PROPER LEADERSHIP, THEY BECAME MORE AND MORE EXTREME. THEY BEGAN TO GO AFTER U.S. ALLIES, EVEN CIVILIANS.
"THEY WERE OUT OF CONTROL, AND IT ALL CAME TO A HEAD SIX MONTHS AGO."
"WHAT HAPPENED?"

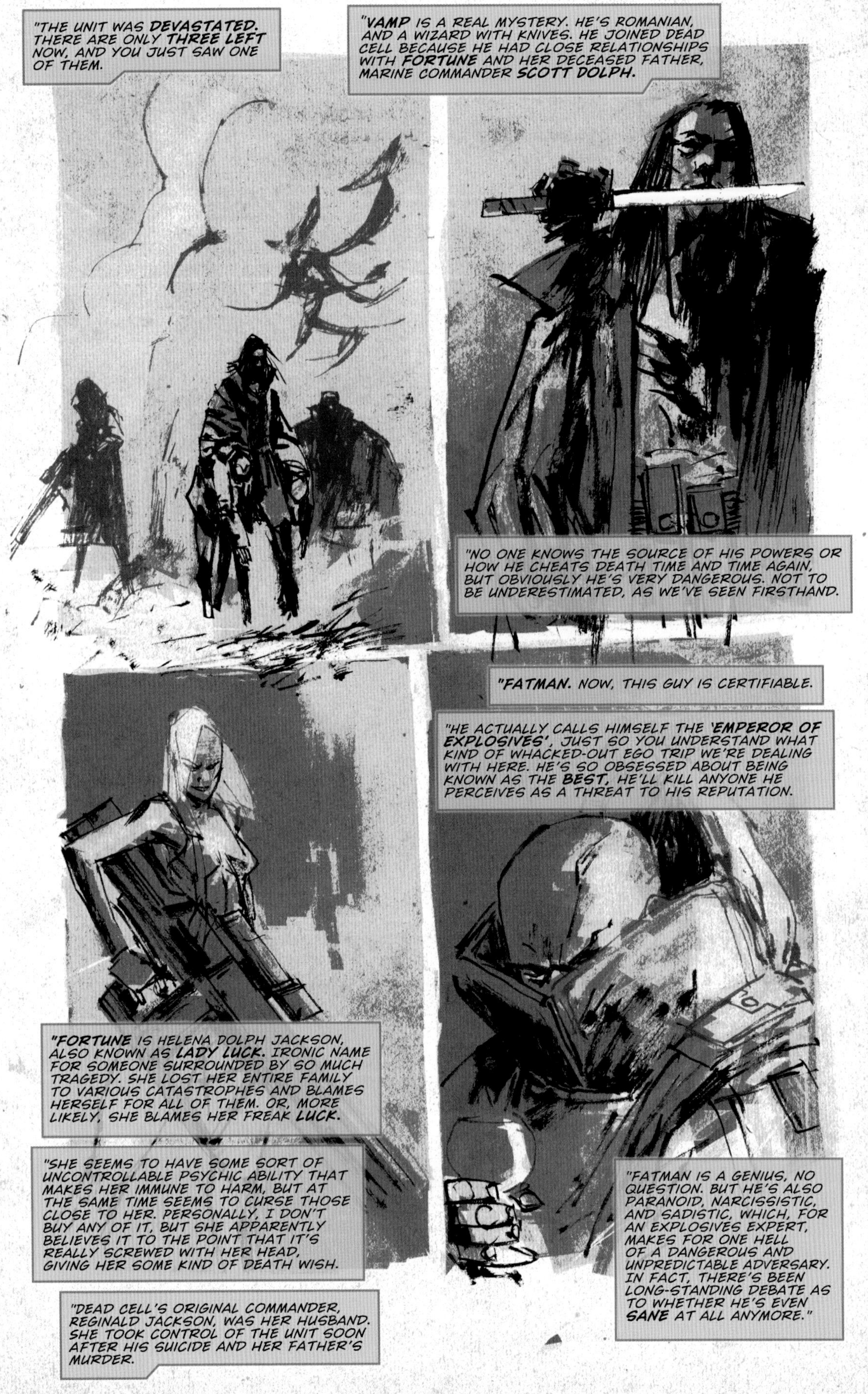
"THE UNIT WAS DEVASTATED. THERE ARE ONLY THREE LEFT NOW, AND YOU JUST SAW ONE OF THEM.
"VAMP IS A REAL MYSTERY. HE'S ROMANIAN, AND A WIZARD WITH KNIVES. HE JOINED DEAD CELL BECAUSE HE HAD CLOSE RELATIONSHIPS WITH FORTUNE AND HER DECEASED FATHER, MARINE COMMANDER SCOTT DOLPH.
"NO ONE KNOWS THE SOURCE OF HIS POWERS OR HOW HE CHEATS DEATH TIME AND TIME AGAIN, BUT OBVIOUSLY HE'S VERY DANGEROUS. NOT TO BE UNDERESTIMATED, AS WE'VE SEEN FIRSTHAND.
"FORTUNE IS HELENA DOLPH JACKSON, ALSO KNOWN AS LADY LUCK. IRONIC NAME FOR SOMEONE SURROUNDED BY SO MUCH TRAGEDY. SHE LOST HER ENTIRE FAMILY TO VARIOUS CATASTROPHES AND BLAMES HERSELF FOR ALL OF THEM. OR, MORE LIKELY, SHE BLAMES HER FREAK LUCK.
"SHE SEEMS TO HAVE SOME SORT OF UNCONTROLLABLE PSYCHIC ABILITY THAT MAKES HER IMMUNE TO HARM, BUT AT THE SAME TIME SEEMS TO CURSE THOSE CLOSE TO HER. PERSONALLY, I DON'T BUY ANY OF IT, BUT SHE APPARENTLY BELIEVES IT TO THE POINT THAT IT'S REALLY SCREWED WITH HER HEAD, GIVING HER SOME KIND OF DEATH WISH.
"DEAD CELL'S ORIGINAL COMMANDER, REGINALD JACKSON, WAS HER HUSBAND. SHE TOOK CONTROL OF THE UNIT SOON AFTER HIS SUICIDE AND HER FATHER'S MURDER.
"FATMAN. NOW, THIS GUY IS CERTIFIABLE.
"HE ACTUALLY CALLS HIMSELF THE 'EMPEROR OF EXPLOSIVES', JUST SO YOU UNDERSTAND WHAT KIND OF WHACKED-OUT EGO TRIP WE'RE DEALING WITH HERE. HE'S SO OBSESSED ABOUT BEING KNOWN AS THE BEST, HE'LL KILL ANYONE HE PERCEIVES AS A THREAT TO HIS REPUTATION.
"FATMAN IS A GENIUS, NO QUESTION. BUT HE'S ALSO PARANOID, NARCISSISTIC, AND SADISTIC, WHICH, FOR AN EXPLOSIVES EXPERT, MAKES FOR ONE HELL OF A DANGEROUS AND UNPREDICTABLE ADVERSARY. IN FACT, THERE'S BEEN LONG-STANDING DEBATE AS TO WHETHER HE'S EVEN SANE AT ALL ANYMORE."

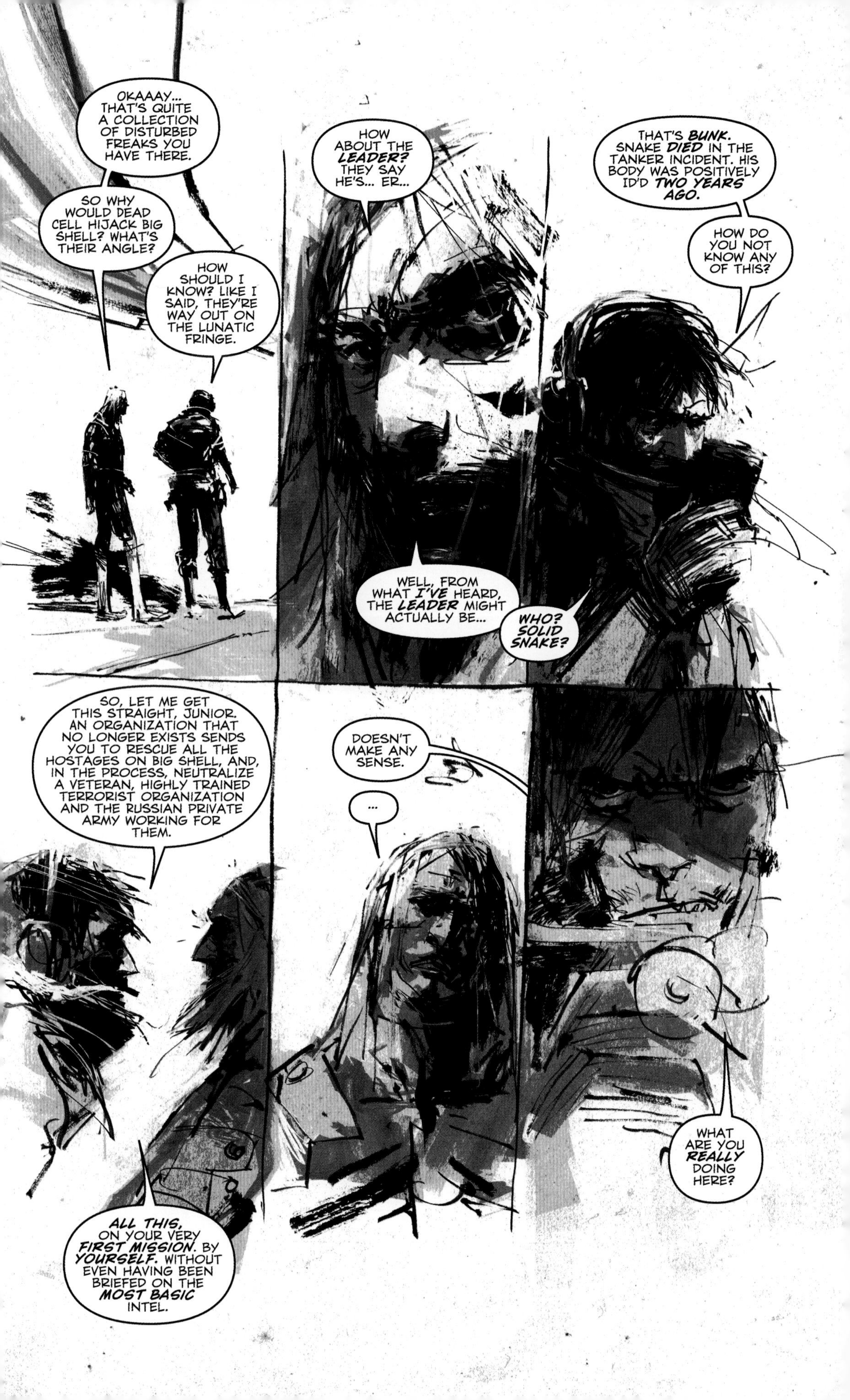
OKAAAY... THAT'S QUITE A COLLECTION OF DISTURBED FREAKS YOU HAVE THERE.
SO WHY WOULD DEAD CELL HIJACK BIG SHELL? WHAT'S THEIR ANGLE?
HOW SHOULD I KNOW? LIKE I SAID, THEY'RE WAY OUT ON THE LUNATIC FRINGE.
HOW ABOUT THE LEADER? THEY SAY HE'S... ER...
WELL, FROM WHAT I'VE HEARD, THE LEADER MIGHT ACTUALLY BE...
WHO? SOLID SNAKE?
THAT'S BUNK. SNAKE DIED IN THE TANKER INCIDENT. HIS BODY WAS POSITIVELY ID'D TWO YEARS AGO.
HOW DO YOU NOT KNOW ANY OF THIS?
SO, LET ME GET THIS STRAIGHT, JUNIOR. AN ORGANIZATION THAT NO LONGER EXISTS SENDS YOU TO RESCUE ALL THE HOSTAGES ON BIG SHELL, AND, IN THE PROCESS, NEUTRALIZE A VETERAN, HIGHLY TRAINED TERRORIST ORGANIZATION AND THE RUSSIAN PRIVATE ARMY WORKING FOR THEM.
ALL THIS, ON YOUR VERY FIRST MISSION. BY YOURSELF. WITHOUT EVEN HAVING BEEN BRIEFED ON THE MOST BASIC INTEL.
DOESN'T MAKE ANY SENSE.
...
WHAT ARE YOU REALLY DOING HERE?

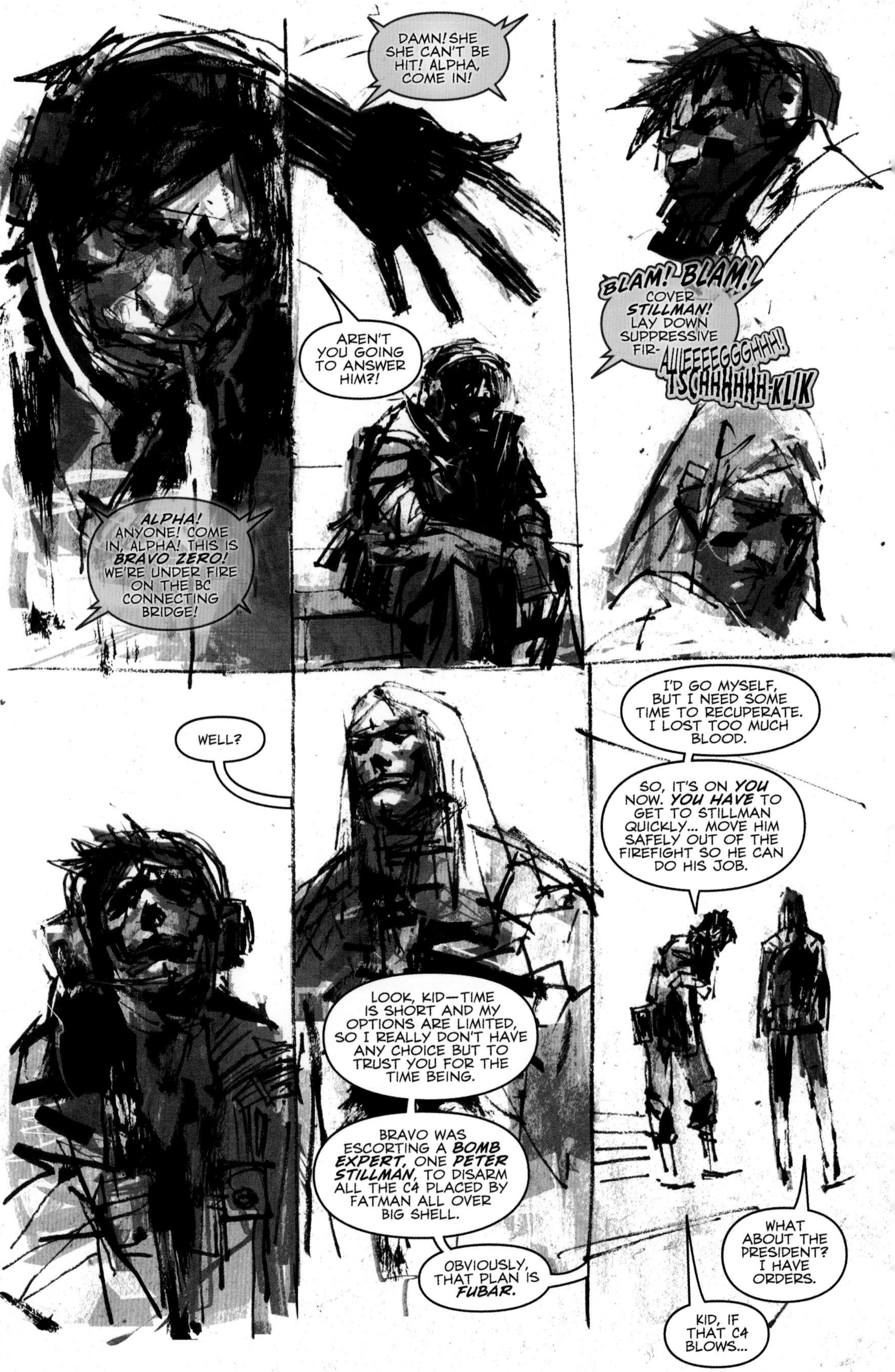
ALPHA! ANYONE! COME IN, ALPHA! THIS IS BRAVO ZERO! WE'RE UNDER FIRE ON THE BC CONNECTING BRIDGE!
DAMN! SHE SHE CAN'T BE HIT! ALPHA, COME IN!
AREN'T YOU GOING TO ANSWER HIM?!
BLAM! BLAM!
COVER STILLMAN! LAY DOWN SUPPRESSIVE FIR-
AIIEEEEGGGHHH!
TSCHHHHHH-KLIK
WELL?
LOOK, KID—TIME IS SHORT AND MY OPTIONS ARE LIMITED, SO I REALLY DON'T HAVE ANY CHOICE BUT TO TRUST YOU FOR THE TIME BEING.
BRAVO WAS ESCORTING A BOMB EXPERT, ONE PETER STILLMAN, TO DISARM ALL THE C4 PLACED BY FATMAN ALL OVER BIG SHELL.
OBVIOUSLY, THAT PLAN IS FUBAR.
I'D GO MYSELF, BUT I NEED SOME TIME TO RECUPERATE. I LOST TOO MUCH BLOOD.
SO, IT'S ON YOU NOW. YOU HAVE TO GET TO STILLMAN QUICKLY... MOVE HIM SAFELY OUT OF THE FIREFIGHT SO HE CAN DO HIS JOB.
WHAT ABOUT THE PRESIDENT? I HAVE ORDERS.
KID, IF THAT C4 BLOWS...

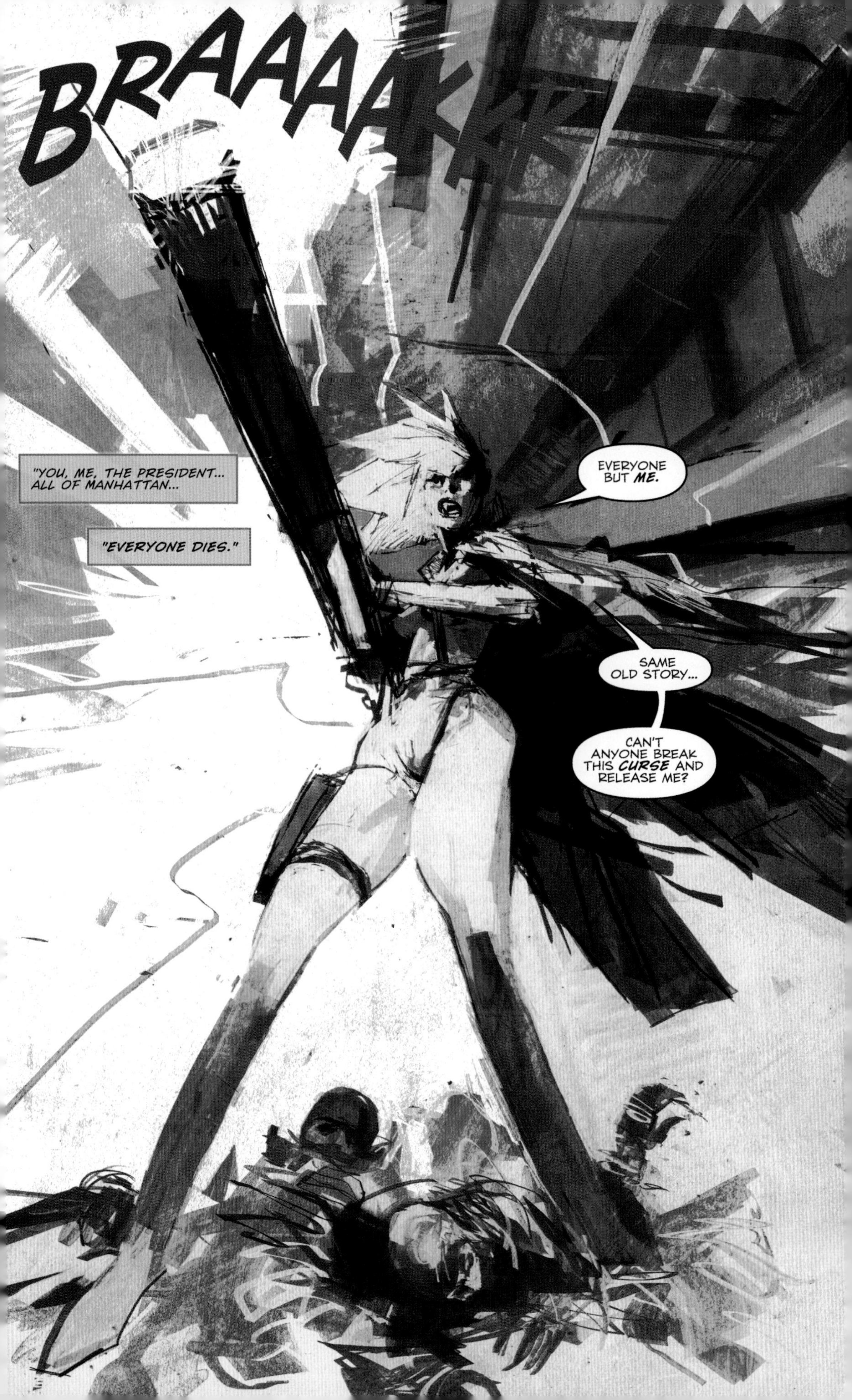
BRAAAAKKK
"YOU, ME, THE PRESIDENT... ALL OF MANHATTAN...
"EVERYONE DIES."
EVERYONE BUT ME.
SAME OLD STORY...
CAN'T ANYONE BREAK THIS CURSE AND RELEASE ME?

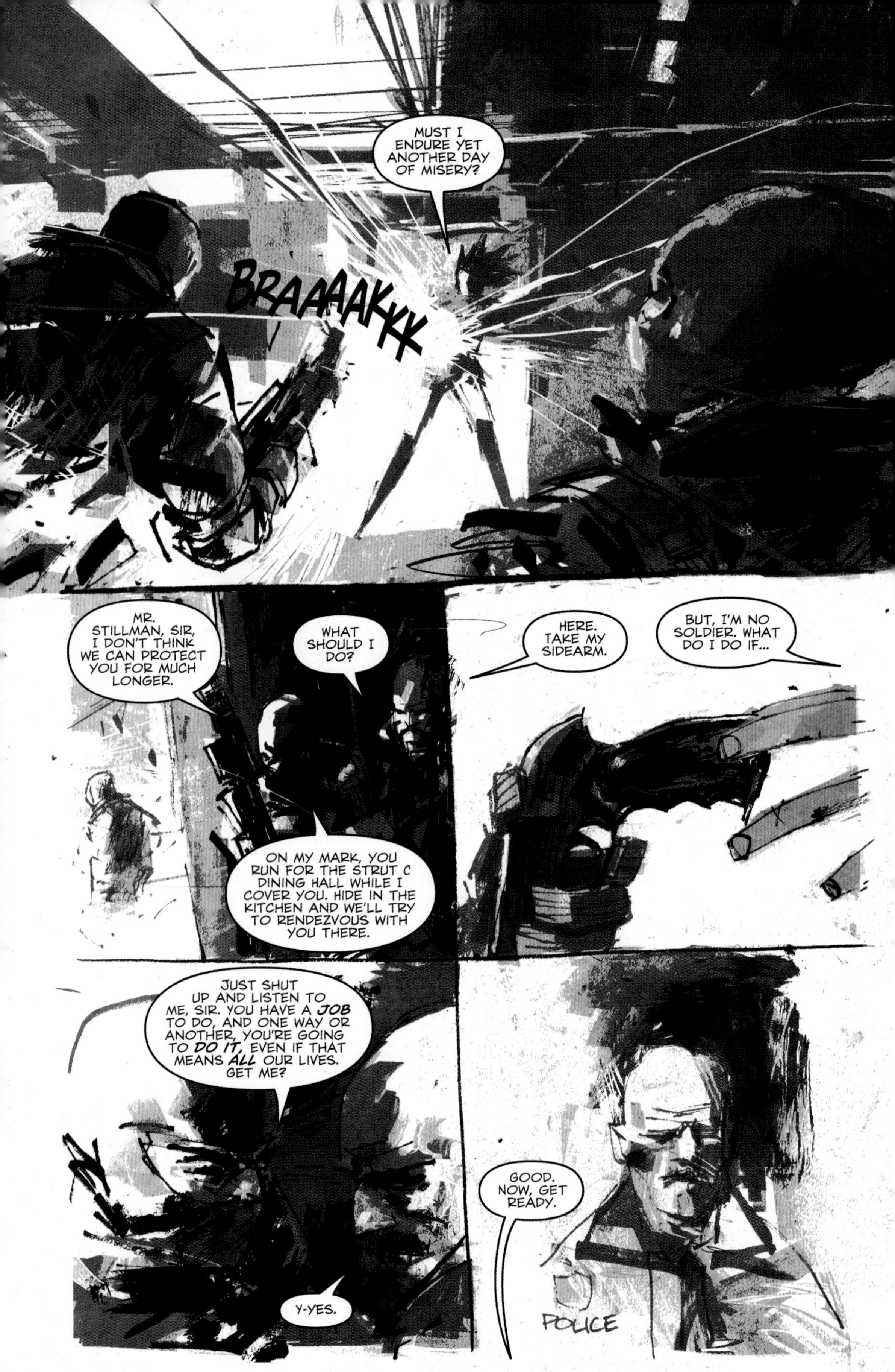
MUST I ENDURE YET ANOTHER DAY OF MISERY?
BRAAAAKKK
MR. STILLMAN, SIR, I DON'T THINK WE CAN PROTECT YOU FOR MUCH LONGER.
WHAT SHOULD I DO?
ON MY MARK, YOU RUN FOR THE STRUT C DINING HALL WHILE I COVER YOU. HIDE IN THE KITCHEN AND WE'LL TRY TO RENDEZVOUS WITH YOU THERE.
HERE. TAKE MY SIDEARM.
BUT, I'M NO SOLDIER. WHAT DO I DO IF...
JUST SHUT UP AND LISTEN TO ME, SIR. YOU HAVE A JOB TO DO, AND ONE WAY OR ANOTHER, YOU'RE GOING TO DO IT, EVEN IF THAT MEANS ALL OUR LIVES. GET ME?
Y-YES.
GOOD. NOW, GET READY.
POLICE

STILLMAN! GO!
BRAAAAKKK
DIE, DAMN YOU! DIE!
BLAM BLAM BLAM BLAM
I WISH.
BRAAAKKK
YOU'RE THE LUCKY ONES TODAY.

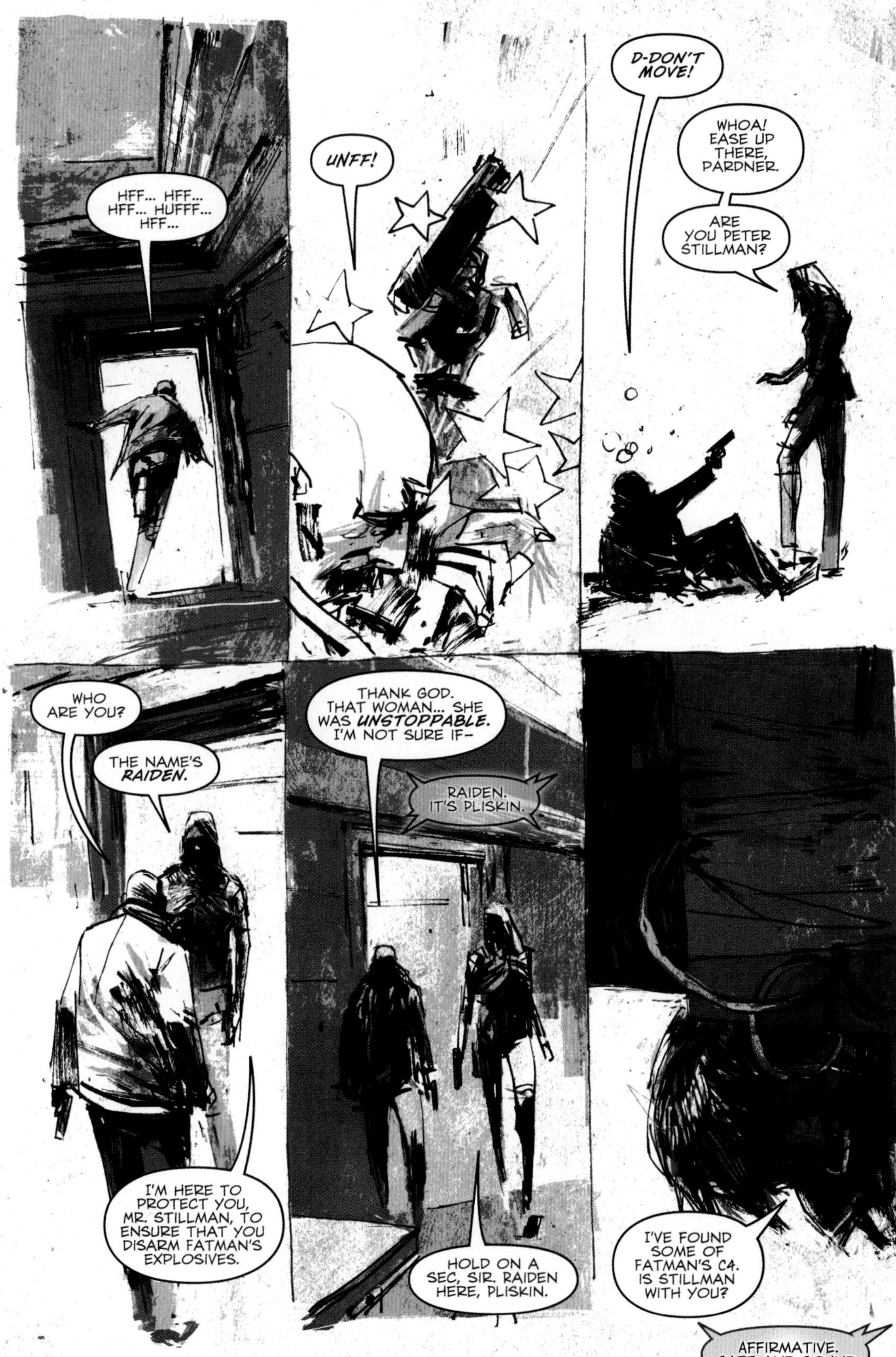
HFF... HFF... HFF... HUFFF... HFF...
UNFF!
D-DON'T MOVE!
WHOA! EASE UP THERE, PARDNER.
ARE YOU PETER STILLMAN?
WHO ARE YOU?
THE NAME'S *RAIDEN.*
I'M HERE TO PROTECT YOU, MR. STILLMAN, TO ENSURE THAT YOU DISARM FATMAN'S EXPLOSIVES.
THANK GOD. THAT WOMAN... SHE WAS *UNSTOPPABLE.* I'M NOT SURE IF–
RAIDEN. IT'S PLISKIN.
HOLD ON A SEC, SIR. RAIDEN HERE, PLISKIN.
I'VE FOUND SOME OF FATMAN'S C4. IS STILLMAN WITH YOU?
AFFIRMATIVE. SAFE AND SOUND.

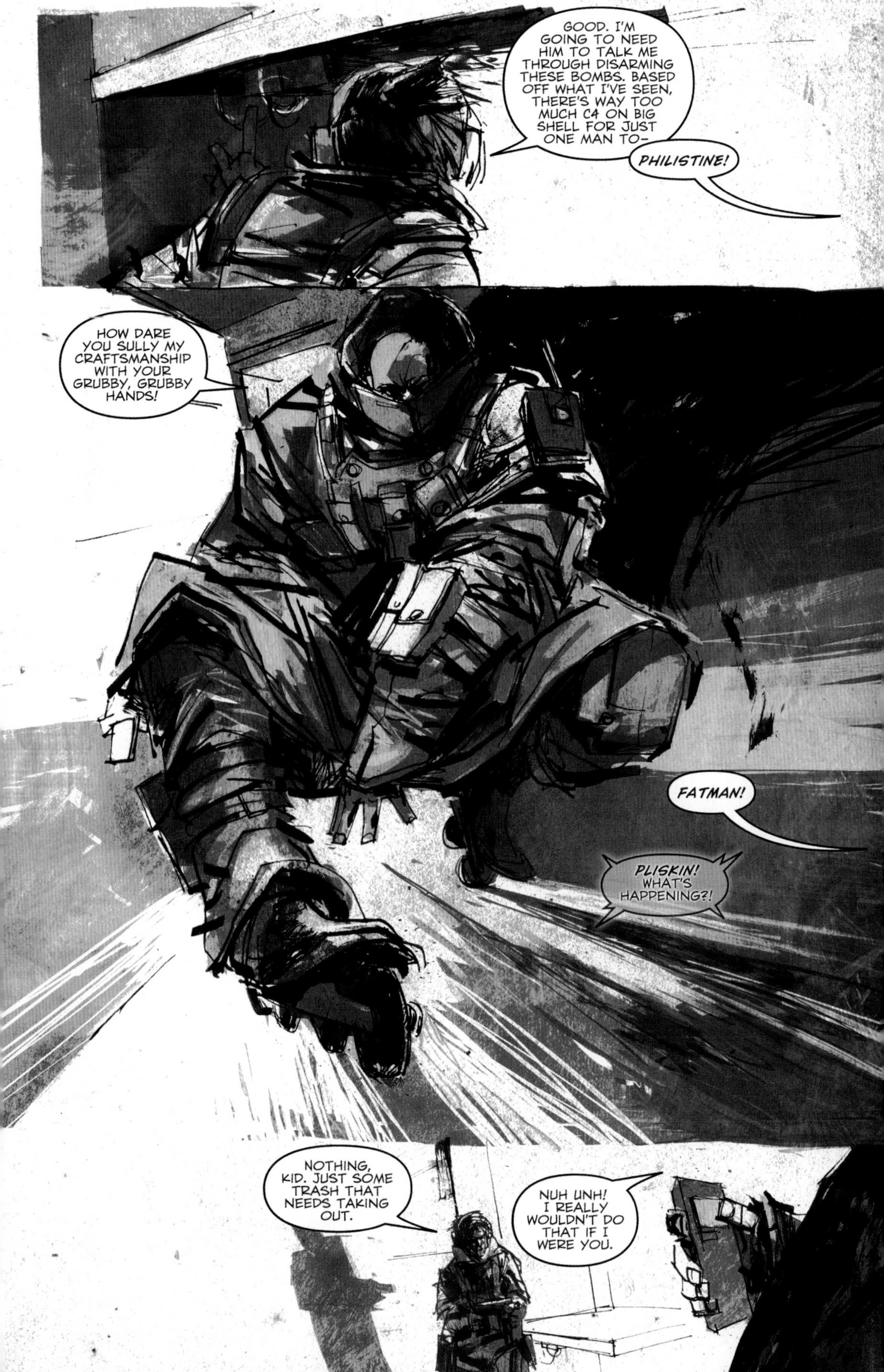

GOOD. I'M GOING TO NEED HIM TO TALK ME THROUGH DISARMING THESE BOMBS. BASED OFF WHAT I'VE SEEN, THERE'S WAY TOO MUCH C4 ON BIG SHELL FOR JUST ONE MAN TO-
PHILISTINE!
HOW DARE YOU SULLY MY CRAFTSMANSHIP WITH YOUR GRUBBY, GRUBBY HANDS!
FATMAN!
PLISKIN! WHAT'S HAPPENING?!
NOTHING, KID. JUST SOME TRASH THAT NEEDS TAKING OUT.
NUH UNH! I REALLY WOULDN'T DO THAT IF I WERE YOU.

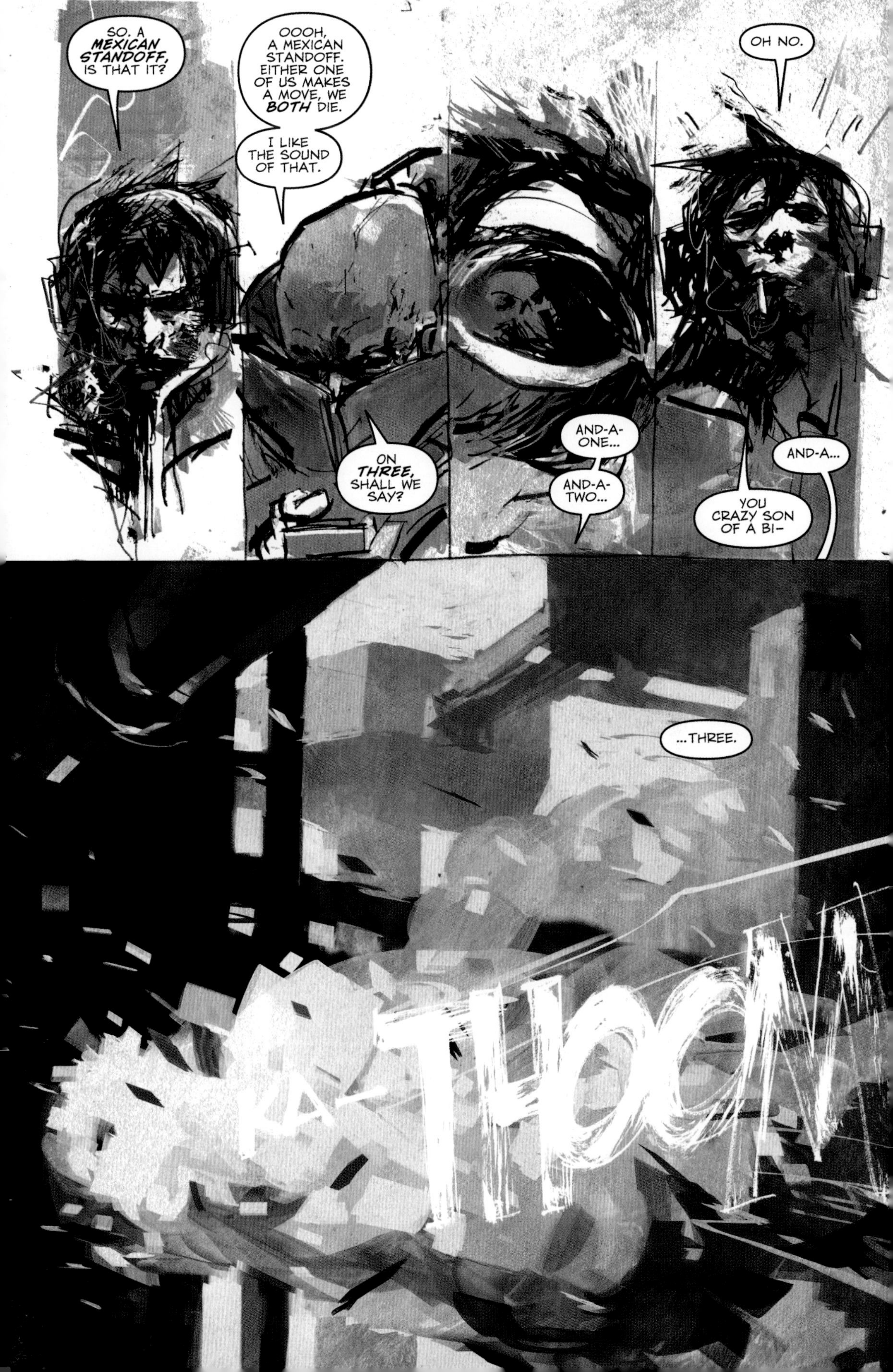
SO. A MEXICAN STANDOFF, IS THAT IT?
OOOH, A MEXICAN STANDOFF. EITHER ONE OF US MAKES A MOVE, WE BOTH DIE.
I LIKE THE SOUND OF THAT.
OH NO.
ON THREE, SHALL WE SAY?
AND-A-ONE...
AND-A-TWO...
AND-A...
YOU CRAZY SON OF A BI–
...THREE.
KA-THOOM

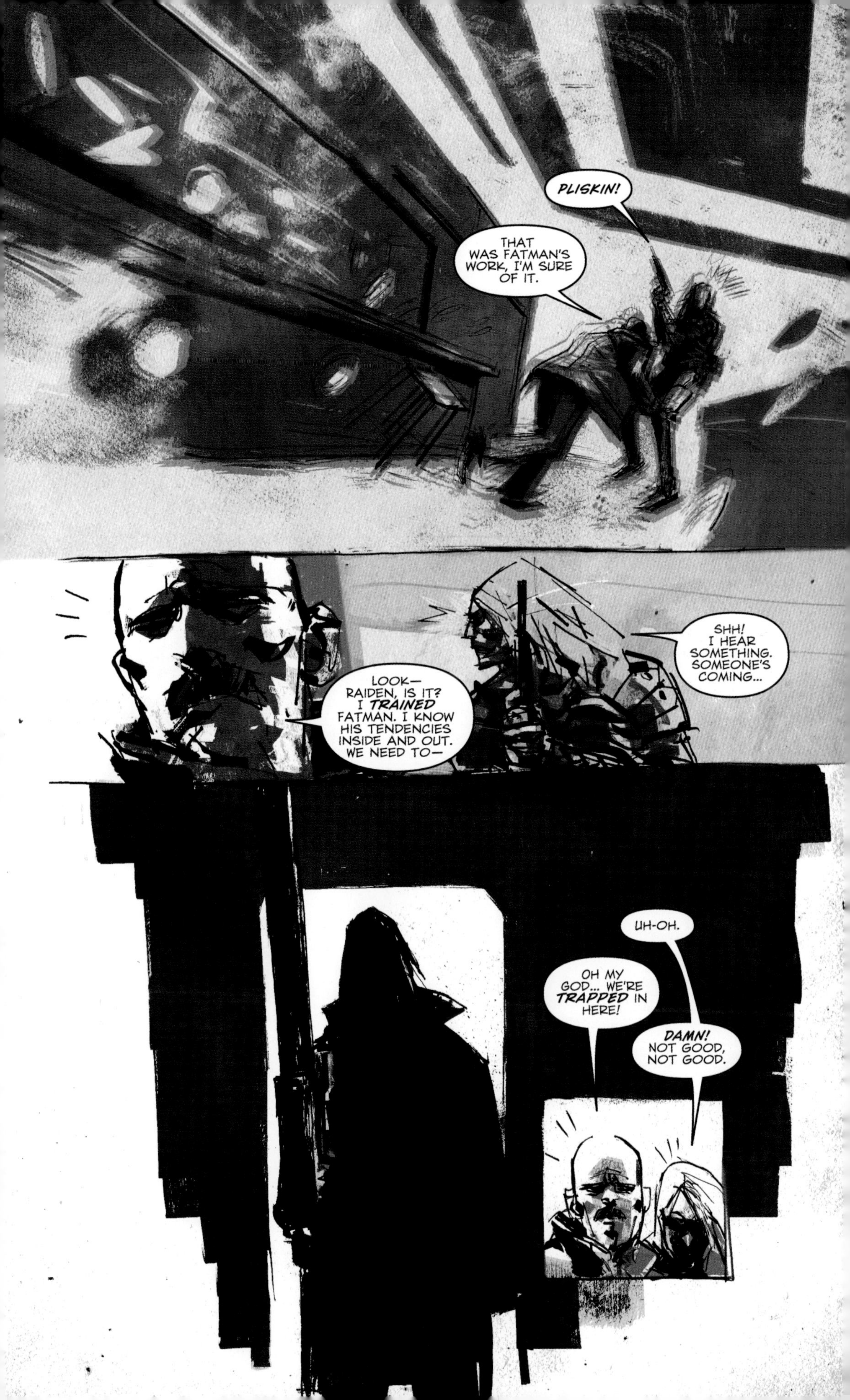
PLISKIN!
THAT WAS FATMAN'S WORK, I'M SURE OF IT.
LOOK— RAIDEN, IS IT? I TRAINED FATMAN. I KNOW HIS TENDENCIES INSIDE AND OUT. WE NEED TO—
SHH! I HEAR SOMETHING. SOMEONE'S COMING...
UH-OH.
OH MY GOD... WE'RE TRAPPED IN HERE!
DAMN! NOT GOOD, NOT GOOD.

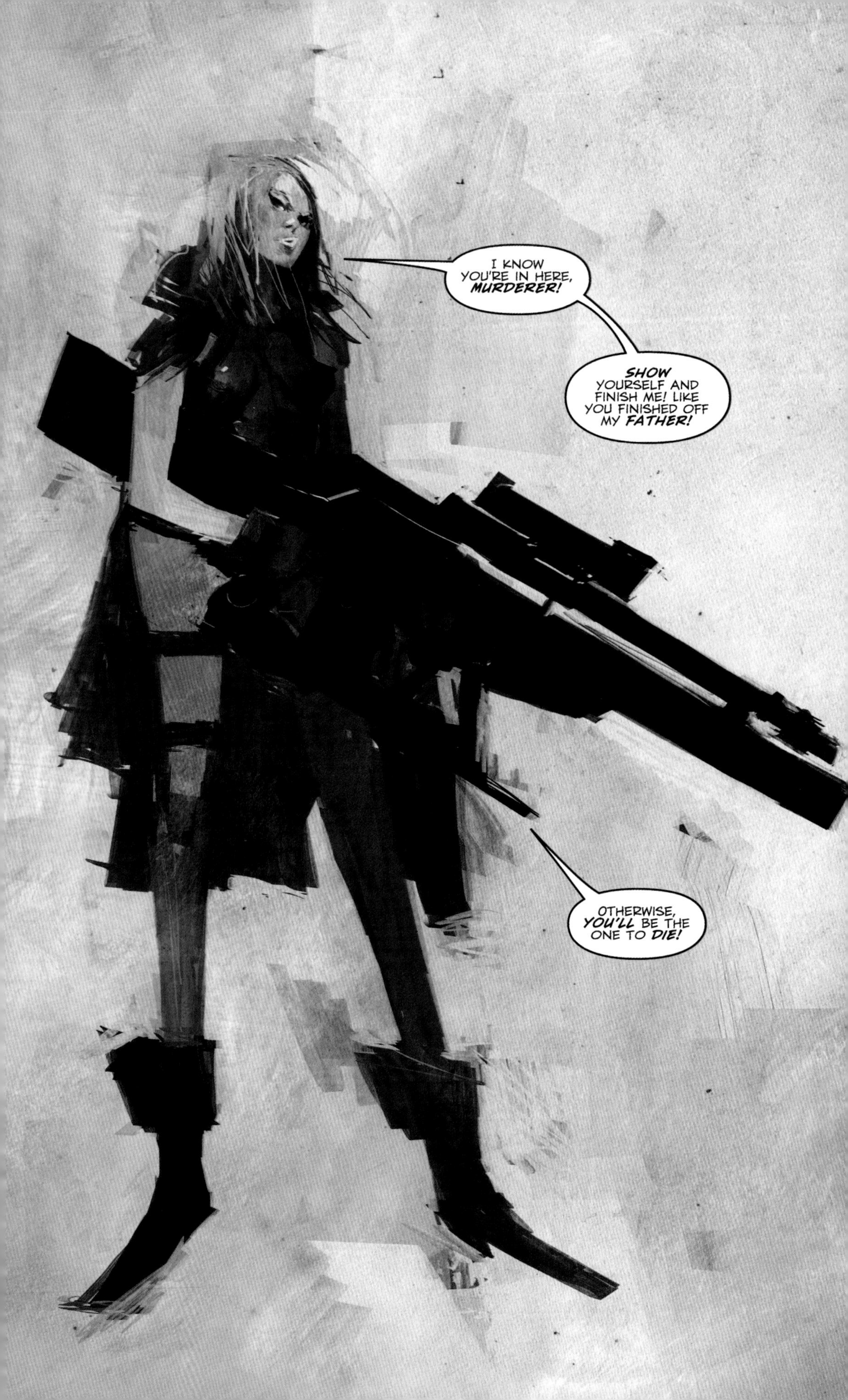
I KNOW YOU'RE IN HERE, **MURDERER!**
SHOW YOURSELF AND FINISH ME! LIKE YOU FINISHED OFF MY **FATHER!**
OTHERWISE, **YOU'LL** BE THE ONE TO **DIE!**

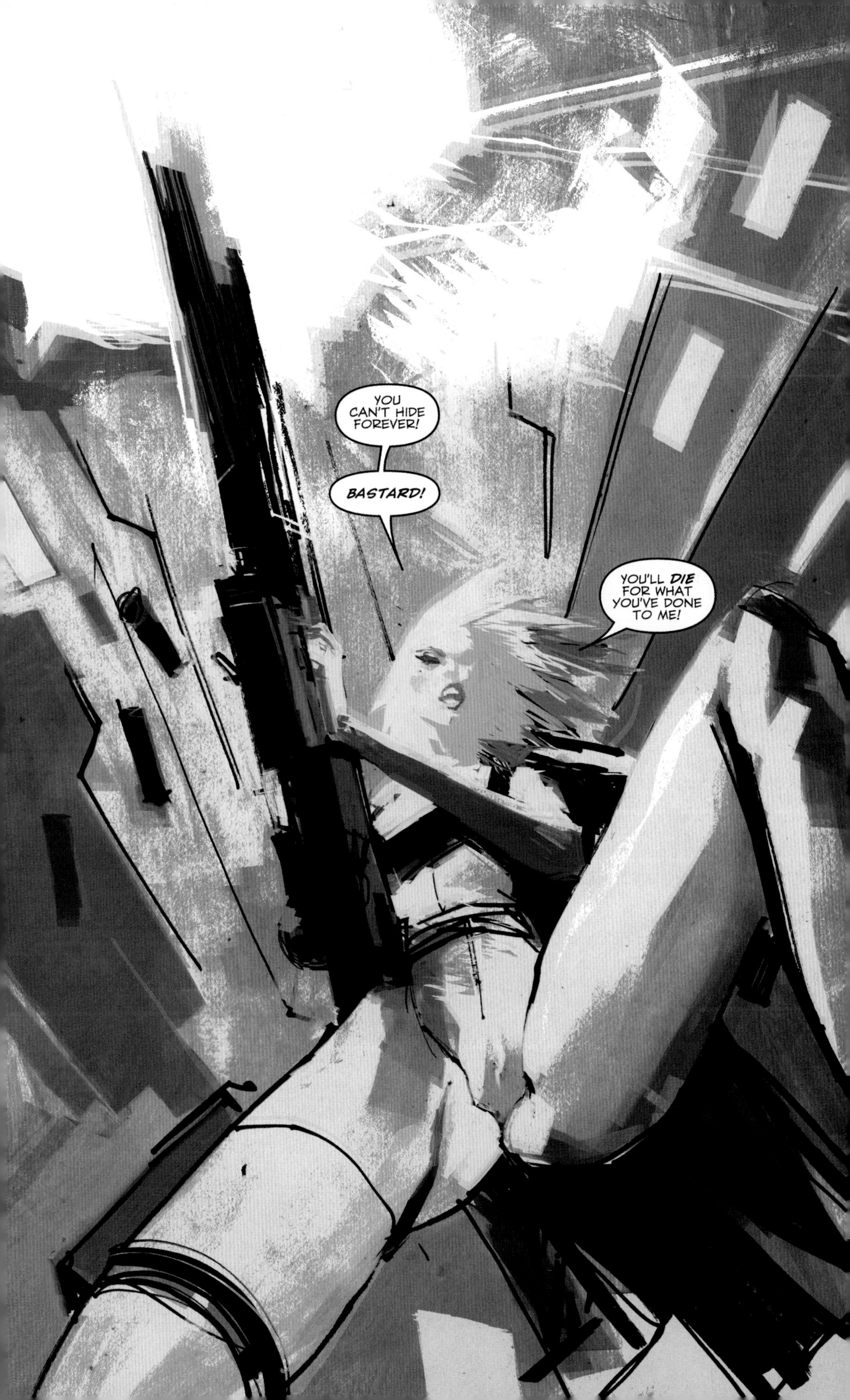
YOU CAN'T HIDE FOREVER!
BASTARD!
YOU'LL DIE FOR WHAT YOU'VE DONE TO ME!

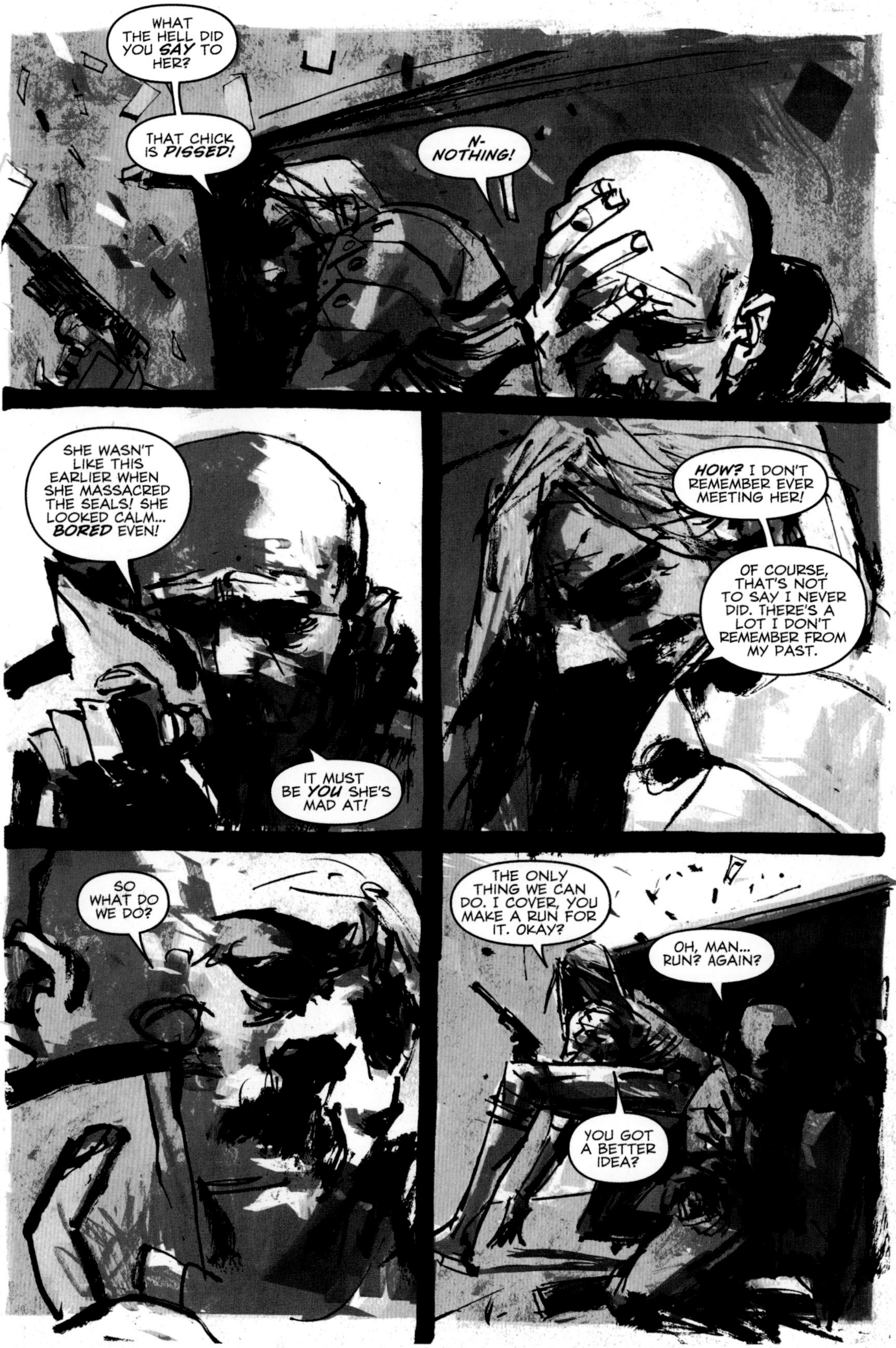
WHAT THE HELL DID YOU *SAY* TO HER?
THAT CHICK IS *PISSED!*
N-NOTHING!
SHE WASN'T LIKE THIS EARLIER WHEN SHE MASSACRED THE SEALS! SHE LOOKED CALM... *BORED* EVEN!
IT MUST BE *YOU* SHE'S MAD AT!
HOW? I DON'T REMEMBER EVER MEETING HER!
OF COURSE, THAT'S NOT TO SAY I NEVER DID. THERE'S A LOT I DON'T REMEMBER FROM MY PAST.
SO WHAT DO WE DO?
THE ONLY THING WE CAN DO. I COVER, YOU MAKE A RUN FOR IT. OKAY?
OH, MAN... RUN? AGAIN?
YOU GOT A BETTER IDEA?

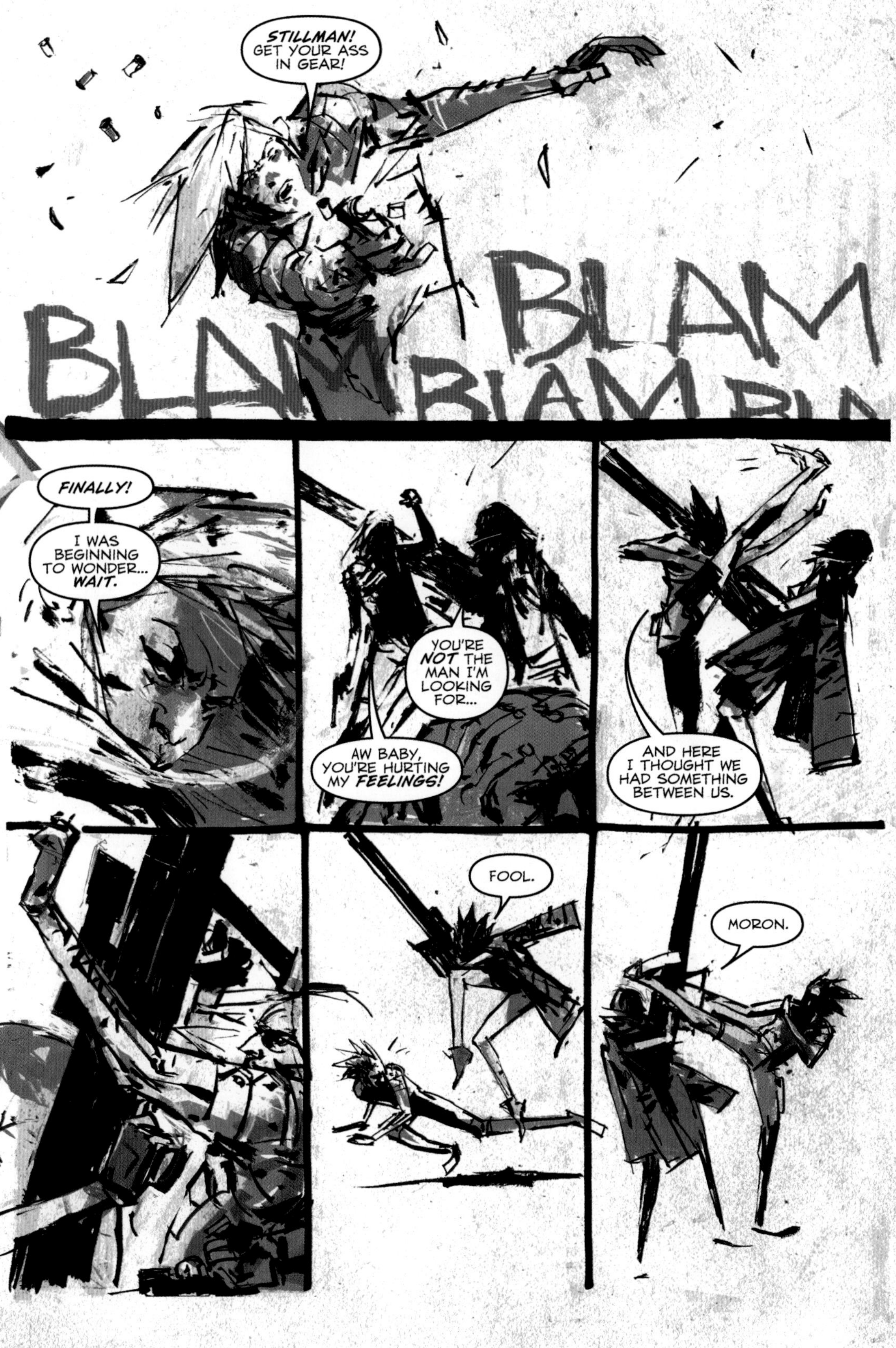
STILLMAN! GET YOUR ASS IN GEAR!
BLAM BLAM BLAM
FINALLY!
I WAS BEGINNING TO WONDER... WAIT.
YOU'RE NOT THE MAN I'M LOOKING FOR...
AW BABY, YOU'RE HURTING MY FEELINGS!
AND HERE I THOUGHT WE HAD SOMETHING BETWEEN US.
FOOL.
MORON.

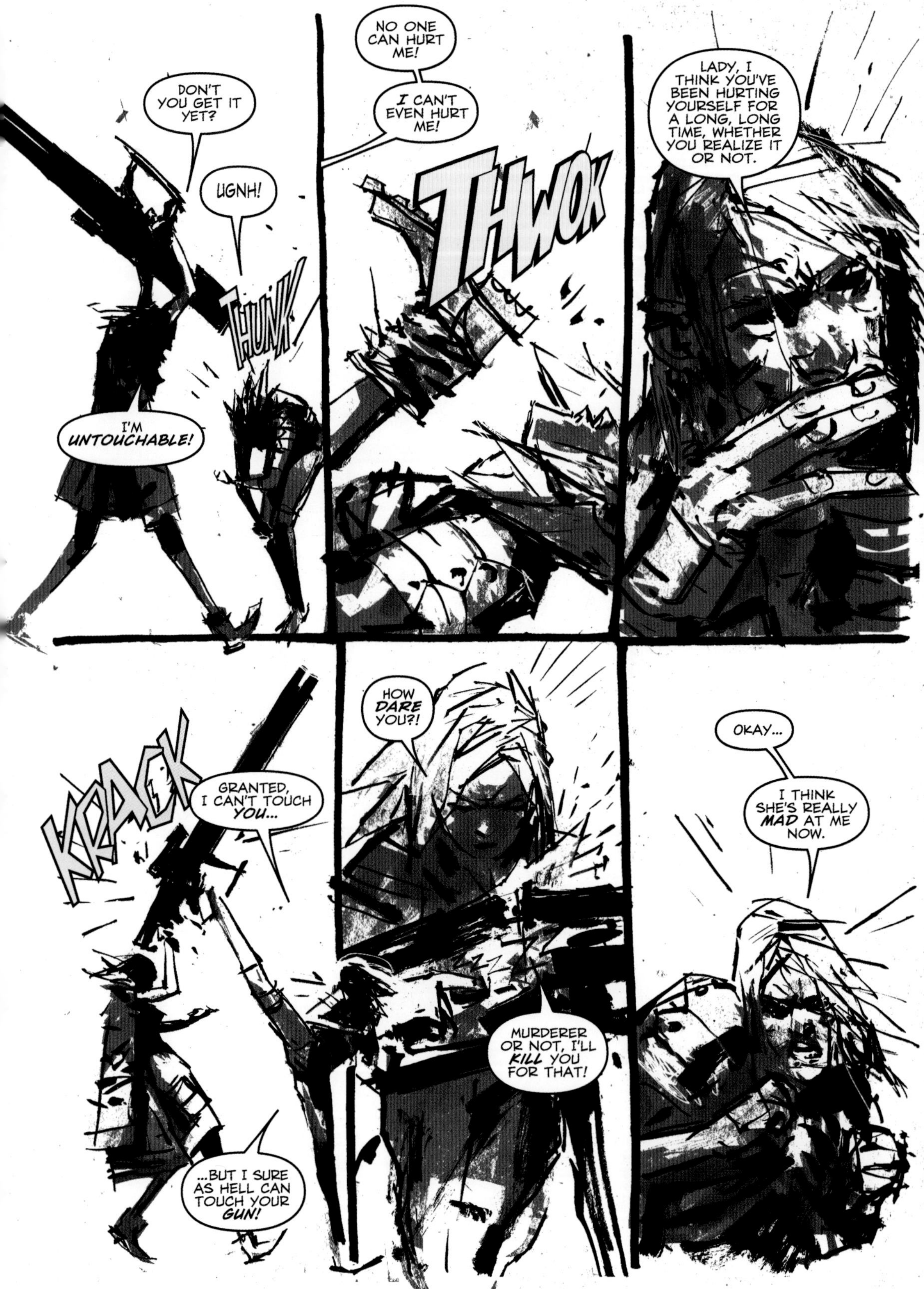
DON'T YOU GET IT YET?
UGNH!
THUNK
I'M UNTOUCHABLE!
NO ONE CAN HURT ME!
I CAN'T EVEN HURT ME!
THWOK
LADY, I THINK YOU'VE BEEN HURTING YOURSELF FOR A LONG, LONG TIME, WHETHER YOU REALIZE IT OR NOT.
KRACK
GRANTED, I CAN'T TOUCH YOU...
...BUT I SURE AS HELL CAN TOUCH YOUR GUN!
HOW DARE YOU?!
MURDERER OR NOT, I'LL KILL YOU FOR THAT!
OKAY...
I THINK SHE'S REALLY MAD AT ME NOW.

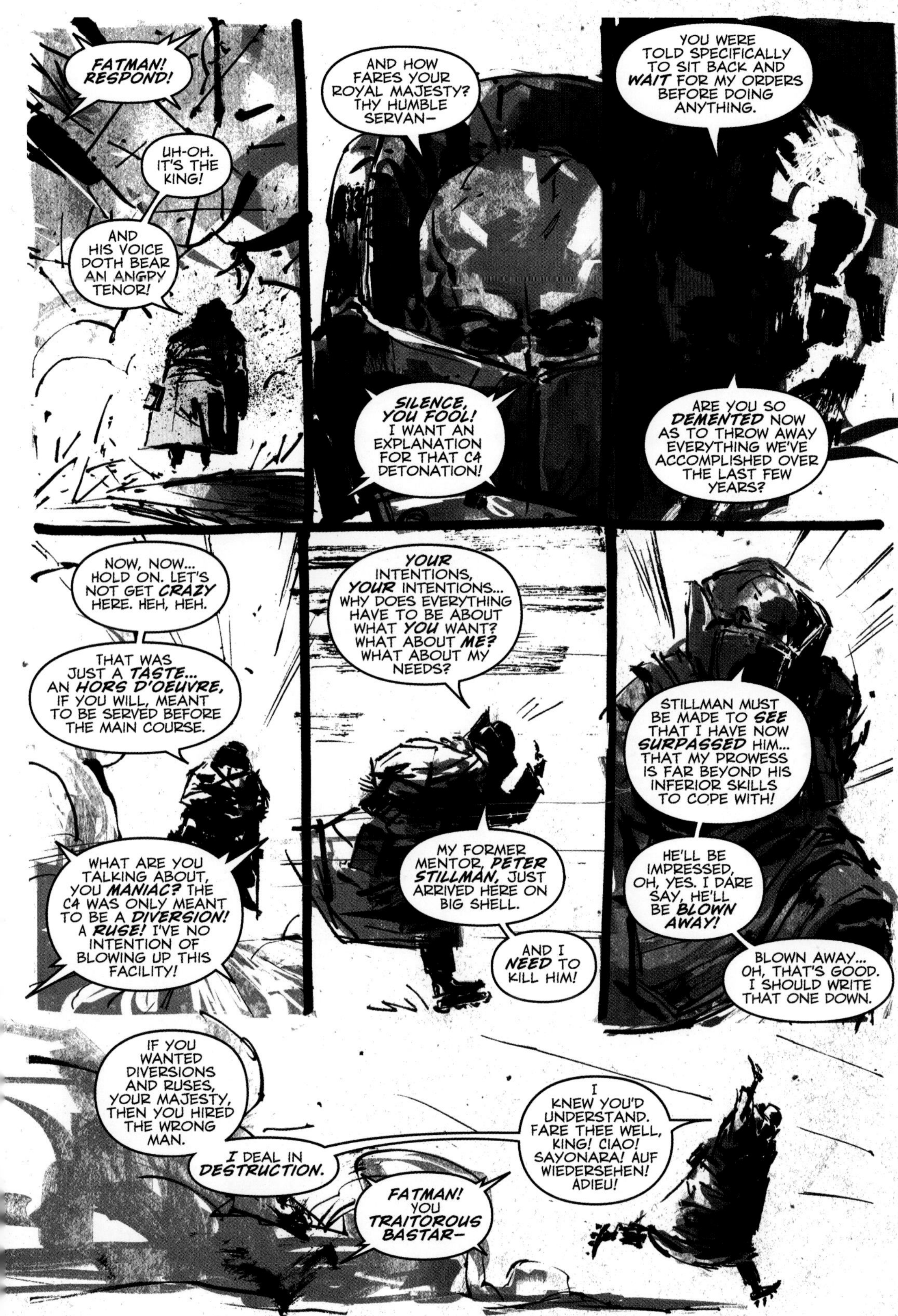
FATMAN! RESPOND!
UH-OH. IT'S THE KING!
AND HIS VOICE DOTH BEAR AN ANGRY TENOR!
AND HOW FARES YOUR ROYAL MAJESTY? THY HUMBLE SERVAN—
SILENCE, YOU FOOL! I WANT AN EXPLANATION FOR THAT C4 DETONATION!
YOU WERE TOLD SPECIFICALLY TO SIT BACK AND WAIT FOR MY ORDERS BEFORE DOING ANYTHING.
ARE YOU SO DEMENTED NOW AS TO THROW AWAY EVERYTHING WE'VE ACCOMPLISHED OVER THE LAST FEW YEARS?
NOW, NOW... HOLD ON. LET'S NOT GET CRAZY HERE. HEH, HEH.
THAT WAS JUST A TASTE... AN HORS D'OEUVRE, IF YOU WILL, MEANT TO BE SERVED BEFORE THE MAIN COURSE.
WHAT ARE YOU TALKING ABOUT, YOU MANIAC? THE C4 WAS ONLY MEANT TO BE A DIVERSION! A RUSE! I'VE NO INTENTION OF BLOWING UP THIS FACILITY!
YOUR INTENTIONS, YOUR INTENTIONS... WHY DOES EVERYTHING HAVE TO BE ABOUT WHAT YOU WANT? WHAT ABOUT ME? WHAT ABOUT MY NEEDS?
MY FORMER MENTOR, PETER STILLMAN, JUST ARRIVED HERE ON BIG SHELL.
AND I NEED TO KILL HIM!
STILLMAN MUST BE MADE TO SEE THAT I HAVE NOW SURPASSED HIM... THAT MY PROWESS IS FAR BEYOND HIS INFERIOR SKILLS TO COPE WITH!
HE'LL BE IMPRESSED, OH, YES. I DARE SAY, HE'LL BE BLOWN AWAY!
BLOWN AWAY... OH, THAT'S GOOD. I SHOULD WRITE THAT ONE DOWN.
IF YOU WANTED DIVERSIONS AND RUSES, YOUR MAJESTY, THEN YOU HIRED THE WRONG MAN.
I DEAL IN DESTRUCTION.
I KNEW YOU'D UNDERSTAND. FARE THEE WELL, KING! CIAO! SAYONARA! AUF WIEDERSEHEN! ADIEU!
FATMAN! YOU TRAITOROUS BASTAR—

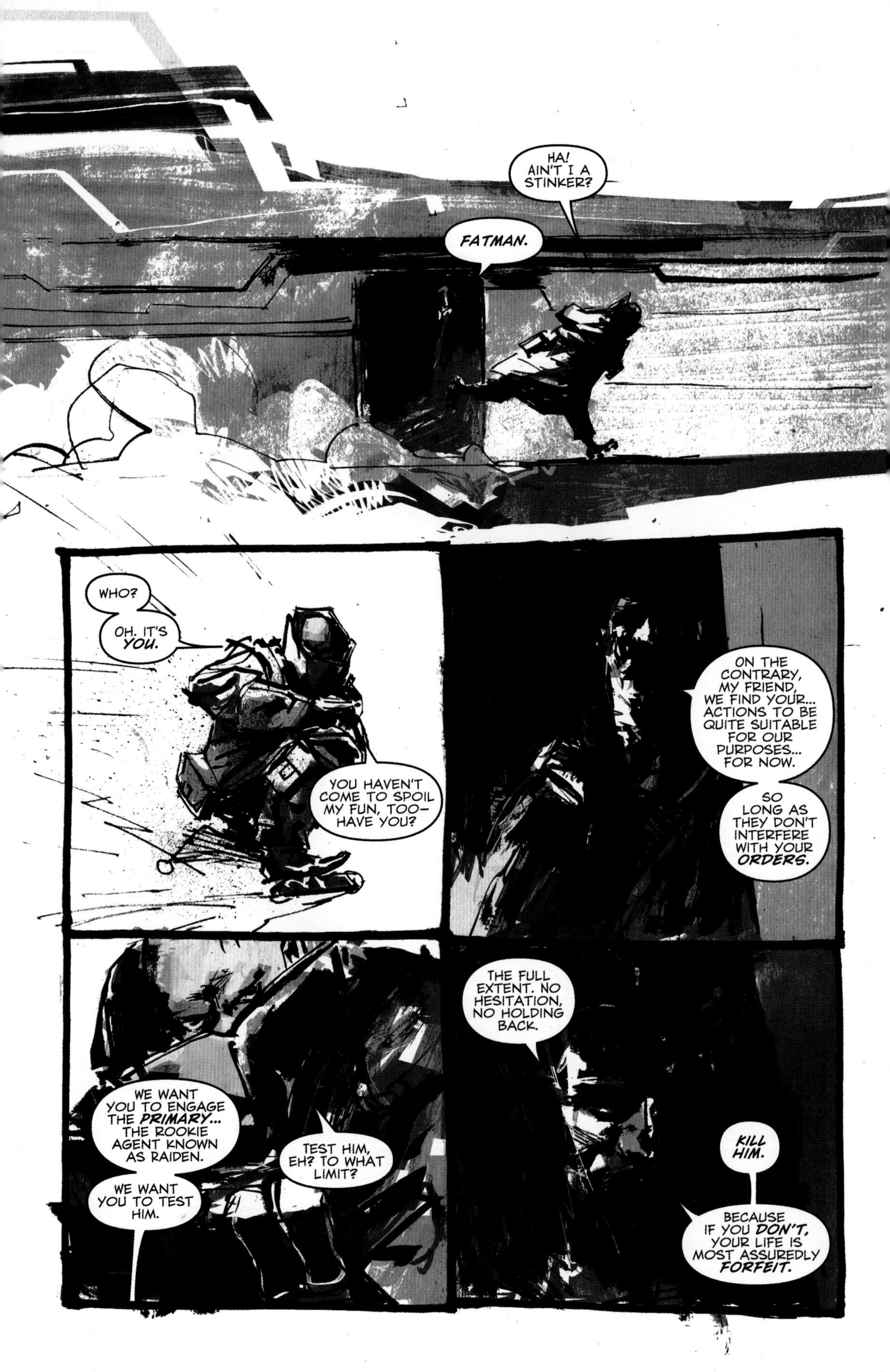
HA! AIN'T I A STINKER?
FATMAN.
WHO?
OH. IT'S *YOU.*
YOU HAVEN'T COME TO SPOIL MY FUN, TOO— HAVE YOU?
ON THE CONTRARY, MY FRIEND, WE FIND YOUR... ACTIONS TO BE QUITE SUITABLE FOR OUR PURPOSES... FOR NOW.
SO LONG AS THEY DON'T INTERFERE WITH YOUR *ORDERS.*
WE WANT YOU TO ENGAGE THE *PRIMARY*... THE ROOKIE AGENT KNOWN AS RAIDEN.
WE WANT YOU TO TEST HIM.
TEST HIM, EH? TO WHAT LIMIT?
THE FULL EXTENT. NO HESITATION, NO HOLDING BACK.
KILL HIM.
BECAUSE IF YOU *DON'T,* YOUR LIFE IS MOST ASSUREDLY *FORFEIT.*

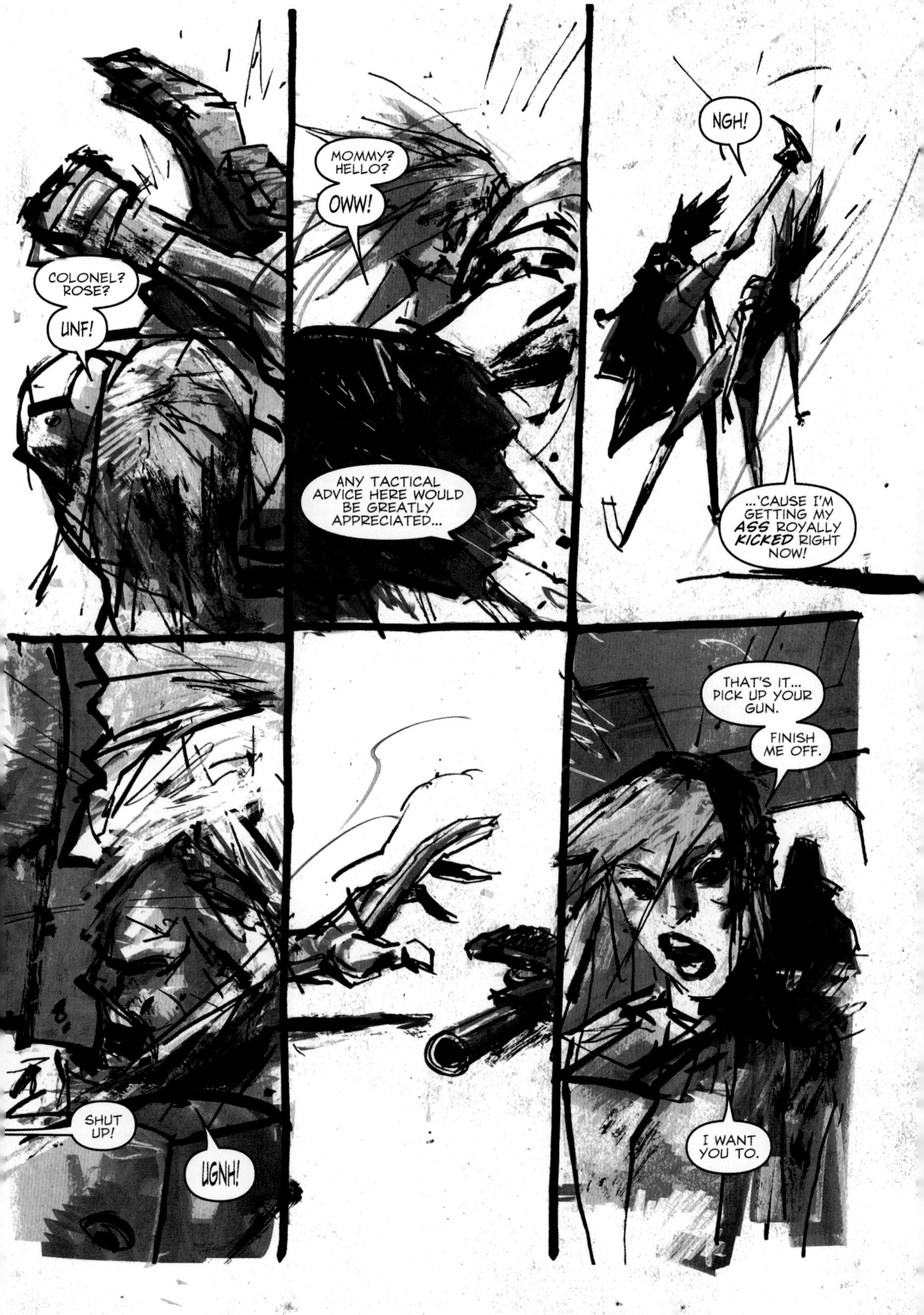
COLONEL? ROSE?
UNF!
MOMMY? HELLO?
OWW!
ANY TACTICAL ADVICE HERE WOULD BE GREATLY APPRECIATED...
NGH!
...'CAUSE I'M GETTING MY ASS ROYALLY KICKED RIGHT NOW!
SHUT UP!
UGNH!
THAT'S IT... PICK UP YOUR GUN.
FINISH ME OFF.
I WANT YOU TO.

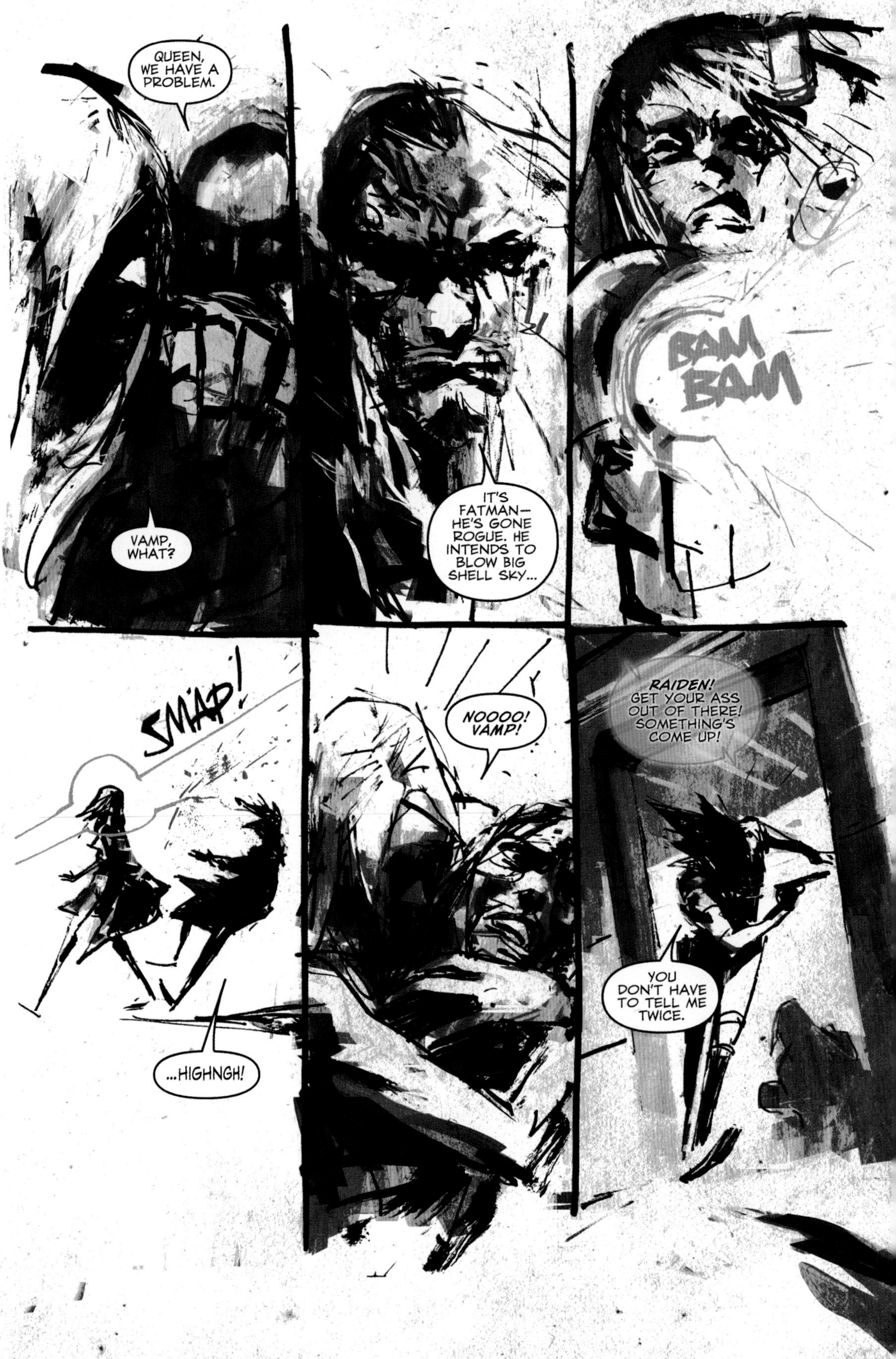
QUEEN, WE HAVE A PROBLEM.
VAMP, WHAT?
IT'S FATMAN— HE'S GONE ROGUE. HE INTENDS TO BLOW BIG SHELL SKY...
BAM BAM
SMAP!
...HIGHNGH!
NOOOO! VAMP!
RAIDEN! GET YOUR ASS OUT OF THERE! SOMETHING'S COME UP!
YOU DON'T HAVE TO TELL ME TWICE.

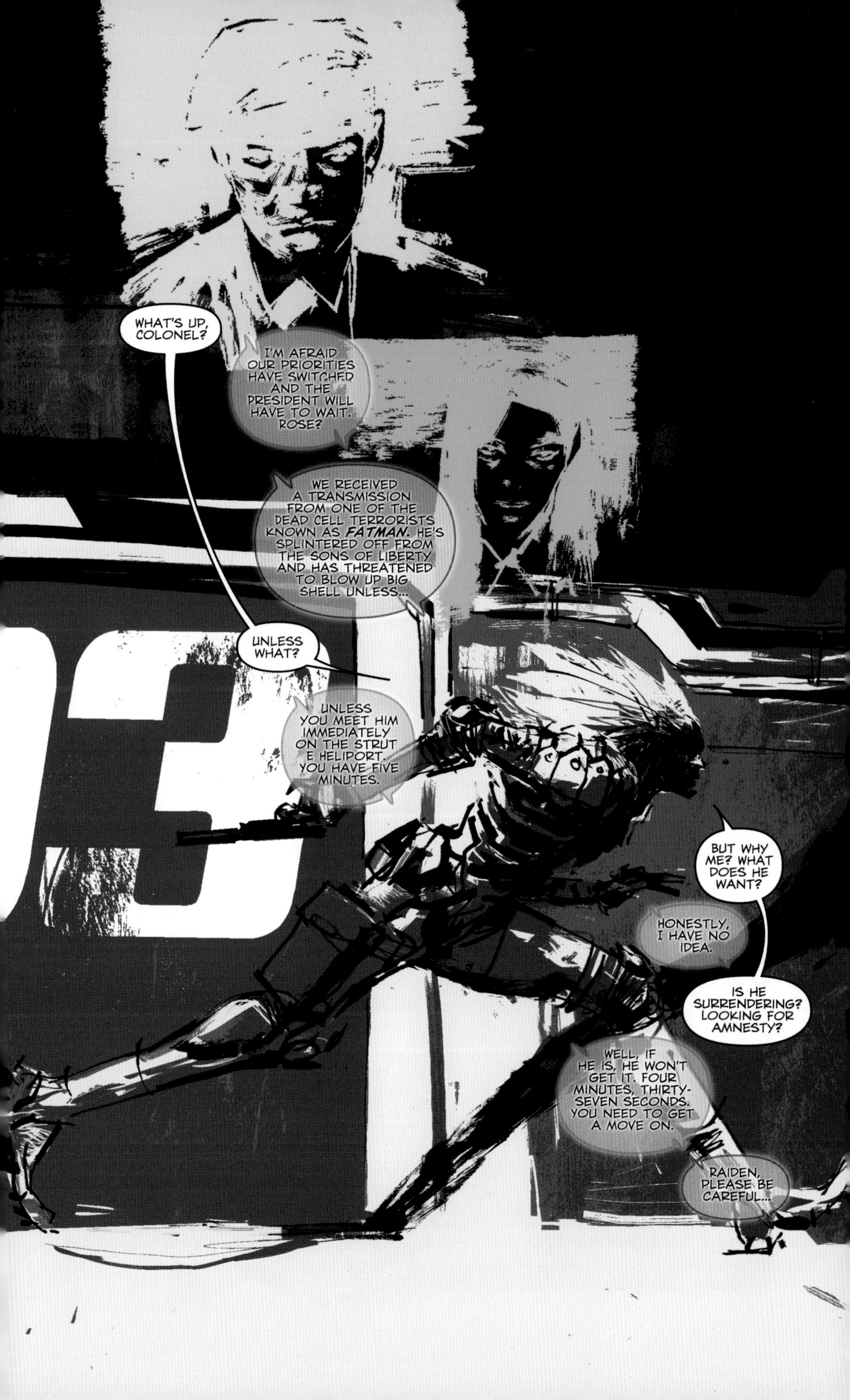

WHAT'S UP, COLONEL?
I'M AFRAID OUR PRIORITIES HAVE SWITCHED AND THE PRESIDENT WILL HAVE TO WAIT. ROSE?
WE RECEIVED A TRANSMISSION FROM ONE OF THE DEAD CELL TERRORISTS KNOWN AS FATMAN. HE'S SPLINTERED OFF FROM THE SONS OF LIBERTY AND HAS THREATENED TO BLOW UP BIG SHELL UNLESS...
UNLESS WHAT?
UNLESS YOU MEET HIM IMMEDIATELY ON THE STRUT E HELIPORT. YOU HAVE FIVE MINUTES.
BUT WHY ME? WHAT DOES HE WANT?
HONESTLY, I HAVE NO IDEA.
IS HE SURRENDERING? LOOKING FOR AMNESTY?
WELL, IF HE IS, HE WON'T GET IT. FOUR MINUTES, THIRTY-SEVEN SECONDS. YOU NEED TO GET A MOVE ON.
RAIDEN, PLEASE BE CAREFUL...

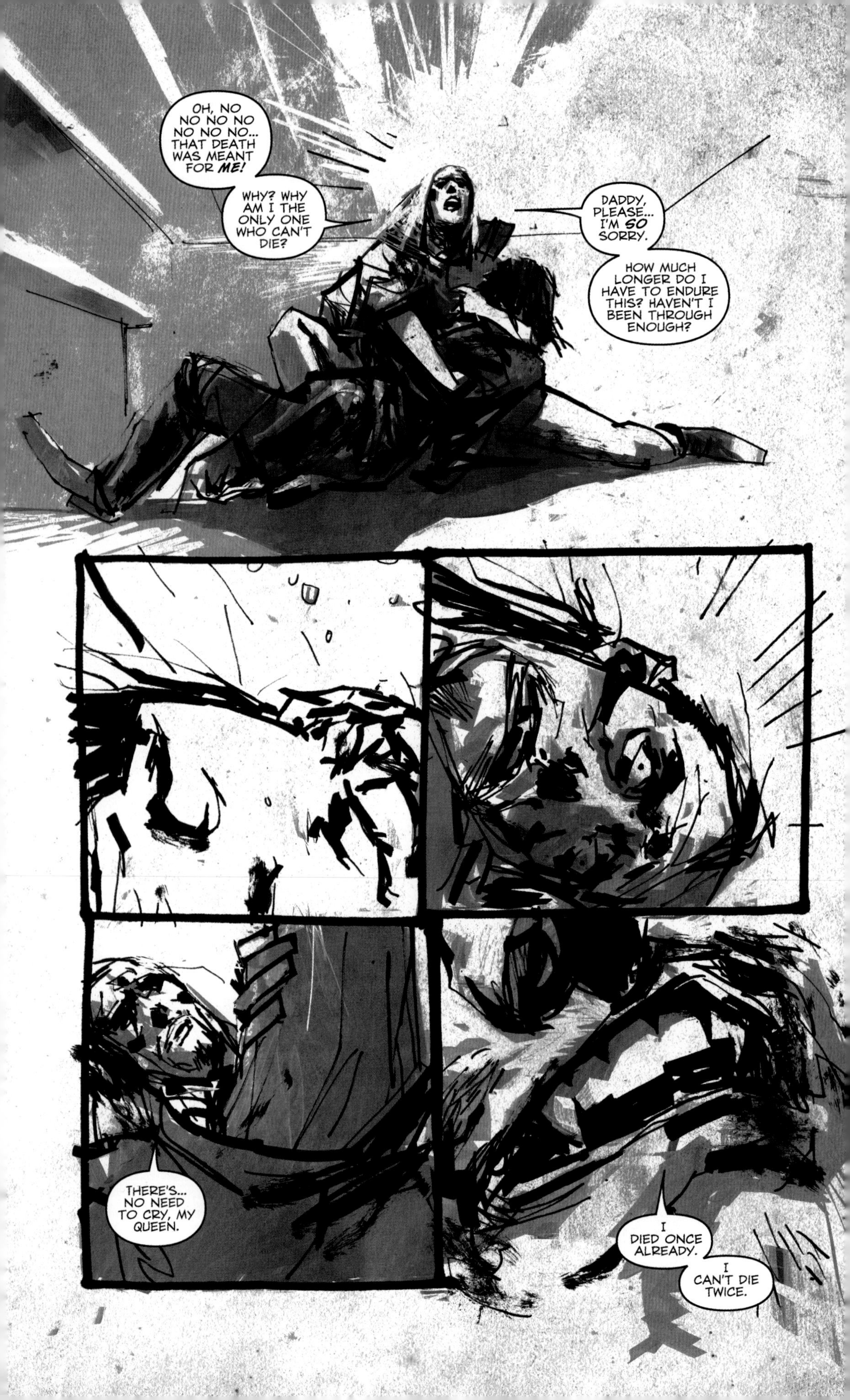
OH, NO NO NO NO NO NO NO... THAT DEATH WAS MEANT FOR *ME!*
WHY? WHY AM I THE ONLY ONE WHO CAN'T DIE?
DADDY, PLEASE... I'M *SO* SORRY.
HOW MUCH LONGER DO I HAVE TO ENDURE THIS? HAVEN'T I BEEN THROUGH ENOUGH?
THERE'S... NO NEED TO CRY, MY QUEEN.
I DIED ONCE ALREADY.
I CAN'T DIE TWICE.

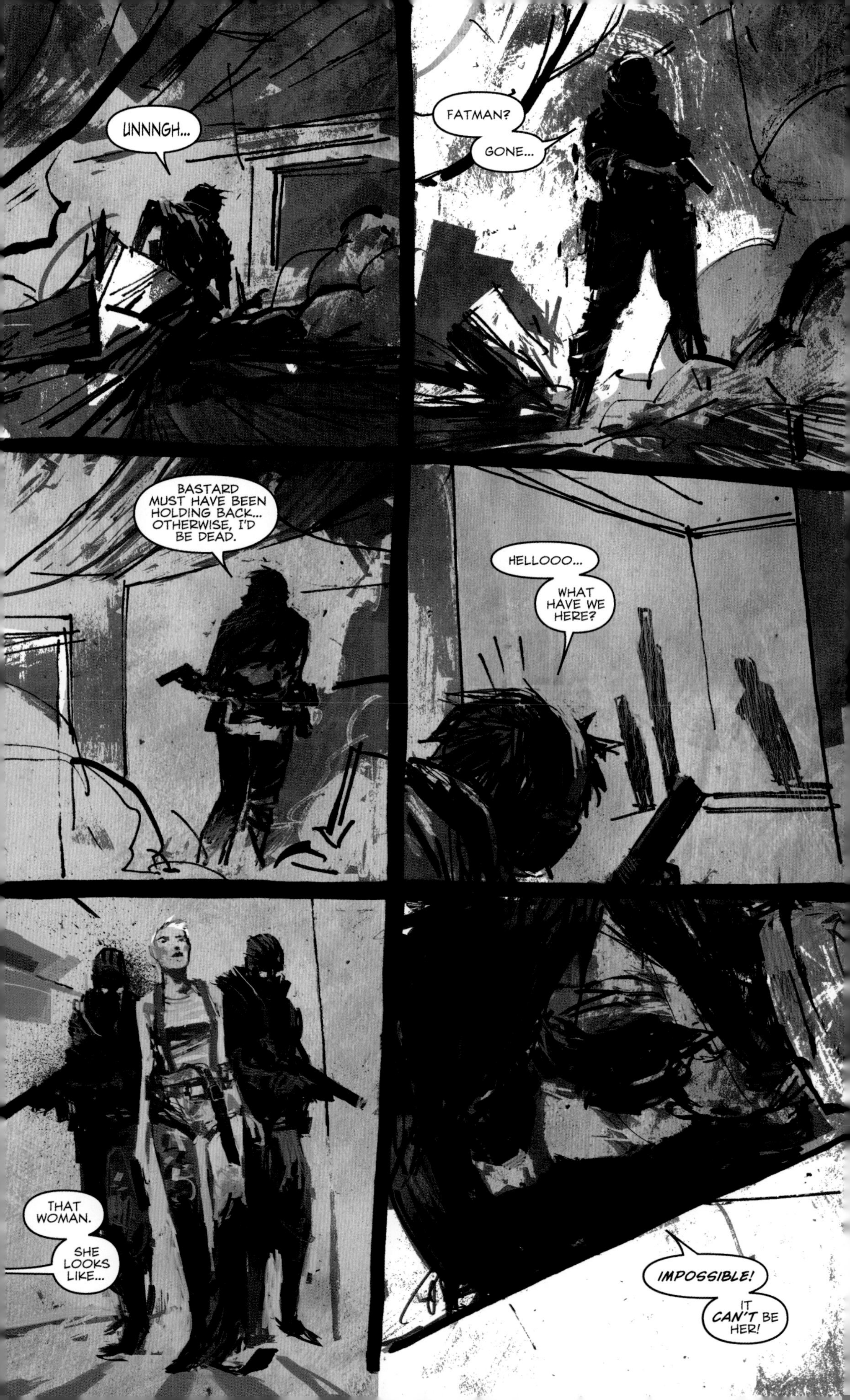
UNNNGH...
FATMAN?
GONE...
BASTARD MUST HAVE BEEN HOLDING BACK... OTHERWISE, I'D BE DEAD.
HELLOOO...
WHAT HAVE WE HERE?
THAT WOMAN.
SHE LOOKS LIKE...
IMPOSSIBLE!
IT *CAN'T* BE HER!

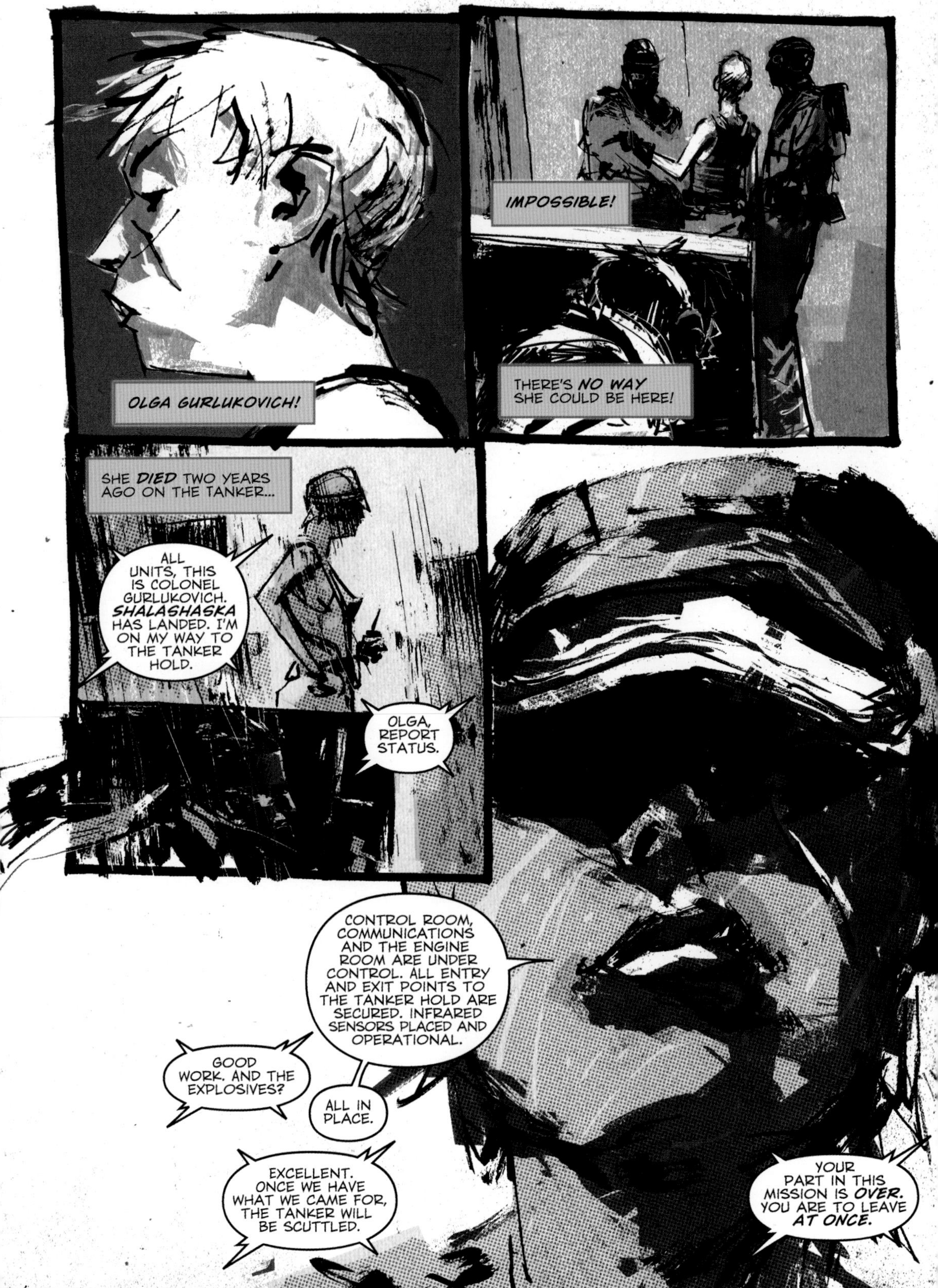
OLGA GURLUKOVICH!
IMPOSSIBLE!
THERE'S NO WAY SHE COULD BE HERE!
SHE DIED TWO YEARS AGO ON THE TANKER...
ALL UNITS, THIS IS COLONEL GURLUKOVICH. SHALASHASKA HAS LANDED. I'M ON MY WAY TO THE TANKER HOLD.
OLGA, REPORT STATUS.
CONTROL ROOM, COMMUNICATIONS AND THE ENGINE ROOM ARE UNDER CONTROL. ALL ENTRY AND EXIT POINTS TO THE TANKER HOLD ARE SECURED. INFRARED SENSORS PLACED AND OPERATIONAL.
GOOD WORK. AND THE EXPLOSIVES?
ALL IN PLACE.
EXCELLENT. ONCE WE HAVE WHAT WE CAME FOR, THE TANKER WILL BE SCUTTLED.
YOUR PART IN THIS MISSION IS OVER. YOU ARE TO LEAVE AT ONCE.

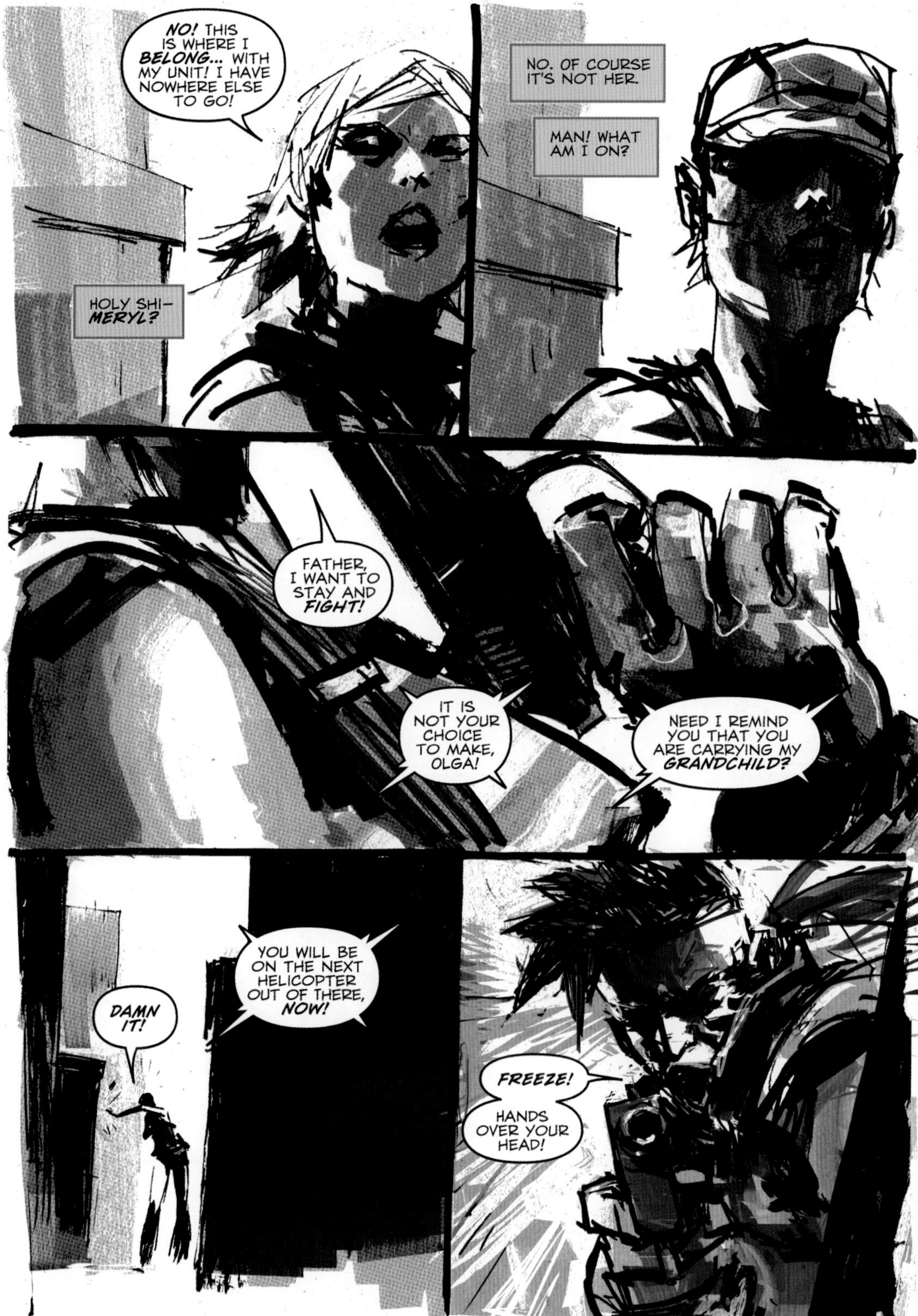
NO! THIS IS WHERE I BELONG... WITH MY UNIT! I HAVE NOWHERE ELSE TO GO!
HOLY SHI— MERYL?
NO. OF COURSE IT'S NOT HER.
MAN! WHAT AM I ON?
FATHER, I WANT TO STAY AND FIGHT!
IT IS NOT YOUR CHOICE TO MAKE, OLGA!
NEED I REMIND YOU THAT YOU ARE CARRYING MY GRANDCHILD?
YOU WILL BE ON THE NEXT HELICOPTER OUT OF THERE, NOW!
DAMN IT!
FREEZE!
HANDS OVER YOUR HEAD!

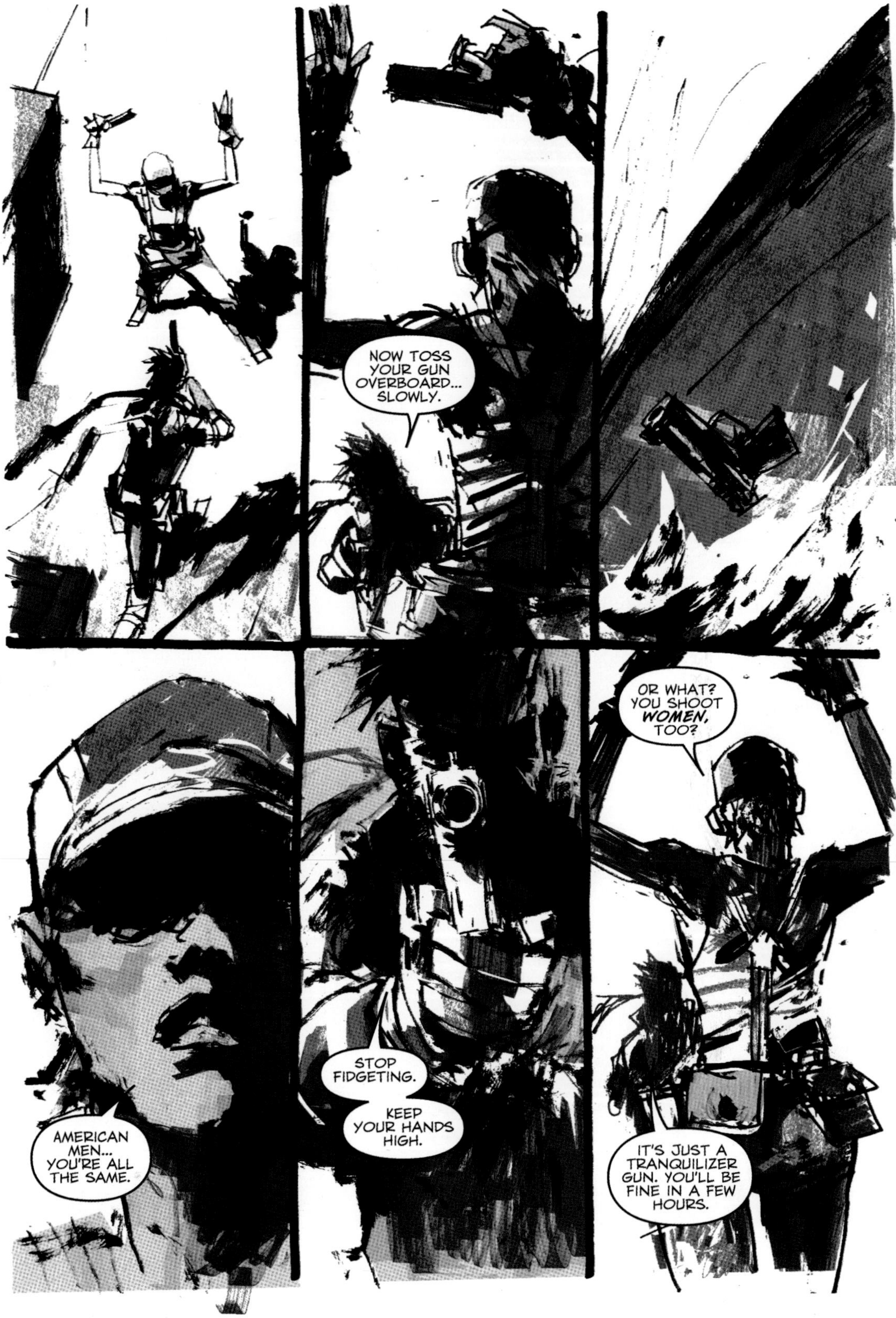
NOW TOSS YOUR GUN OVERBOARD... SLOWLY.
AMERICAN MEN... YOU'RE ALL THE SAME.
STOP FIDGETING.
KEEP YOUR HANDS HIGH.
OR WHAT? YOU SHOOT WOMEN, TOO?
IT'S JUST A TRANQUILIZER GUN. YOU'LL BE FINE IN A FEW HOURS.

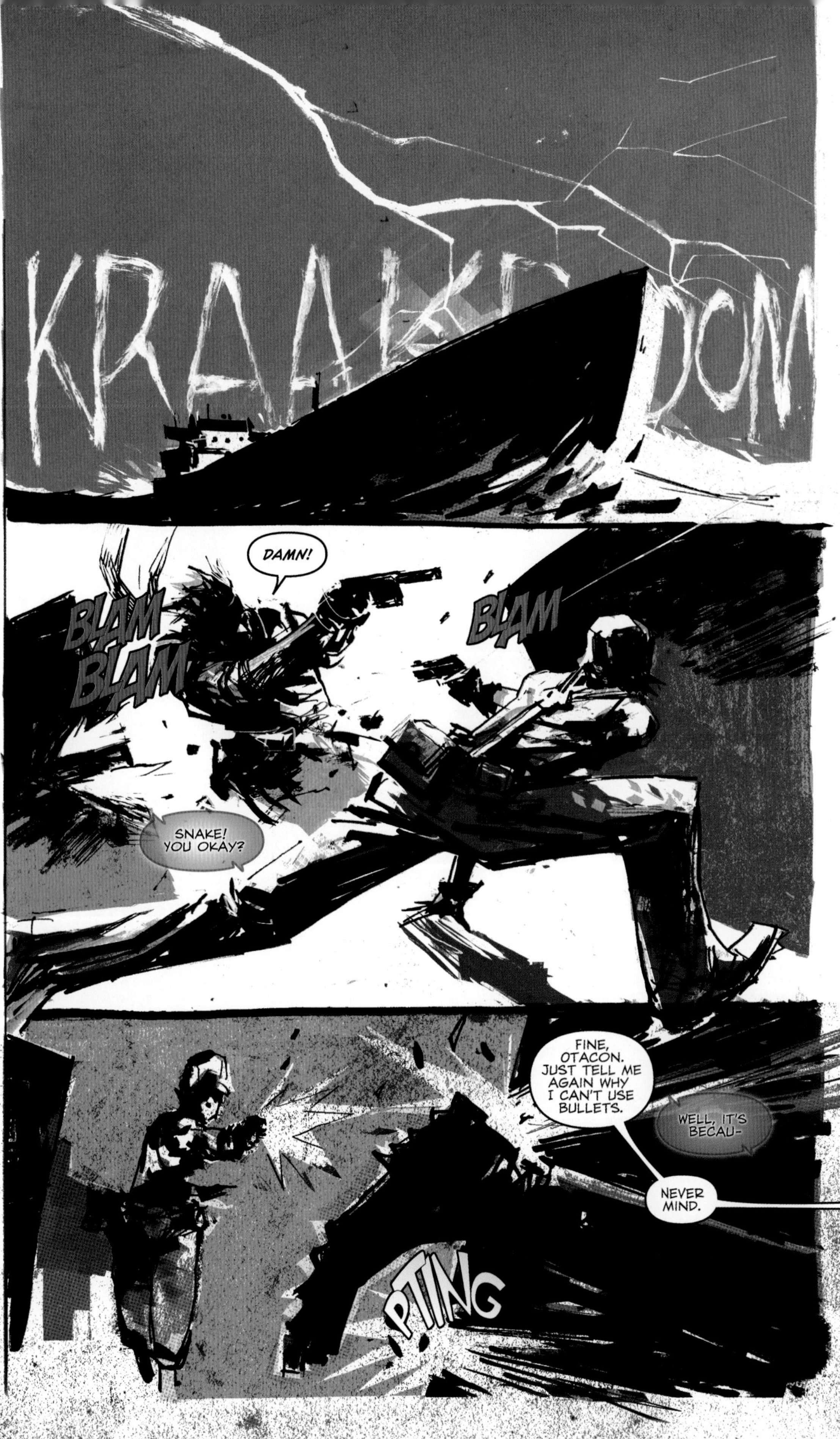
DAMN!
BLAM
BLAM
BLAM
SNAKE! YOU OKAY?
FINE, OTACON. JUST TELL ME AGAIN WHY I CAN'T USE BULLETS.
WELL, IT'S BECAU-
NEVER MIND.
PTING

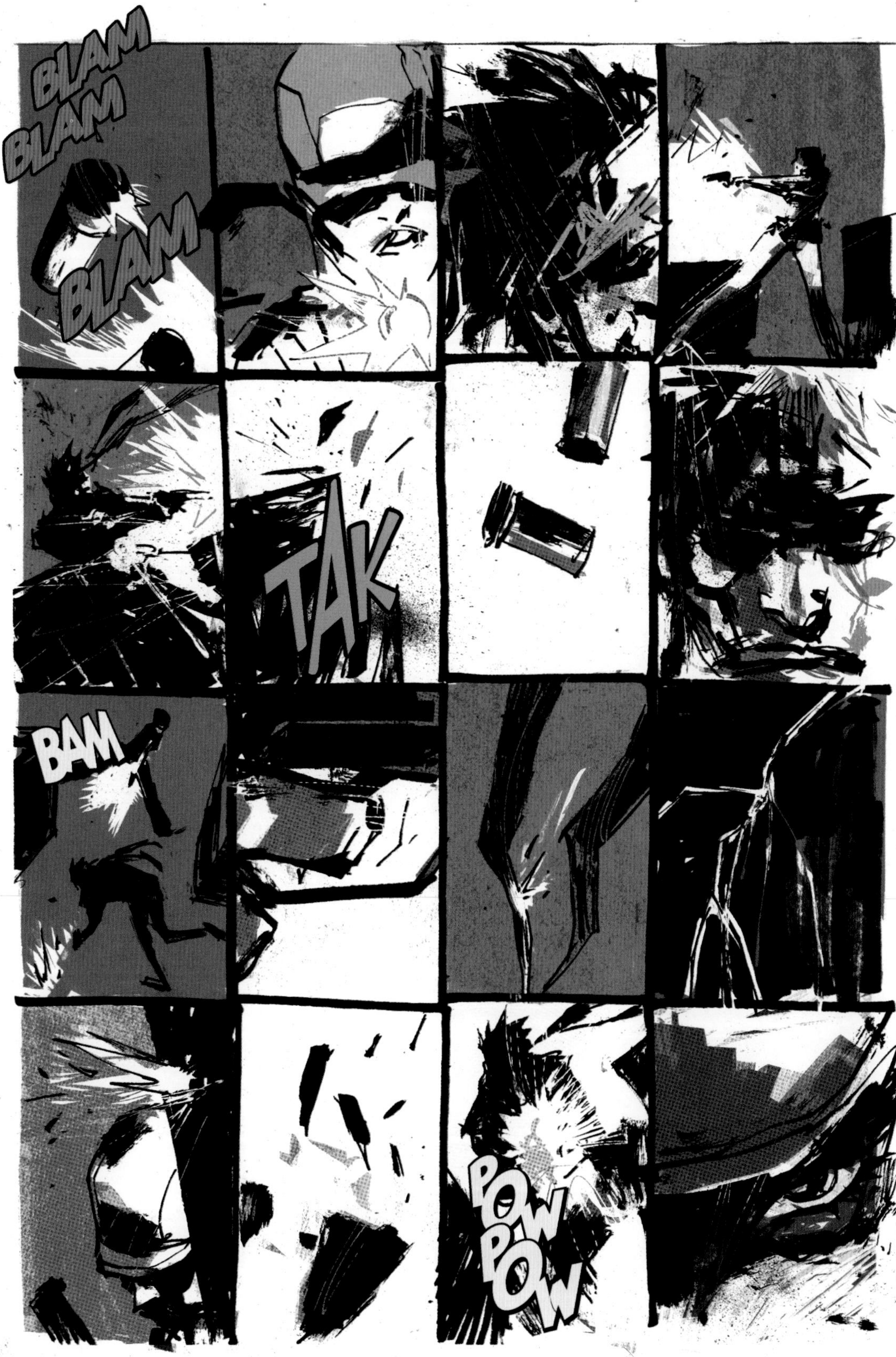
BLAM
BLAM
BLAM
TAK
BAM
POW
POW

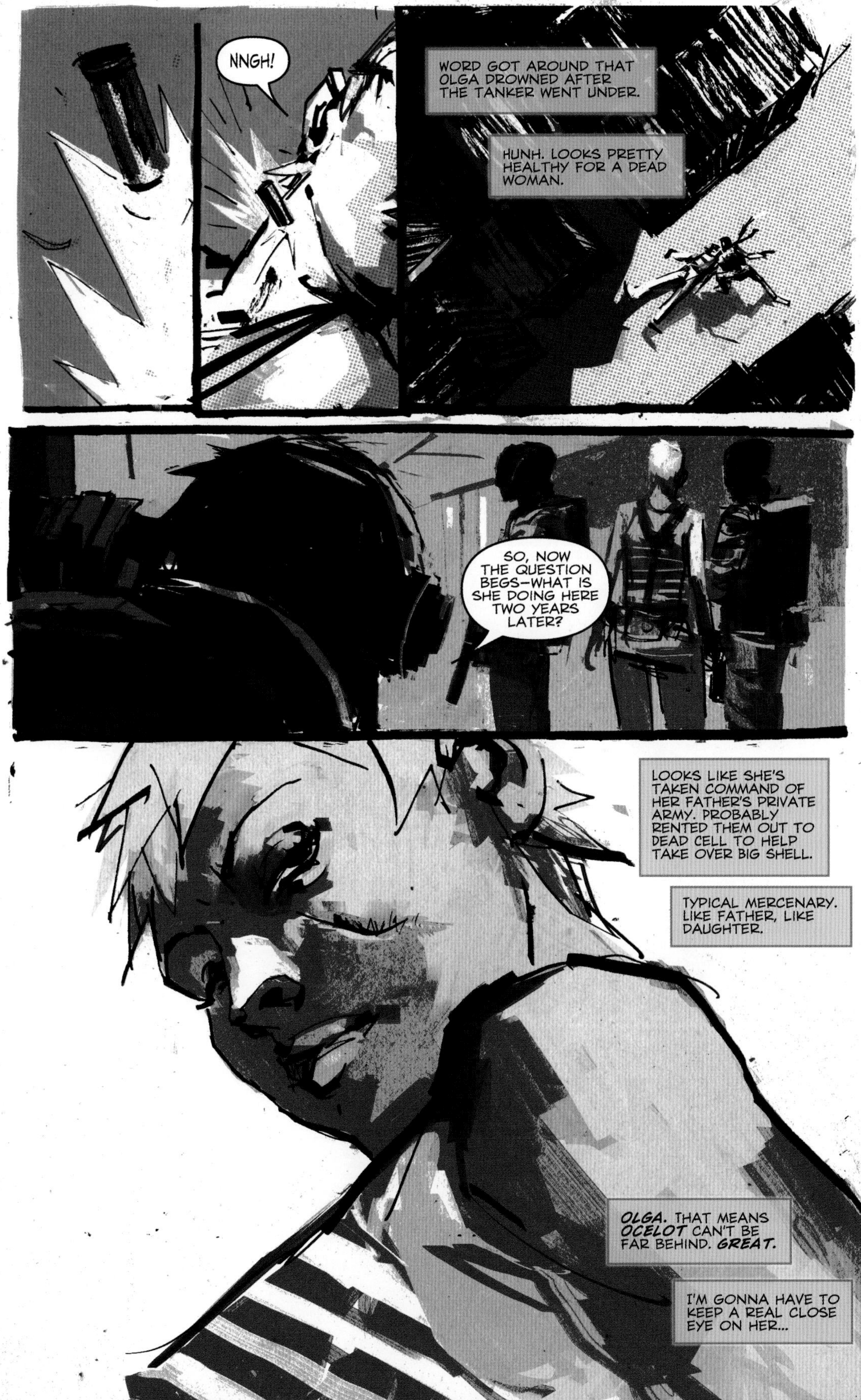
NNGH!
WORD GOT AROUND THAT OLGA DROWNED AFTER THE TANKER WENT UNDER.
HUNH. LOOKS PRETTY HEALTHY FOR A DEAD WOMAN.
SO, NOW THE QUESTION BEGS—WHAT IS SHE DOING HERE TWO YEARS LATER?
LOOKS LIKE SHE'S TAKEN COMMAND OF HER FATHER'S PRIVATE ARMY. PROBABLY RENTED THEM OUT TO DEAD CELL TO HELP TAKE OVER BIG SHELL.
TYPICAL MERCENARY. LIKE FATHER, LIKE DAUGHTER.
OLGA. THAT MEANS OCELOT CAN'T BE FAR BEHIND. GREAT.
I'M GONNA HAVE TO KEEP A REAL CLOSE EYE ON HER...

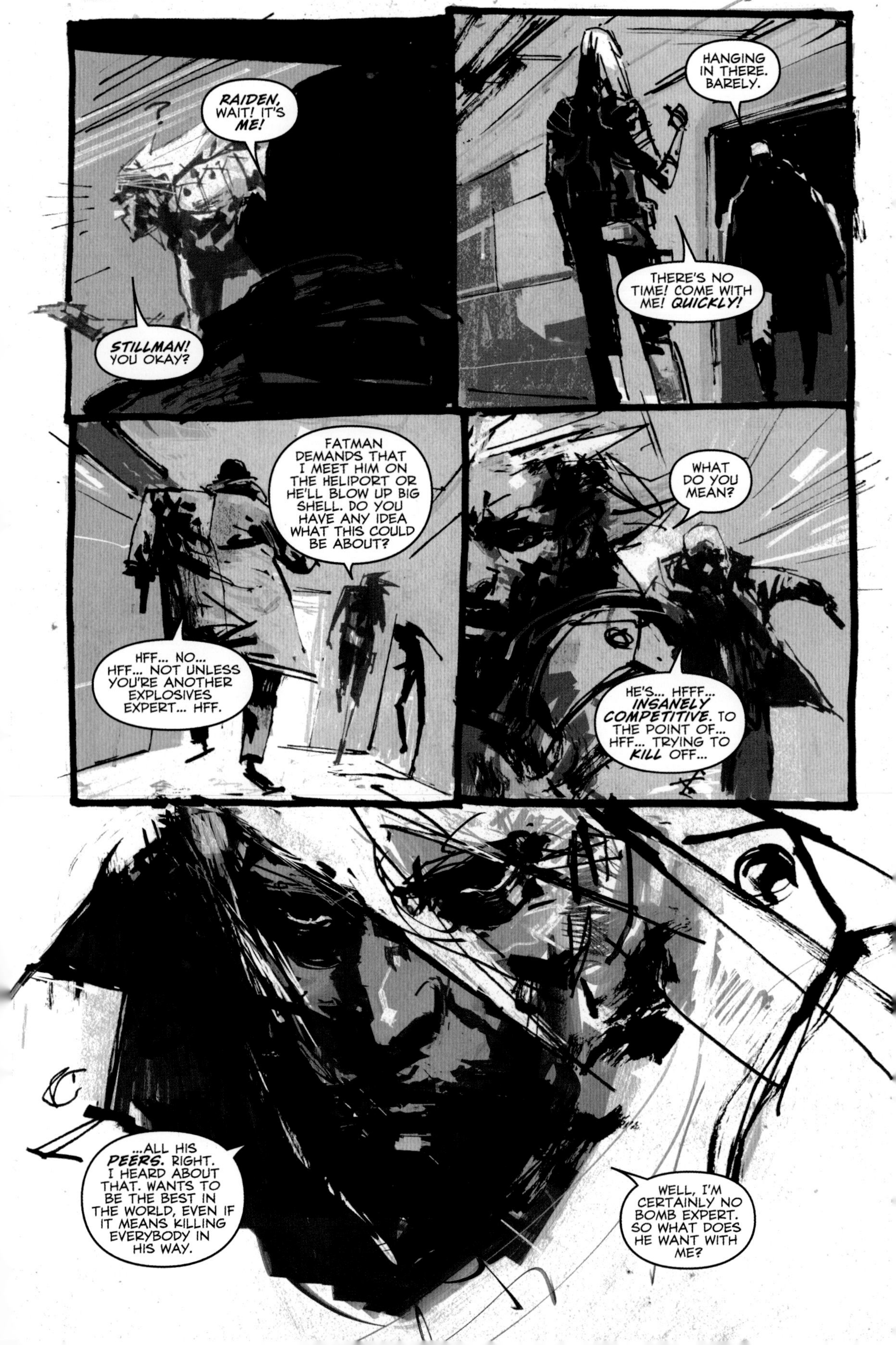
RAIDEN, WAIT! IT'S ME!
?
STILLMAN! YOU OKAY?
HANGING IN THERE. BARELY.
THERE'S NO TIME! COME WITH ME! QUICKLY!
FATMAN DEMANDS THAT I MEET HIM ON THE HELIPORT OR HE'LL BLOW UP BIG SHELL. DO YOU HAVE ANY IDEA WHAT THIS COULD BE ABOUT?
HFF... NO... HFF... NOT UNLESS YOU'RE ANOTHER EXPLOSIVES EXPERT... HFF.
WHAT DO YOU MEAN?
HE'S... HFFF... INSANELY COMPETITIVE. TO THE POINT OF... HFF... TRYING TO KILL OFF...
...ALL HIS PEERS. RIGHT. I HEARD ABOUT THAT. WANTS TO BE THE BEST IN THE WORLD, EVEN IF IT MEANS KILLING EVERYBODY IN HIS WAY.
WELL, I'M CERTAINLY NO BOMB EXPERT. SO WHAT DOES HE WANT WITH ME?

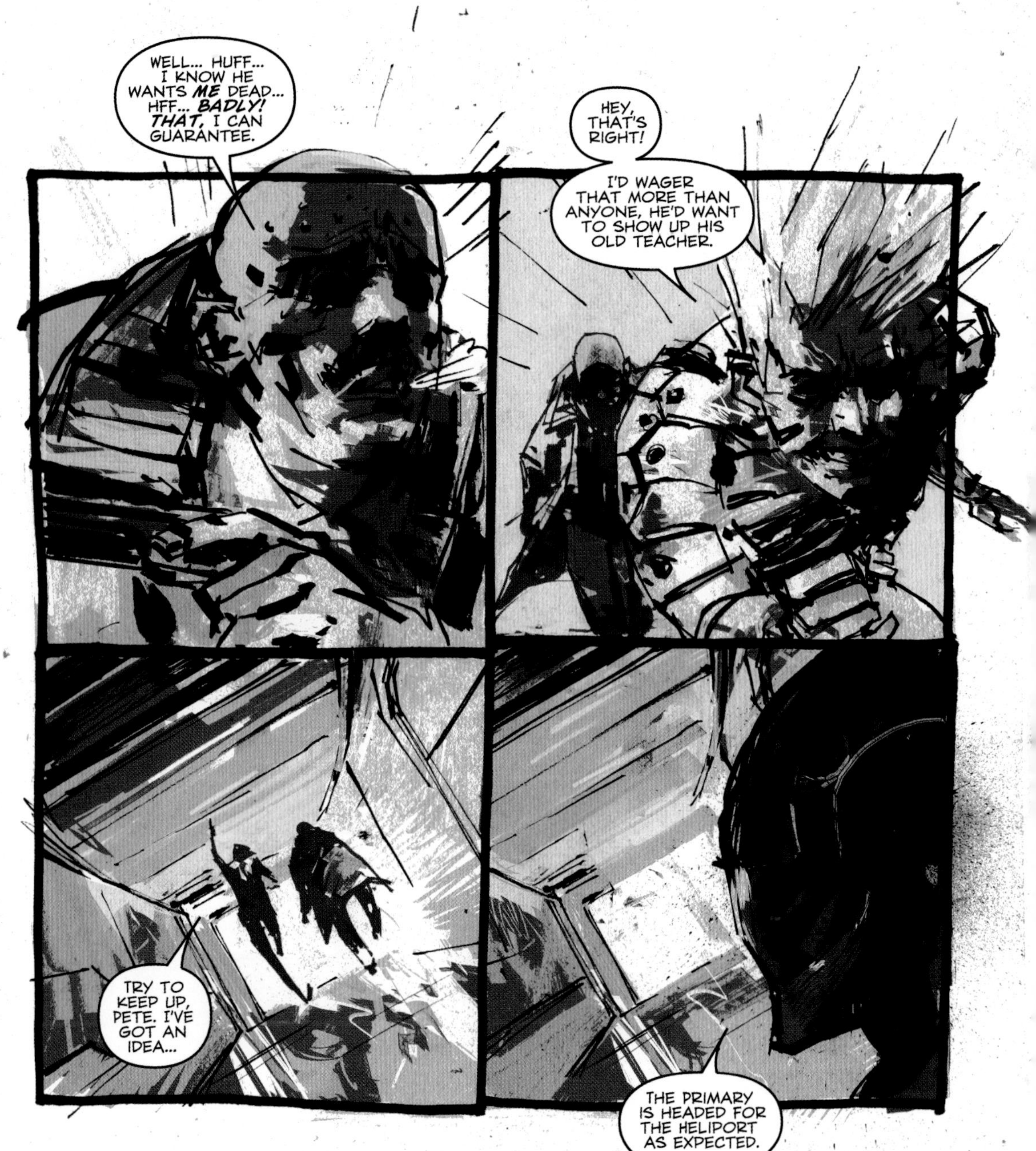
WELL... HUFF... I KNOW HE WANTS *ME* DEAD... HFF... *BADLY!* *THAT,* I CAN GUARANTEE.
HEY, THAT'S RIGHT!
I'D WAGER THAT MORE THAN ANYONE, HE'D WANT TO SHOW UP HIS OLD TEACHER.
TRY TO KEEP UP, PETE. I'VE GOT AN IDEA...
THE PRIMARY IS HEADED FOR THE HELIPORT AS EXPECTED.

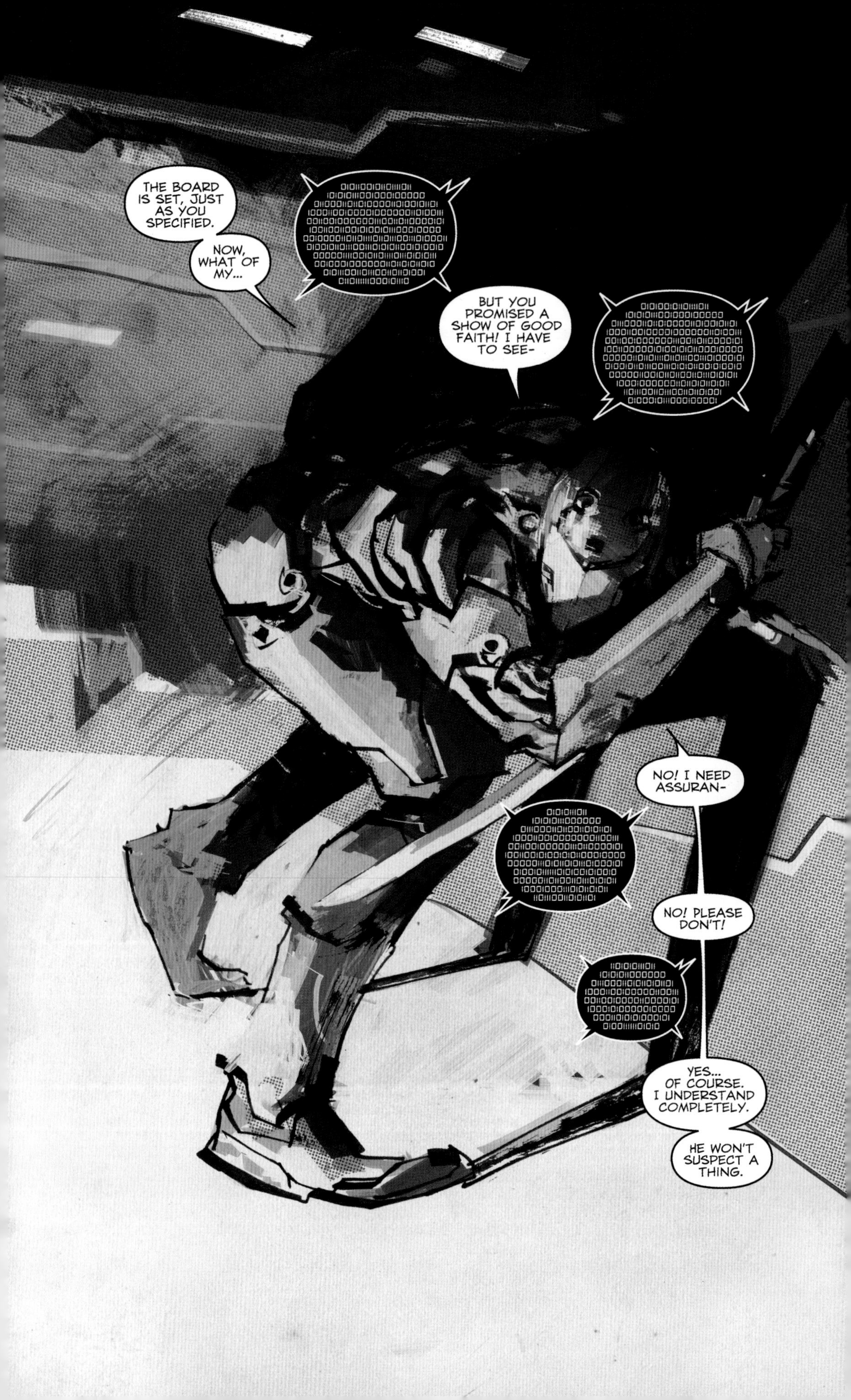
THE BOARD IS SET, JUST AS YOU SPECIFIED.
NOW, WHAT OF MY...
BUT YOU PROMISED A SHOW OF GOOD FAITH! I HAVE TO SEE-
NO! I NEED ASSURAN-
NO! PLEASE DON'T!
YES... OF COURSE. I UNDERSTAND COMPLETELY.
HE WON'T SUSPECT A THING.

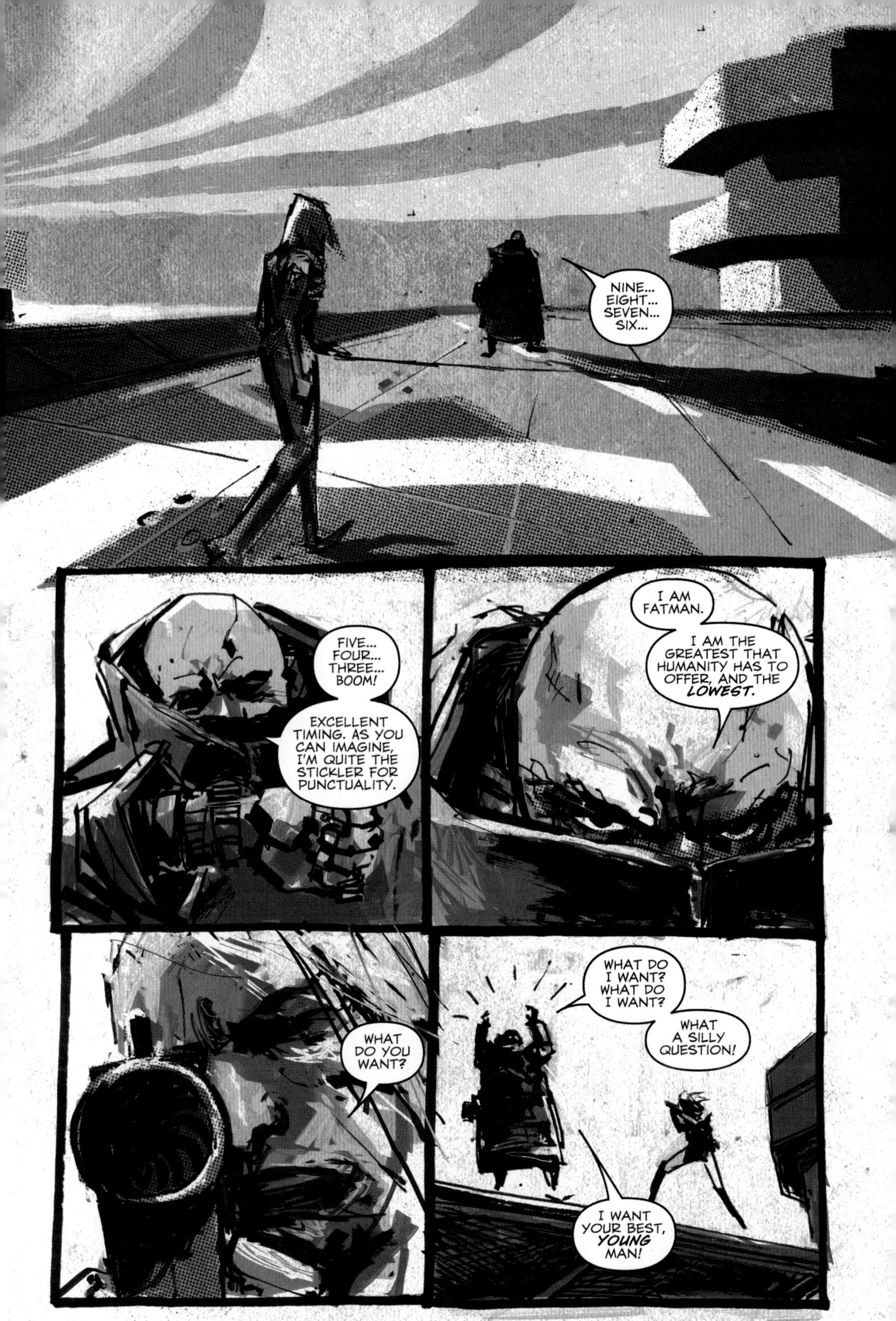
NINE... EIGHT... SEVEN... SIX...
FIVE... FOUR... THREE... BOOM!
EXCELLENT TIMING. AS YOU CAN IMAGINE, I'M QUITE THE STICKLER FOR PUNCTUALITY.
I AM FATMAN.
I AM THE GREATEST THAT HUMANITY HAS TO OFFER, AND THE LOWEST.
WHAT DO YOU WANT?
WHAT DO I WANT? WHAT DO I WANT?
WHAT A SILLY QUESTION!
I WANT YOUR BEST, YOUNG MAN!

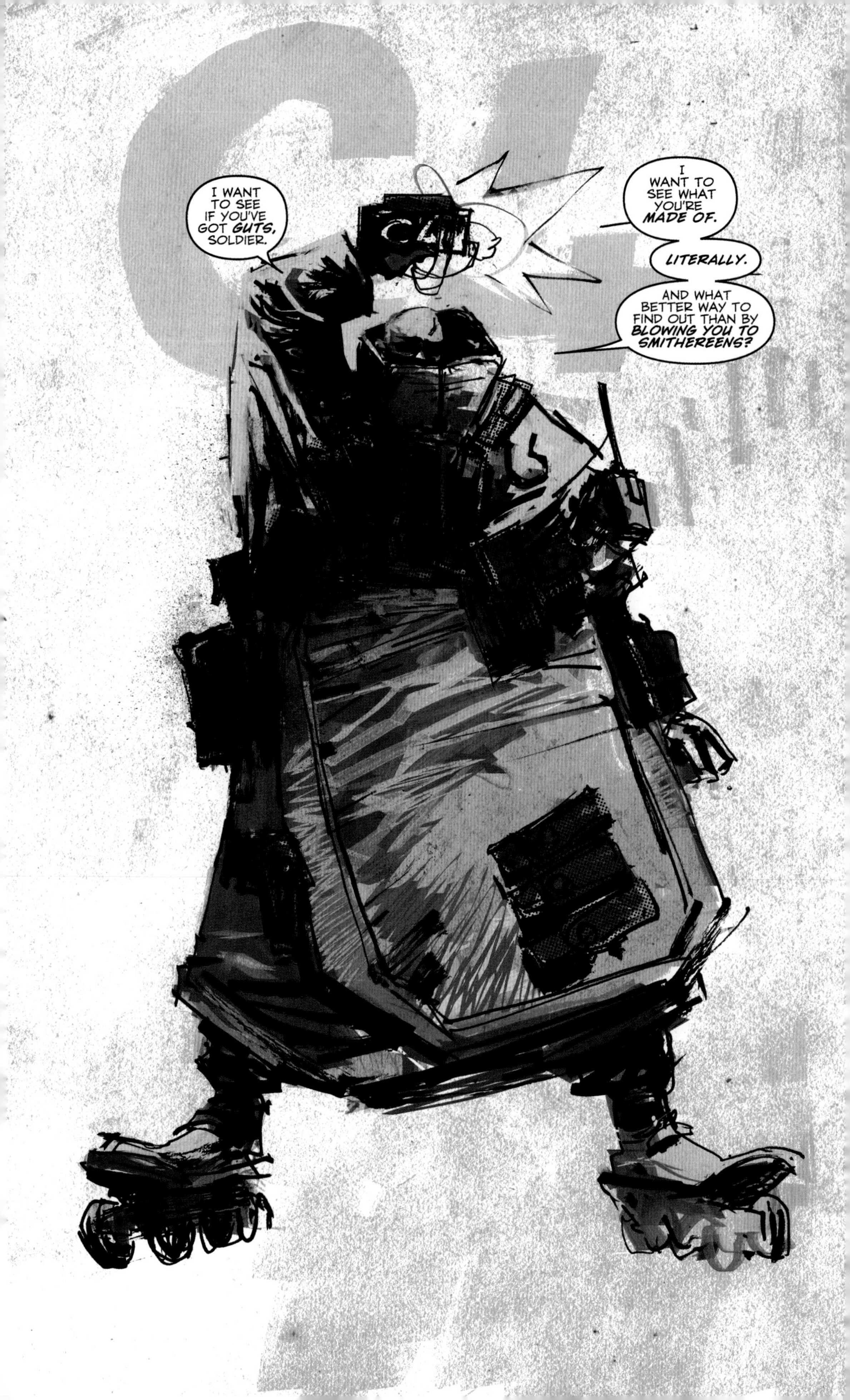
I WANT TO SEE IF YOU'VE GOT GUTS, SOLDIER.
I WANT TO SEE WHAT YOU'RE MADE OF.
LITERALLY.
AND WHAT BETTER WAY TO FIND OUT THAN BY BLOWING YOU TO SMITHEREENS?

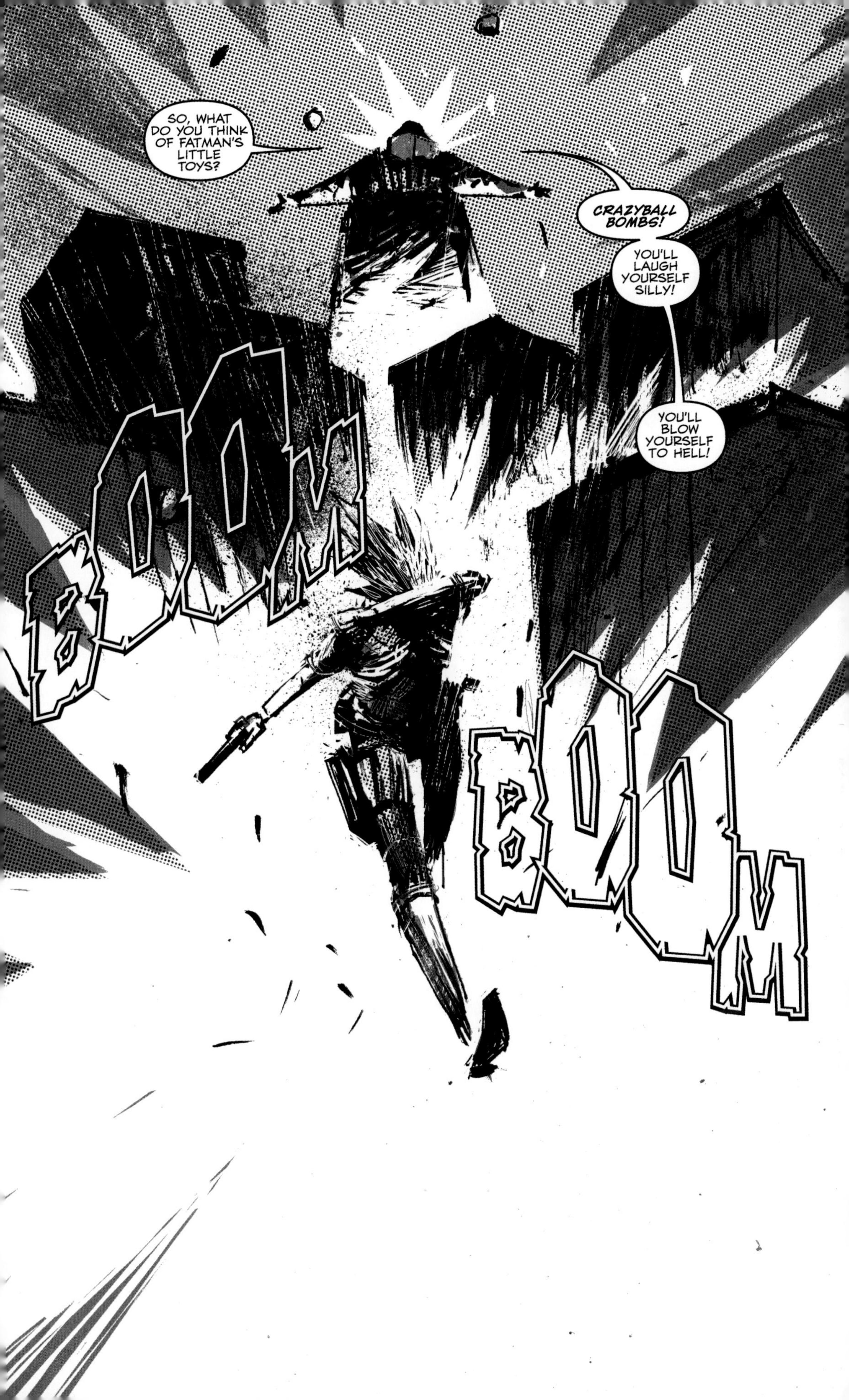
SO, WHAT DO YOU THINK OF FATMAN'S LITTLE TOYS?
CRAZYBALL BOMBS!
YOU'LL LAUGH YOURSELF SILLY!
YOU'LL BLOW YOURSELF TO HELL!
BOOM
BOOM

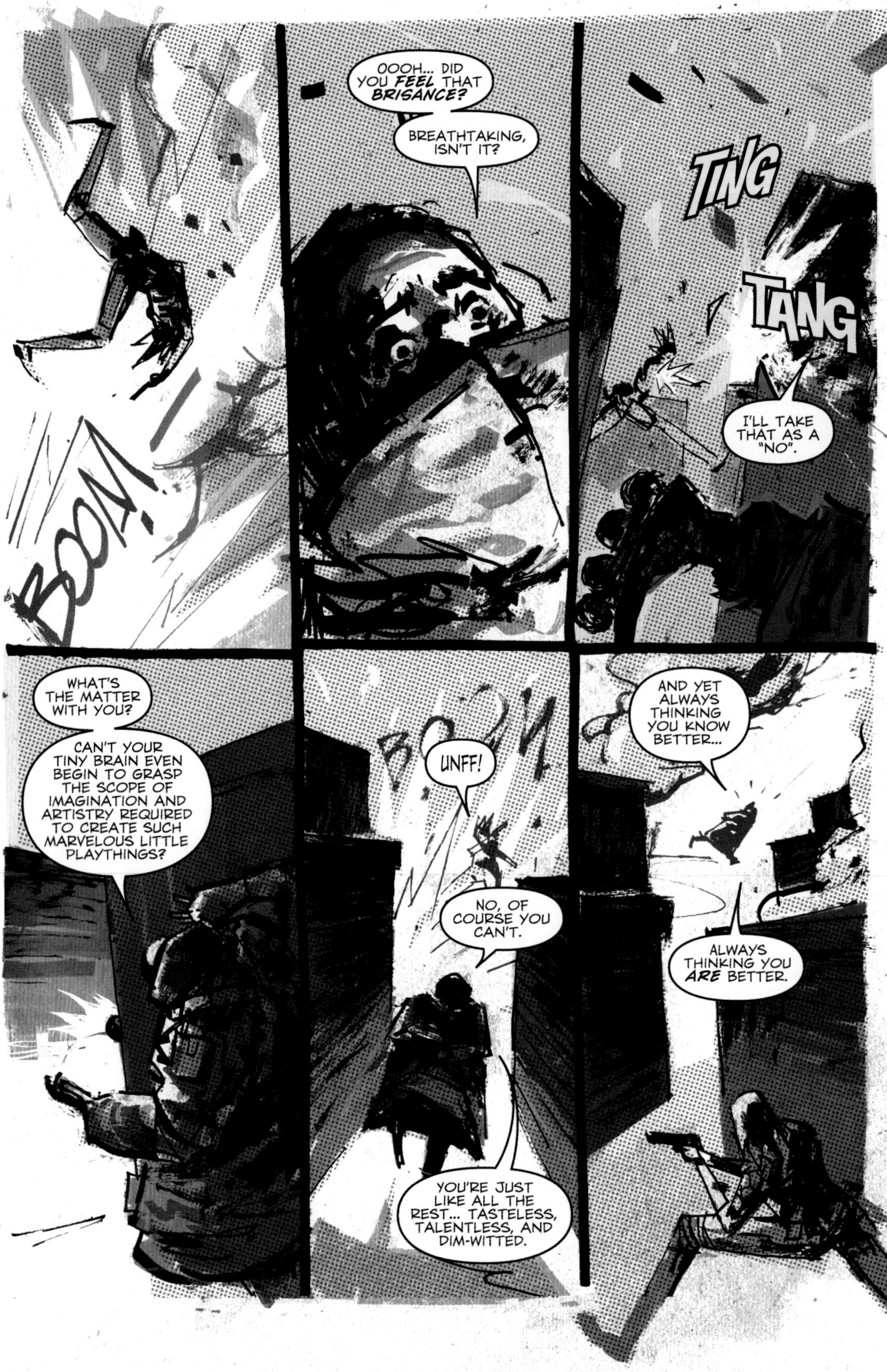
BOOM!
OOOH... DID YOU FEEL THAT BRISANCE?
BREATHTAKING, ISN'T IT?
TING
TANG
I'LL TAKE THAT AS A "NO".
WHAT'S THE MATTER WITH YOU?
CAN'T YOUR TINY BRAIN EVEN BEGIN TO GRASP THE SCOPE OF IMAGINATION AND ARTISTRY REQUIRED TO CREATE SUCH MARVELOUS LITTLE PLAYTHINGS?
UNFF!
NO, OF COURSE YOU CAN'T.
YOU'RE JUST LIKE ALL THE REST... TASTELESS, TALENTLESS, AND DIM-WITTED.
AND YET ALWAYS THINKING YOU KNOW BETTER...
ALWAYS THINKING YOU ARE BETTER.

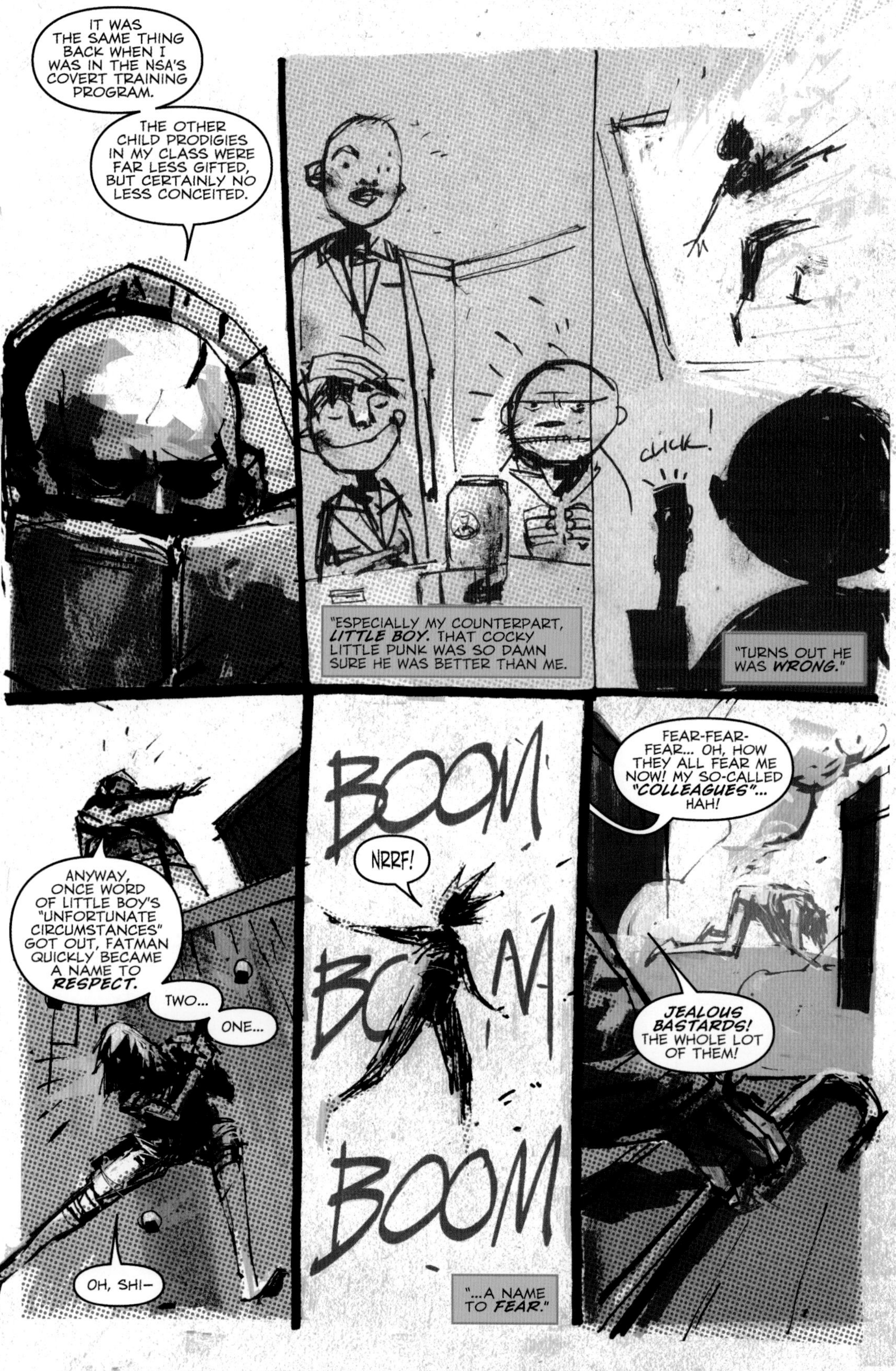
IT WAS THE SAME THING BACK WHEN I WAS IN THE NSA'S COVERT TRAINING PROGRAM.
THE OTHER CHILD PRODIGIES IN MY CLASS WERE FAR LESS GIFTED, BUT CERTAINLY NO LESS CONCEITED.
"ESPECIALLY MY COUNTERPART, LITTLE BOY. THAT COCKY LITTLE PUNK WAS SO DAMN SURE HE WAS BETTER THAN ME.
CLICK!
"TURNS OUT HE WAS WRONG."
ANYWAY, ONCE WORD OF LITTLE BOY'S "UNFORTUNATE CIRCUMSTANCES" GOT OUT, FATMAN QUICKLY BECAME A NAME TO RESPECT.
TWO...
ONE...
OH, SHI–
BOOM
NRRF!
BOOM
BOOM
"...A NAME TO FEAR."
FEAR-FEAR-FEAR... OH, HOW THEY ALL FEAR ME NOW! MY SO-CALLED "COLLEAGUES"... HAH!
JEALOUS BASTARDS! THE WHOLE LOT OF THEM!

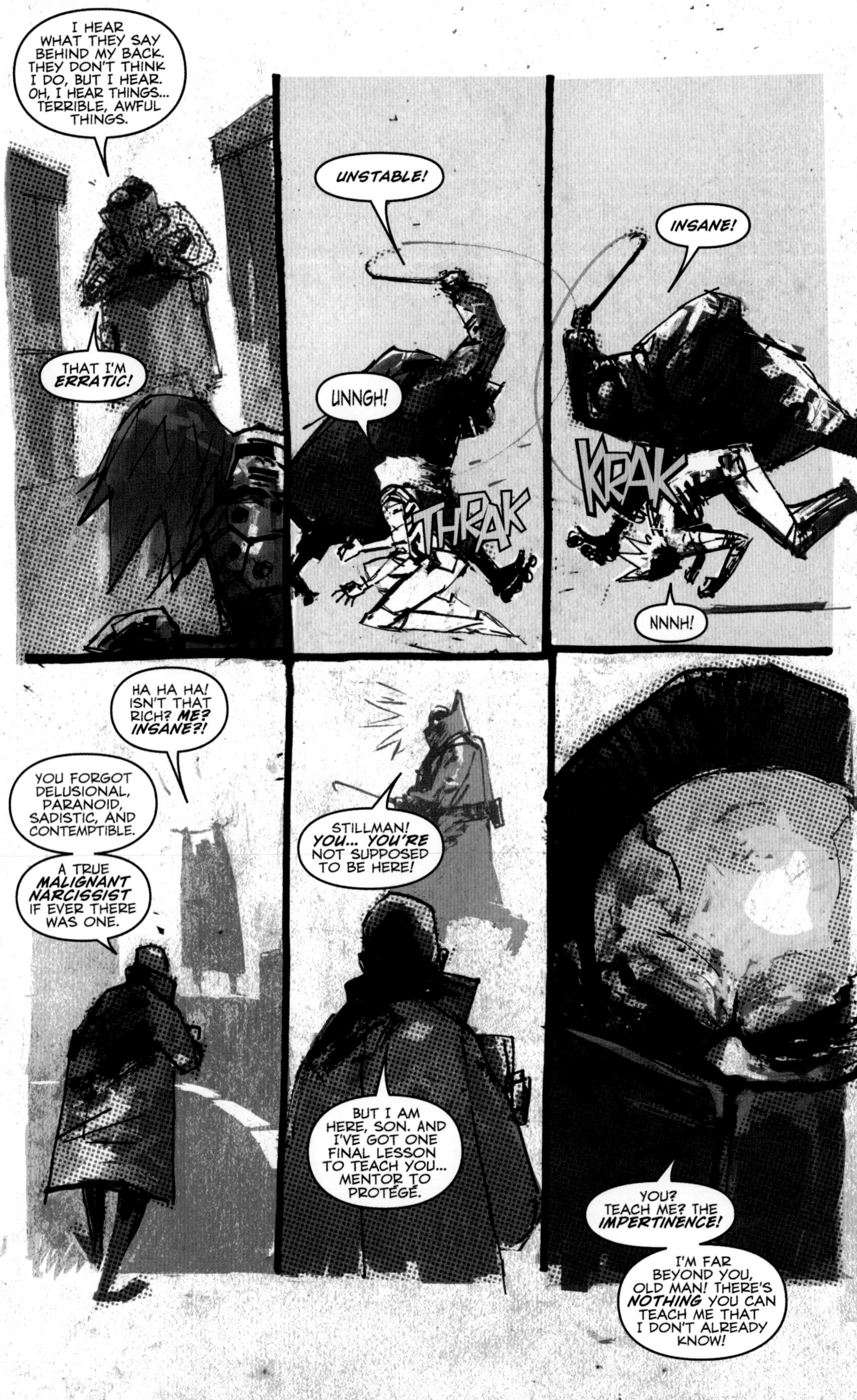
I HEAR WHAT THEY SAY BEHIND MY BACK. THEY DON'T THINK I DO, BUT I HEAR. OH, I HEAR THINGS... TERRIBLE, AWFUL THINGS.
THAT I'M *ERRATIC!*
UNSTABLE!
UNNGH!
THRAK
INSANE!
KRAK
NNNH!
HA HA HA! ISN'T THAT RICH? *ME? INSANE?!*
YOU FORGOT DELUSIONAL, PARANOID, SADISTIC, AND CONTEMPTIBLE.
A TRUE *MALIGNANT NARCISSIST* IF EVER THERE WAS ONE.
STILLMAN! *YOU... YOU'RE* NOT SUPPOSED TO BE HERE!
BUT I AM HERE, SON. AND I'VE GOT ONE FINAL LESSON TO TEACH YOU... MENTOR TO PROTÉGÉ.
YOU? TEACH ME? THE *IMPERTINENCE!*
I'M FAR BEYOND YOU, OLD MAN! THERE'S *NOTHING* YOU CAN TEACH ME THAT I DON'T ALREADY KNOW!

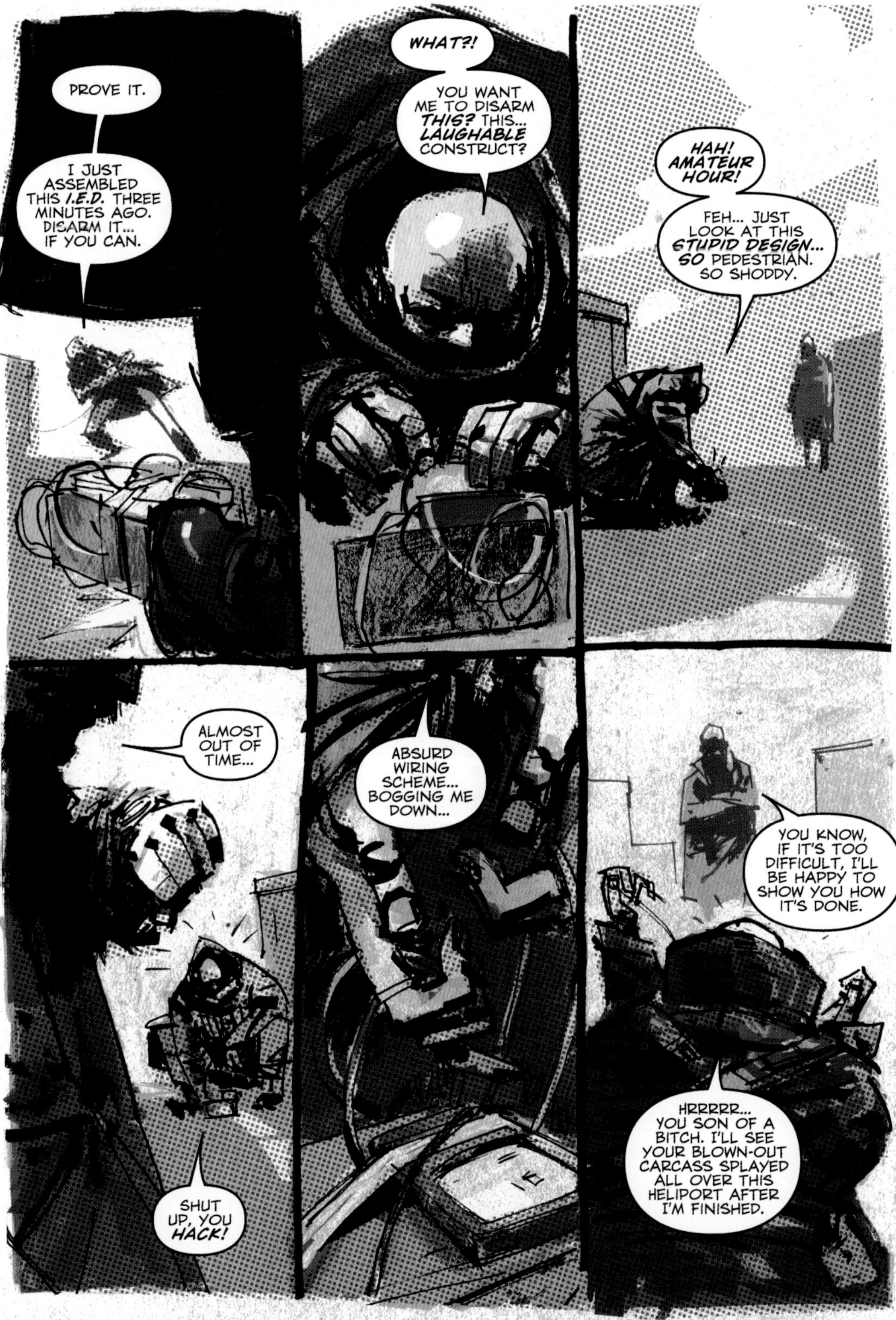
PROVE IT.
I JUST ASSEMBLED THIS I.E.D. THREE MINUTES AGO. DISARM IT... IF YOU CAN.
WHAT?!
YOU WANT ME TO DISARM THIS? THIS... LAUGHABLE CONSTRUCT?
HAH! AMATEUR HOUR!
FEH... JUST LOOK AT THIS STUPID DESIGN... SO PEDESTRIAN. SO SHODDY.
ALMOST OUT OF TIME...
SHUT UP, YOU HACK!
ABSURD WIRING SCHEME... BOGGING ME DOWN...
YOU KNOW, IF IT'S TOO DIFFICULT, I'LL BE HAPPY TO SHOW YOU HOW IT'S DONE.
HRRRRR... YOU SON OF A BITCH. I'LL SEE YOUR BLOWN-OUT CARCASS SPLAYED ALL OVER THIS HELIPORT AFTER I'M FINISHED.

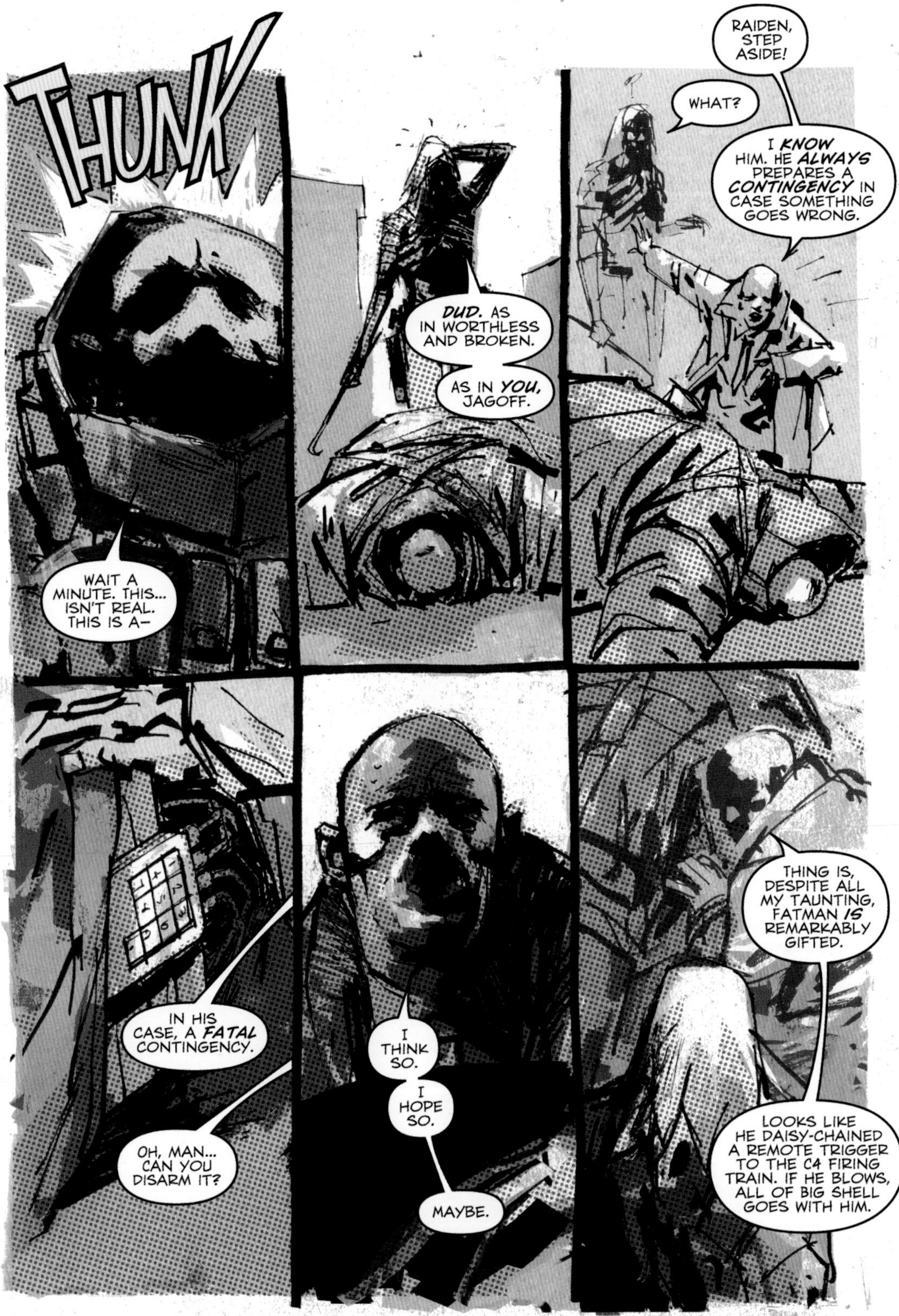
THUNK
WAIT A MINUTE. THIS... ISN'T REAL. THIS IS A–
DUD. AS IN WORTHLESS AND BROKEN.
AS IN YOU, JAGOFF.
RAIDEN, STEP ASIDE!
WHAT?
I KNOW HIM. HE ALWAYS PREPARES A CONTINGENCY IN CASE SOMETHING GOES WRONG.
IN HIS CASE, A FATAL CONTINGENCY.
OH, MAN... CAN YOU DISARM IT?
I THINK SO.
I HOPE SO.
MAYBE.
THING IS, DESPITE ALL MY TAUNTING, FATMAN IS REMARKABLY GIFTED.
LOOKS LIKE HE DAISY-CHAINED A REMOTE TRIGGER TO THE C4 FIRING TRAIN. IF HE BLOWS, ALL OF BIG SHELL GOES WITH HIM.

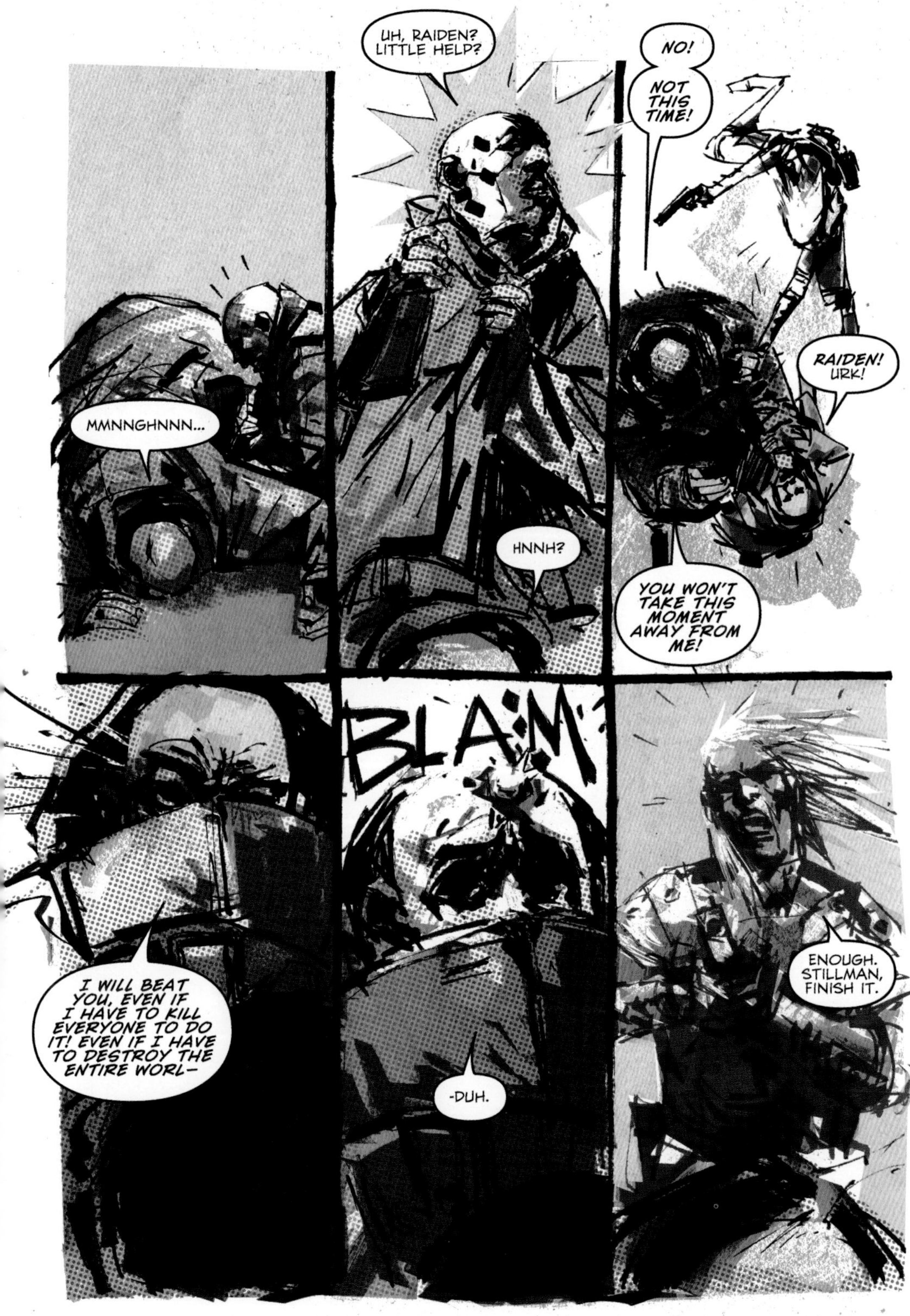
MMNNGHNNN...
UH, RAIDEN? LITTLE HELP?
HNNH?
NO!
NOT THIS TIME!
RAIDEN! URK!
YOU WON'T TAKE THIS MOMENT AWAY FROM ME!
I WILL BEAT YOU, EVEN IF I HAVE TO KILL EVERYONE TO DO IT! EVEN IF I HAVE TO DESTROY THE ENTIRE WORL—
BLAM
-DUH.
ENOUGH. STILLMAN, FINISH IT.

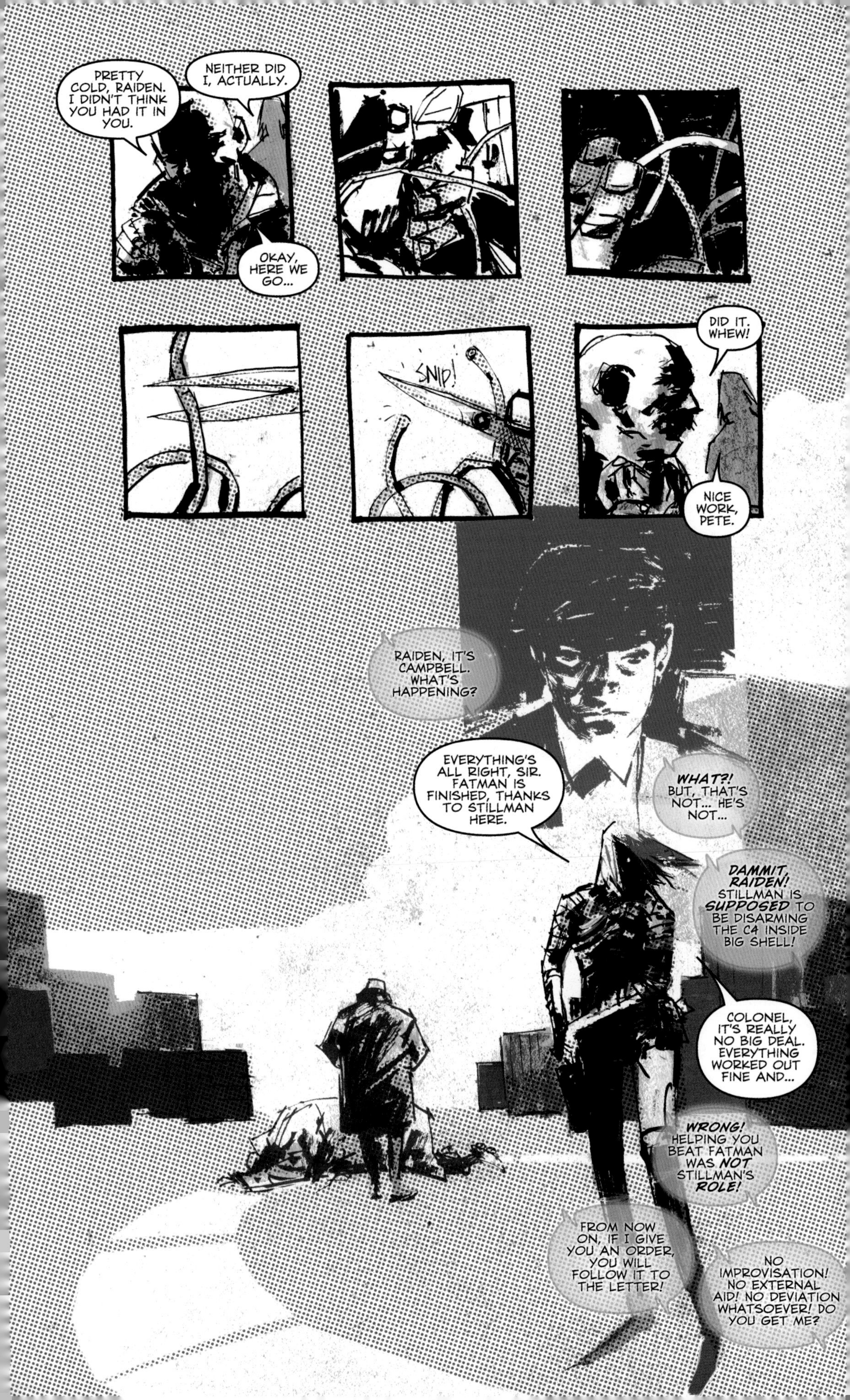
PRETTY COLD, RAIDEN. I DIDN'T THINK YOU HAD IT IN YOU.
NEITHER DID I, ACTUALLY.
OKAY, HERE WE GO...
SNIP!
DID IT. WHEW!
NICE WORK, PETE.
RAIDEN, IT'S CAMPBELL. WHAT'S HAPPENING?
EVERYTHING'S ALL RIGHT, SIR. FATMAN IS FINISHED, THANKS TO STILLMAN HERE.
WHAT?! BUT, THAT'S NOT... HE'S NOT...
DAMMIT, RAIDEN! STILLMAN IS SUPPOSED TO BE DISARMING THE C4 INSIDE BIG SHELL!
COLONEL, IT'S REALLY NO BIG DEAL. EVERYTHING WORKED OUT FINE AND...
WRONG! HELPING YOU BEAT FATMAN WAS NOT STILLMAN'S ROLE!
FROM NOW ON, IF I GIVE YOU AN ORDER, YOU WILL FOLLOW IT TO THE LETTER!
NO IMPROVISATION! NO EXTERNAL AID! NO DEVIATION WHATSOEVER! DO YOU GET ME?

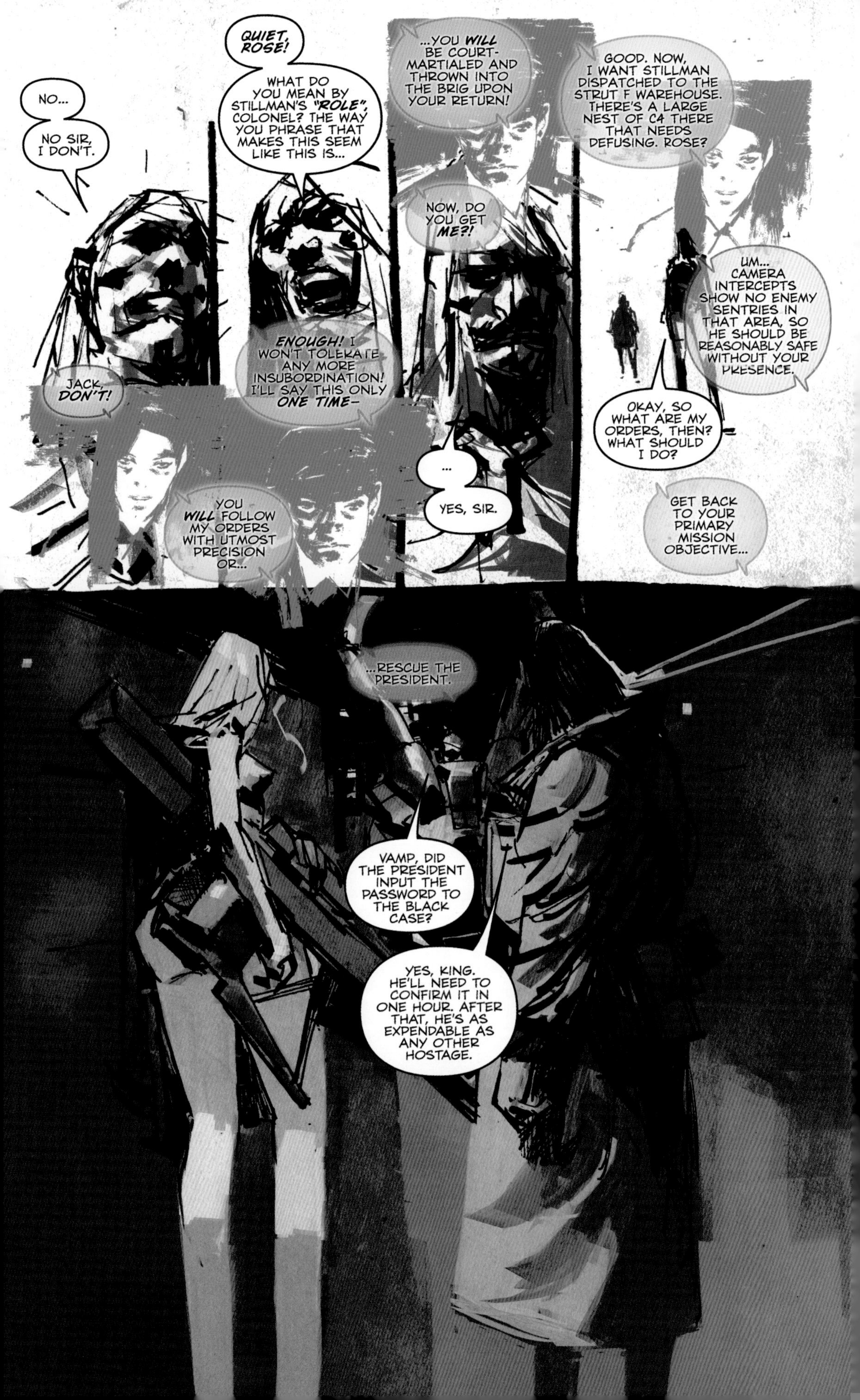
NO...
NO SIR, I DON'T.
QUIET, ROSE!
WHAT DO YOU MEAN BY STILLMAN'S "ROLE", COLONEL? THE WAY YOU PHRASE THAT MAKES THIS SEEM LIKE THIS IS...
ENOUGH! I WON'T TOLERATE ANY MORE INSUBORDINATION! I'LL SAY THIS ONLY ONE TIME–
JACK, DON'T!
YOU WILL FOLLOW MY ORDERS WITH UTMOST PRECISION OR...
...YOU WILL BE COURT-MARTIALED AND THROWN INTO THE BRIG UPON YOUR RETURN!
NOW, DO YOU GET ME?!
...
YES, SIR.
GOOD. NOW, I WANT STILLMAN DISPATCHED TO THE STRUT F WAREHOUSE. THERE'S A LARGE NEST OF C4 THERE THAT NEEDS DEFUSING. ROSE?
UM... CAMERA INTERCEPTS SHOW NO ENEMY SENTRIES IN THAT AREA, SO HE SHOULD BE REASONABLY SAFE WITHOUT YOUR PRESENCE.
OKAY, SO WHAT ARE MY ORDERS, THEN? WHAT SHOULD I DO?
GET BACK TO YOUR PRIMARY MISSION OBJECTIVE...
...RESCUE THE PRESIDENT.
VAMP, DID THE PRESIDENT INPUT THE PASSWORD TO THE BLACK CASE?
YES, KING. HE'LL NEED TO CONFIRM IT IN ONE HOUR. AFTER THAT, HE'S AS EXPENDABLE AS ANY OTHER HOSTAGE.

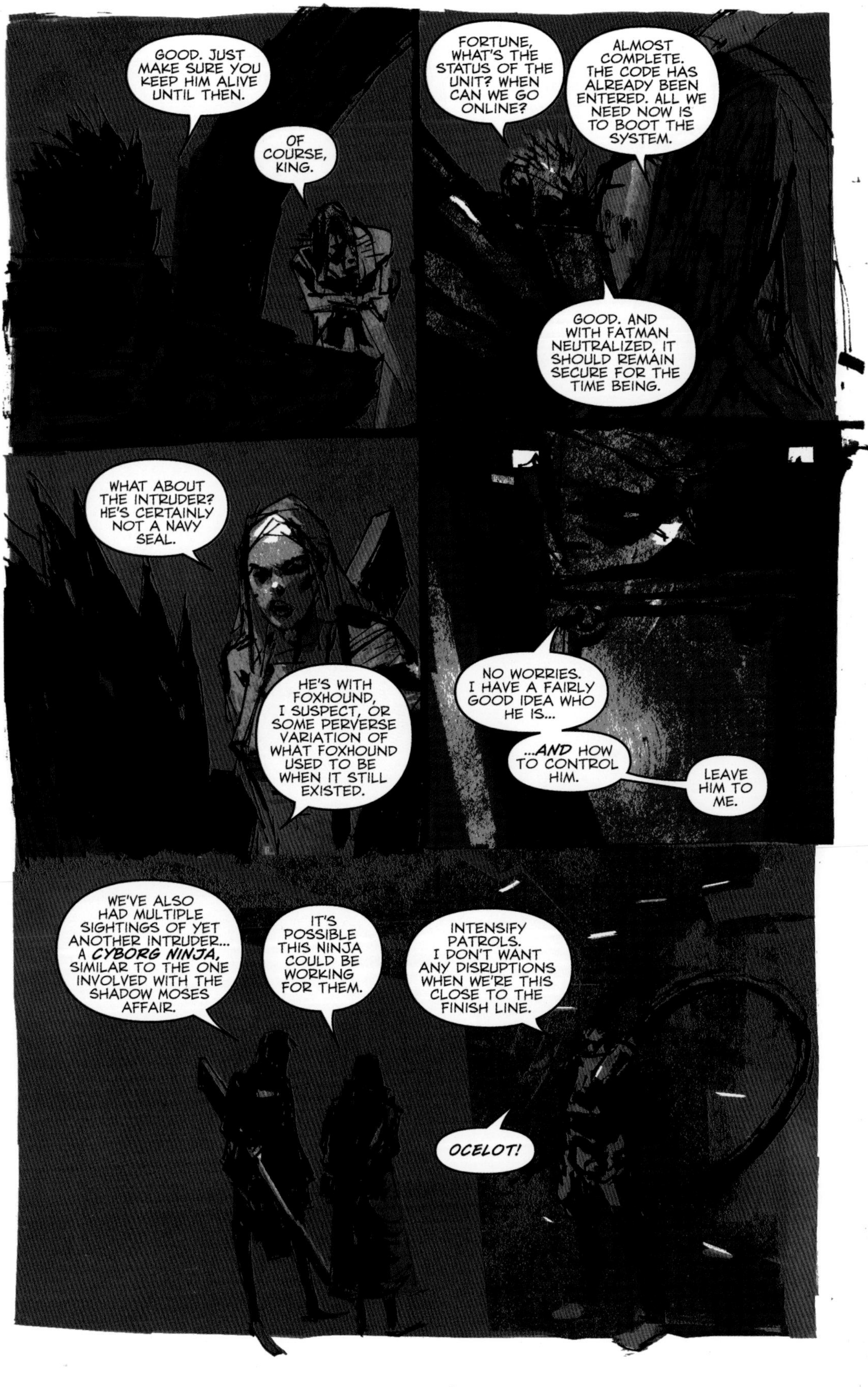
GOOD. JUST MAKE SURE YOU KEEP HIM ALIVE UNTIL THEN.
OF COURSE, KING.
FORTUNE, WHAT'S THE STATUS OF THE UNIT? WHEN CAN WE GO ONLINE?
ALMOST COMPLETE. THE CODE HAS ALREADY BEEN ENTERED. ALL WE NEED NOW IS TO BOOT THE SYSTEM.
GOOD. AND WITH FATMAN NEUTRALIZED, IT SHOULD REMAIN SECURE FOR THE TIME BEING.
WHAT ABOUT THE INTRUDER? HE'S CERTAINLY NOT A NAVY SEAL.
HE'S WITH FOXHOUND, I SUSPECT, OR SOME PERVERSE VARIATION OF WHAT FOXHOUND USED TO BE WHEN IT STILL EXISTED.
NO WORRIES. I HAVE A FAIRLY GOOD IDEA WHO HE IS...
...*AND* HOW TO CONTROL HIM.
LEAVE HIM TO ME.
WE'VE ALSO HAD MULTIPLE SIGHTINGS OF YET ANOTHER INTRUDER... A *CYBORG NINJA*, SIMILAR TO THE ONE INVOLVED WITH THE SHADOW MOSES AFFAIR.
IT'S POSSIBLE THIS NINJA COULD BE WORKING FOR THEM.
INTENSIFY PATROLS. I DON'T WANT ANY DISRUPTIONS WHEN WE'RE THIS CLOSE TO THE FINISH LINE.
OCELOT!

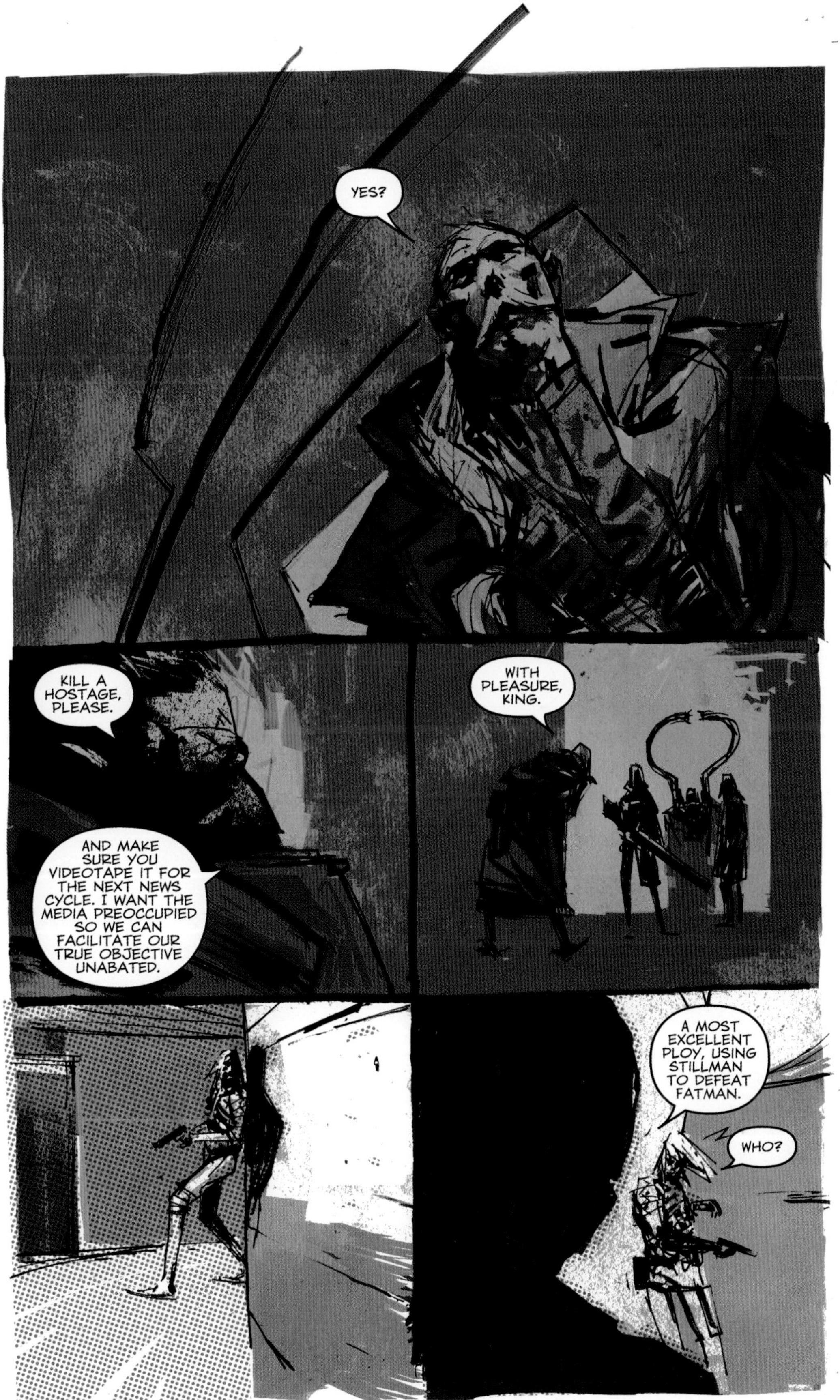
YES?
KILL A HOSTAGE, PLEASE.
AND MAKE SURE YOU VIDEOTAPE IT FOR THE NEXT NEWS CYCLE. I WANT THE MEDIA PREOCCUPIED SO WE CAN FACILITATE OUR TRUE OBJECTIVE UNABATED.
WITH PLEASURE, KING.
A MOST EXCELLENT PLOY, USING STILLMAN TO DEFEAT FATMAN.
WHO?

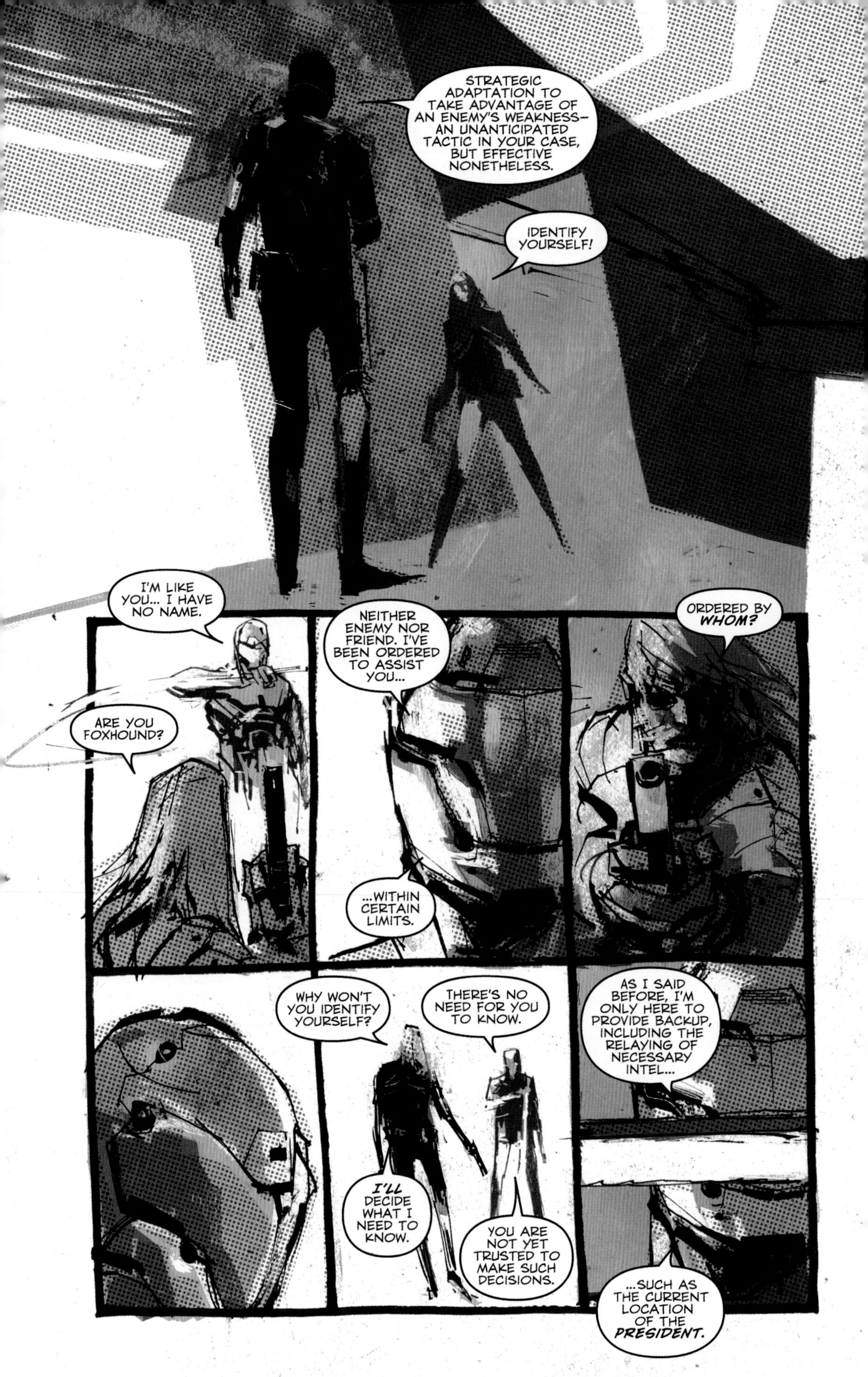
STRATEGIC ADAPTATION TO TAKE ADVANTAGE OF AN ENEMY'S WEAKNESS— AN UNANTICIPATED TACTIC IN YOUR CASE, BUT EFFECTIVE NONETHELESS.
IDENTIFY YOURSELF!
I'M LIKE YOU... I HAVE NO NAME.
ARE YOU FOXHOUND?
NEITHER ENEMY NOR FRIEND. I'VE BEEN ORDERED TO ASSIST YOU...
...WITHIN CERTAIN LIMITS.
ORDERED BY *WHOM?*
WHY WON'T YOU IDENTIFY YOURSELF?
THERE'S NO NEED FOR YOU TO KNOW.
I'LL DECIDE WHAT I NEED TO KNOW.
YOU ARE NOT YET TRUSTED TO MAKE SUCH DECISIONS.
AS I SAID BEFORE, I'M ONLY HERE TO PROVIDE BACKUP, INCLUDING THE RELAYING OF NECESSARY INTEL...
...SUCH AS THE CURRENT LOCATION OF THE *PRESIDENT.*

WHAT? WHERE IS HE?
HE WAS MOVED TO THE FIRST FLOOR OF SHELL 2'S CORE SECTION—A HIGHLY SECURE AREA.
WHY ARE YOU TELLING ME THIS?
MUST I REPEAT MYSELF?
THERE'S NO REASON FOR ME TO BELIEVE ANYTHING YOU SAY. YOU UNDERSTAND THAT?
IF YOU HAVE ANY OTHER LEADS, YOU'RE FREE TO FOLLOW THEM.
BUT I SUGGEST YOU MOVE QUICKLY. THE SONS OF LIBERTY HAVE NUCLEAR WEAPONS.
NUKES?! DEAD CELL HAS NUKES?

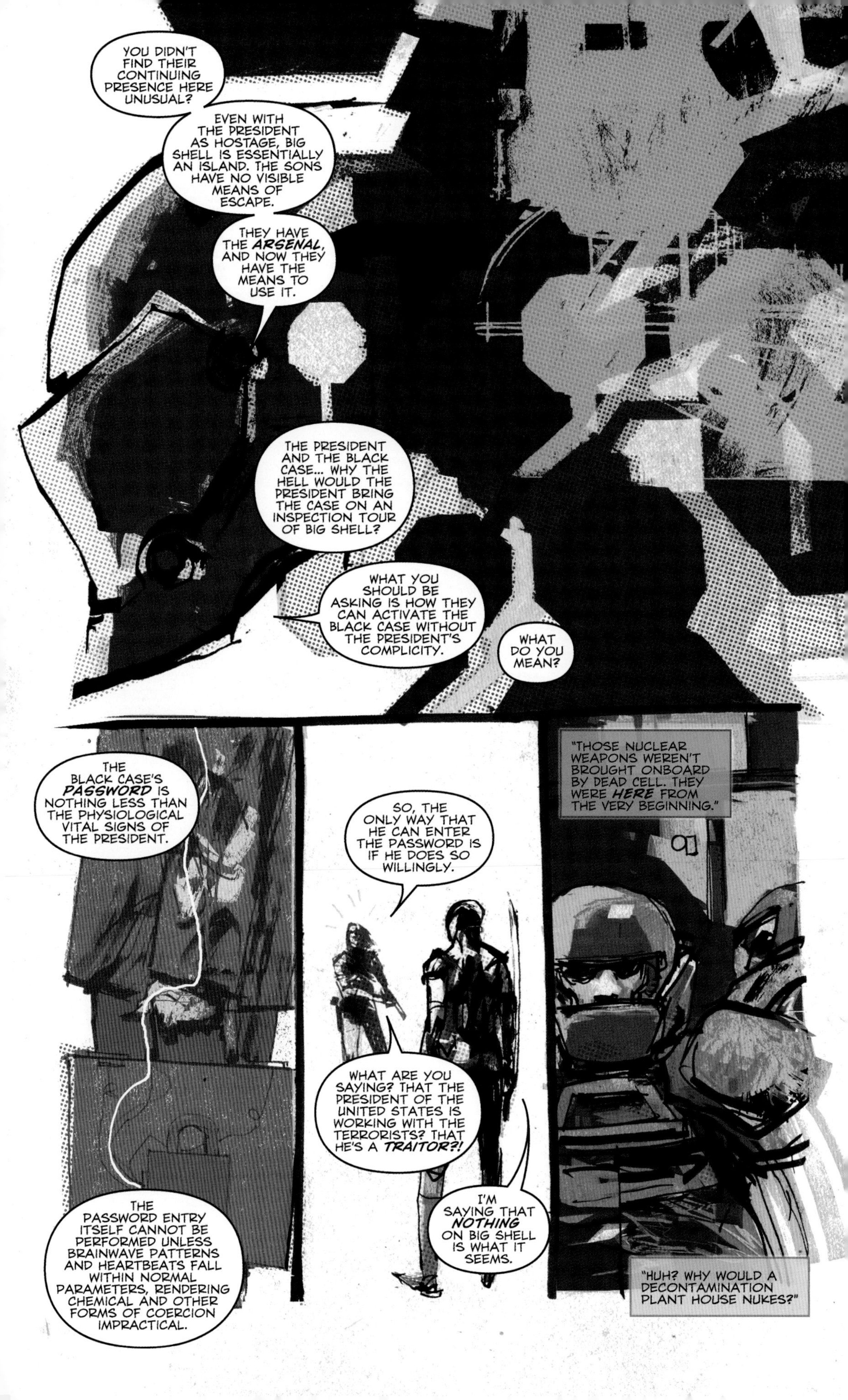
YOU DIDN'T FIND THEIR CONTINUING PRESENCE HERE UNUSUAL?
EVEN WITH THE PRESIDENT AS HOSTAGE, BIG SHELL IS ESSENTIALLY AN ISLAND. THE SONS HAVE NO VISIBLE MEANS OF ESCAPE.
THEY HAVE THE ARSENAL, AND NOW THEY HAVE THE MEANS TO USE IT.
THE PRESIDENT AND THE BLACK CASE... WHY THE HELL WOULD THE PRESIDENT BRING THE CASE ON AN INSPECTION TOUR OF BIG SHELL?
WHAT YOU SHOULD BE ASKING IS HOW THEY CAN ACTIVATE THE BLACK CASE WITHOUT THE PRESIDENT'S COMPLICITY.
WHAT DO YOU MEAN?
THE BLACK CASE'S PASSWORD IS NOTHING LESS THAN THE PHYSIOLOGICAL VITAL SIGNS OF THE PRESIDENT.
THE PASSWORD ENTRY ITSELF CANNOT BE PERFORMED UNLESS BRAINWAVE PATTERNS AND HEARTBEATS FALL WITHIN NORMAL PARAMETERS, RENDERING CHEMICAL AND OTHER FORMS OF COERCION IMPRACTICAL.
SO, THE ONLY WAY THAT HE CAN ENTER THE PASSWORD IS IF HE DOES SO WILLINGLY.
WHAT ARE YOU SAYING? THAT THE PRESIDENT OF THE UNITED STATES IS WORKING WITH THE TERRORISTS? THAT HE'S A TRAITOR?!
I'M SAYING THAT NOTHING ON BIG SHELL IS WHAT IT SEEMS.
"THOSE NUCLEAR WEAPONS WEREN'T BROUGHT ONBOARD BY DEAD CELL. THEY WERE HERE FROM THE VERY BEGINNING."
"HUH? WHY WOULD A DECONTAMINATION PLANT HOUSE NUKES?"

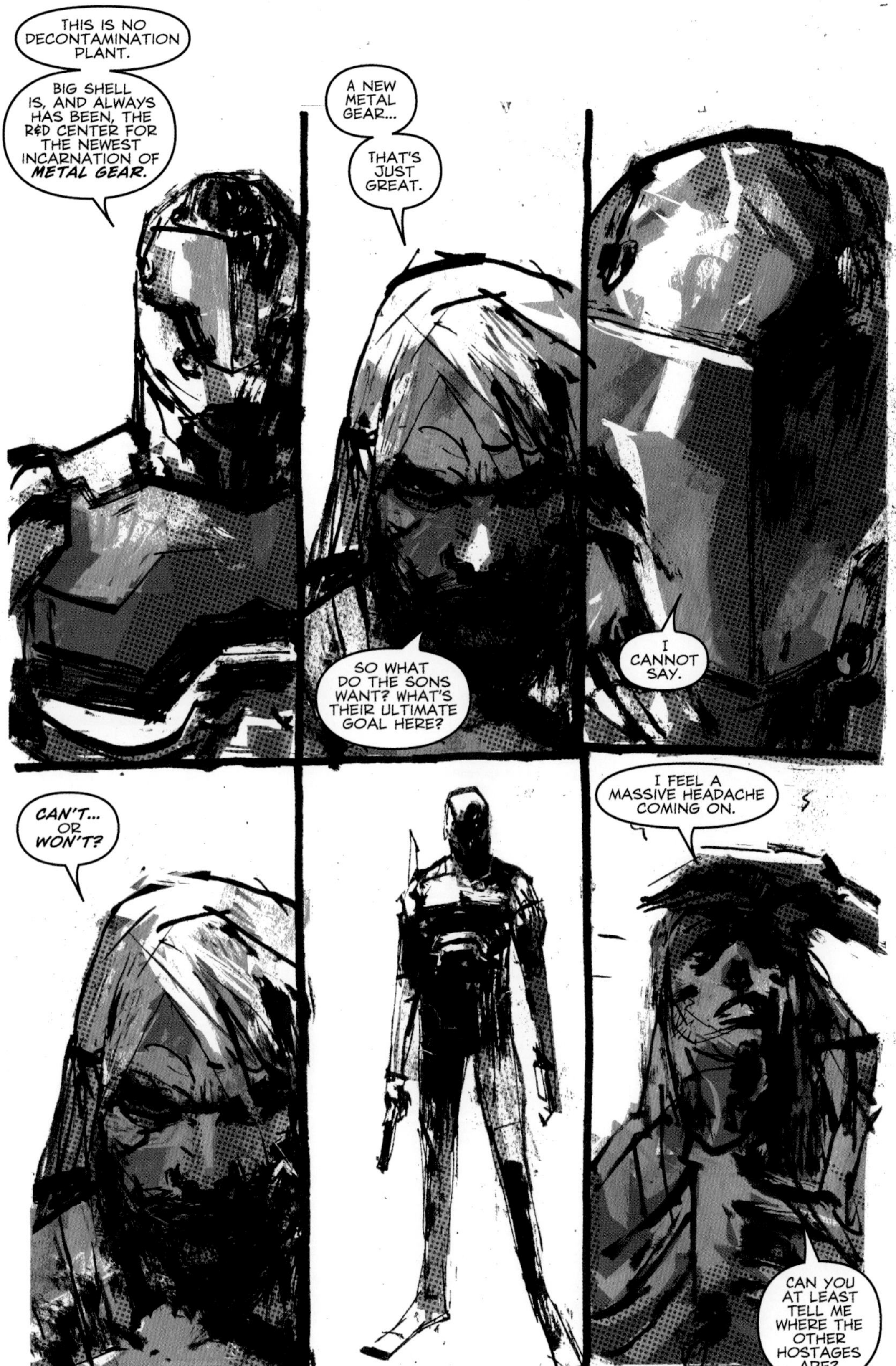
THIS IS NO DECONTAMINATION PLANT.
BIG SHELL IS, AND ALWAYS HAS BEEN, THE R&D CENTER FOR THE NEWEST INCARNATION OF METAL GEAR.
A NEW METAL GEAR...
THAT'S JUST GREAT.
SO WHAT DO THE SONS WANT? WHAT'S THEIR ULTIMATE GOAL HERE?
I CANNOT SAY.
CAN'T... OR WON'T?
I FEEL A MASSIVE HEADACHE COMING ON.
CAN YOU AT LEAST TELL ME WHERE THE OTHER HOSTAGES ARE?

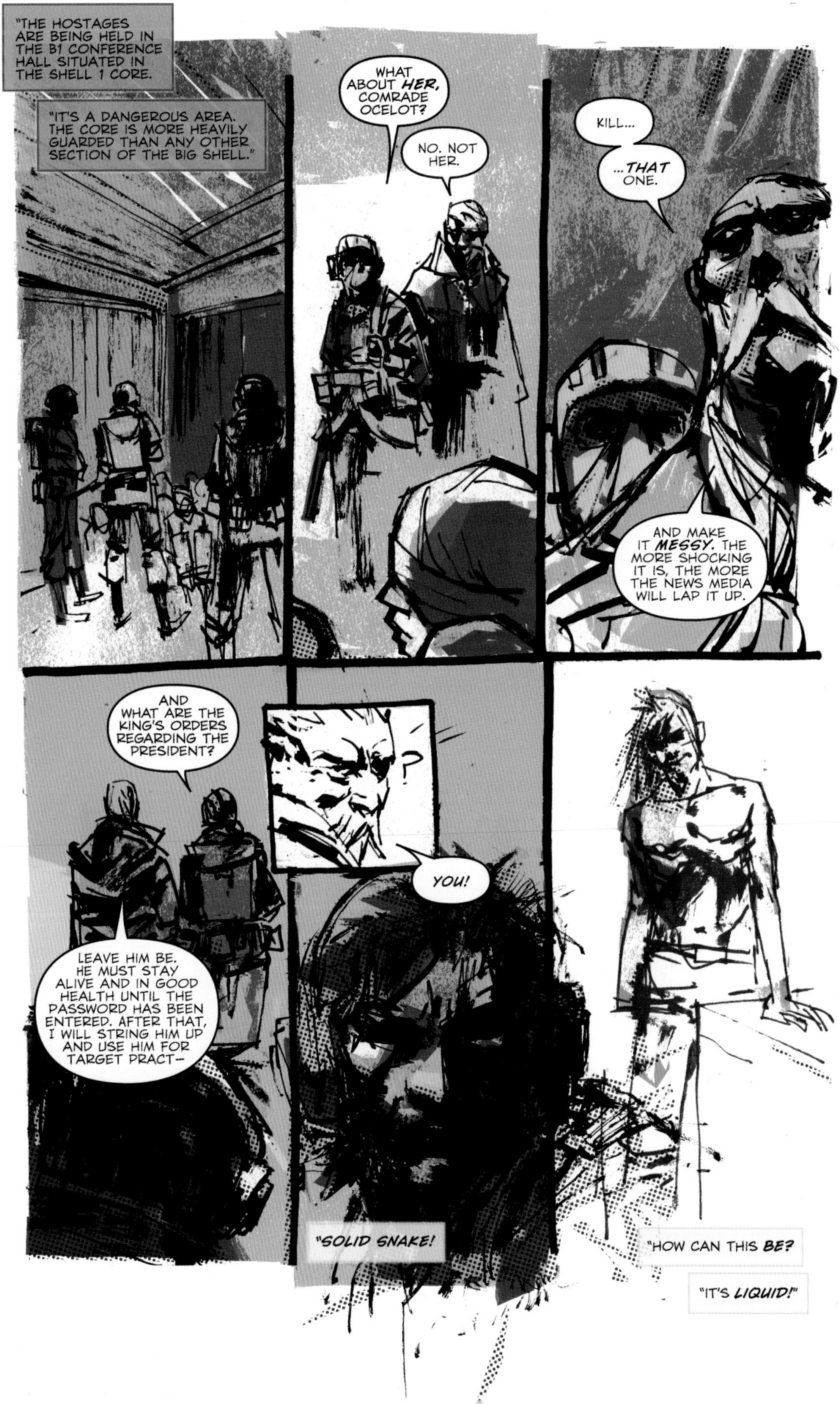
"THE HOSTAGES ARE BEING HELD IN THE B1 CONFERENCE HALL SITUATED IN THE SHELL 1 CORE.
"IT'S A DANGEROUS AREA. THE CORE IS MORE HEAVILY GUARDED THAN ANY OTHER SECTION OF THE BIG SHELL."
WHAT ABOUT HER, COMRADE OCELOT?
NO. NOT HER.
KILL...
...THAT ONE.
AND MAKE IT MESSY. THE MORE SHOCKING IT IS, THE MORE THE NEWS MEDIA WILL LAP IT UP.
AND WHAT ARE THE KING'S ORDERS REGARDING THE PRESIDENT?
LEAVE HIM BE. HE MUST STAY ALIVE AND IN GOOD HEALTH UNTIL THE PASSWORD HAS BEEN ENTERED. AFTER THAT, I WILL STRING HIM UP AND USE HIM FOR TARGET PRACT—
?
YOU!
"SOLID SNAKE!
"HOW CAN THIS BE?
"IT'S LIQUID!"

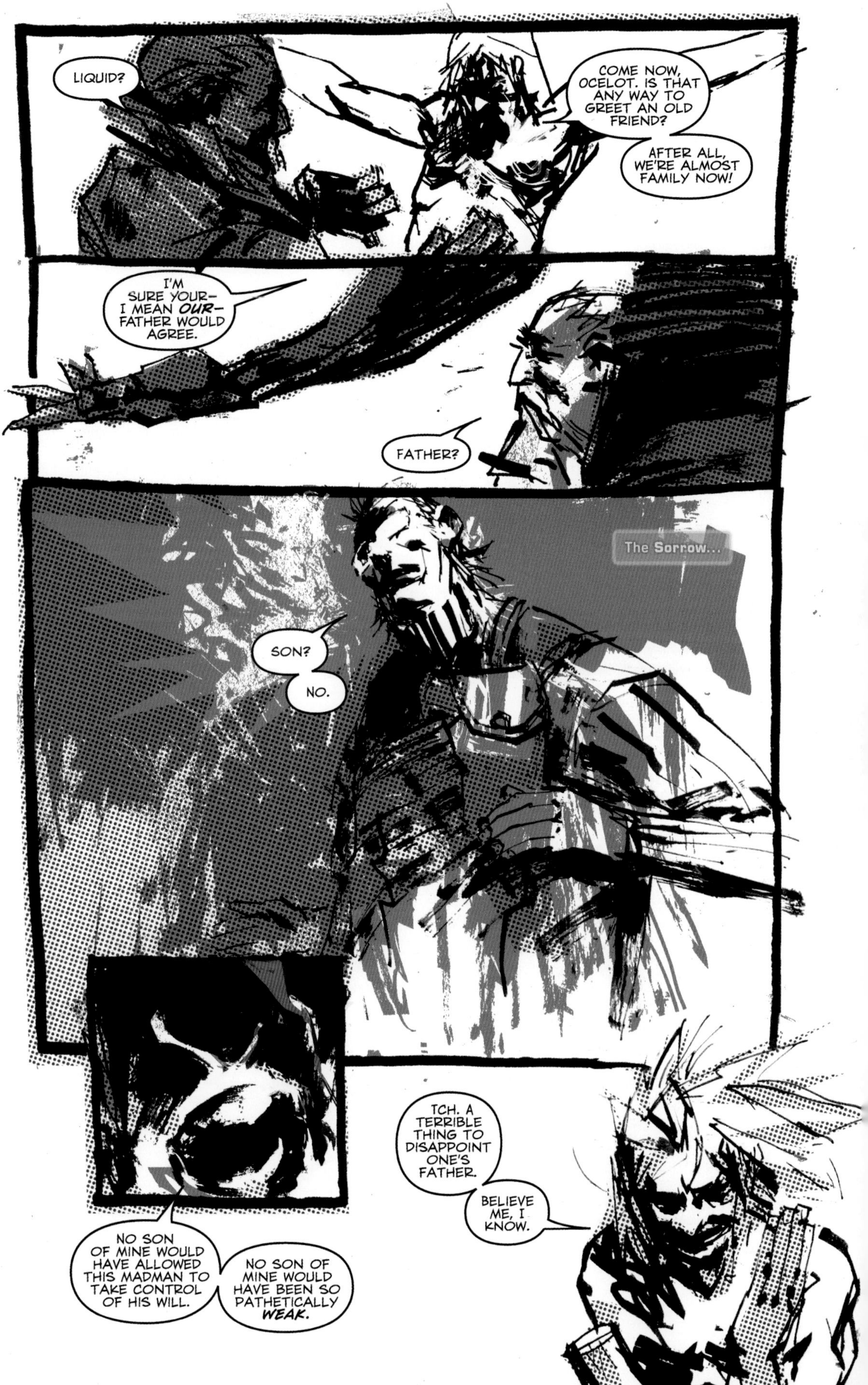

LIQUID?
COME NOW, OCELOT. IS THAT ANY WAY TO GREET AN OLD FRIEND?
AFTER ALL, WE'RE ALMOST FAMILY NOW!
I'M SURE YOUR- I MEAN ***OUR***- FATHER WOULD AGREE.
FATHER?
The Sorrow...
SON?
NO.
NO SON OF MINE WOULD HAVE ALLOWED THIS MADMAN TO TAKE CONTROL OF HIS WILL.
NO SON OF MINE WOULD HAVE BEEN SO PATHETICALLY ***WEAK.***
TCH. A TERRIBLE THING TO DISAPPOINT ONE'S FATHER.
BELIEVE ME, I KNOW.

SHUT UP!
ARE YOU TALKING TO ME, OR YOURSELF?
MADNESS...
JUST GO AWAY! BOTH OF YOU!
LET ME BE!
VERY WELL, OCELOT. JUST KNOW THAT I HOLD THE UPPER HAND NOW.
REMEMBER THAT WELL, OR YOU'LL LIVE TO REGRET IT...
...REGRET IT TO YOUR EVERLASTING SORROW.

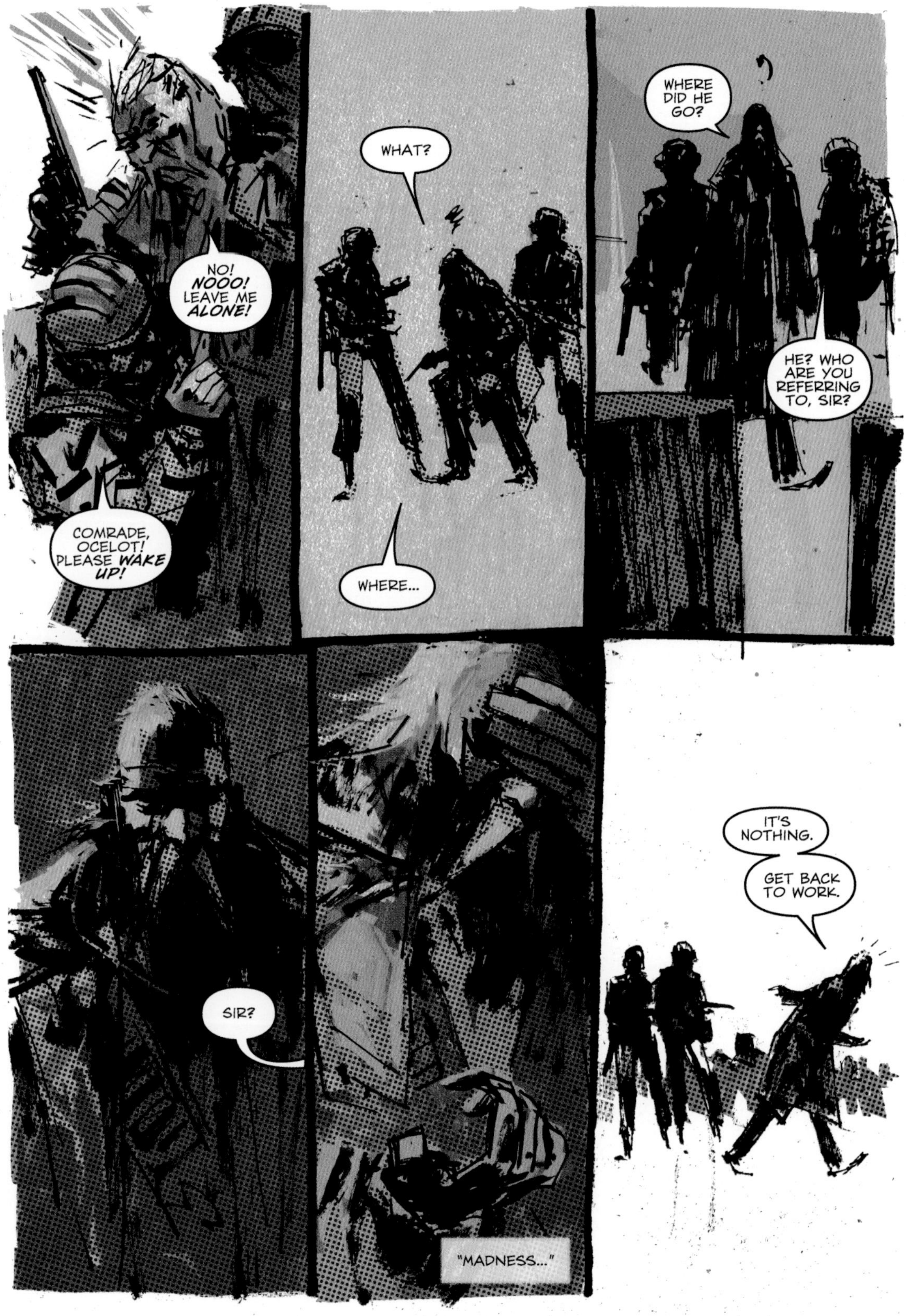
NO! NOOO! LEAVE ME ALONE!
COMRADE, OCELOT! PLEASE WAKE UP!
WHAT?
WHERE...
WHERE DID HE GO?
HE? WHO ARE YOU REFERRING TO, SIR?
SIR?
"MADNESS..."
IT'S NOTHING.
GET BACK TO WORK.

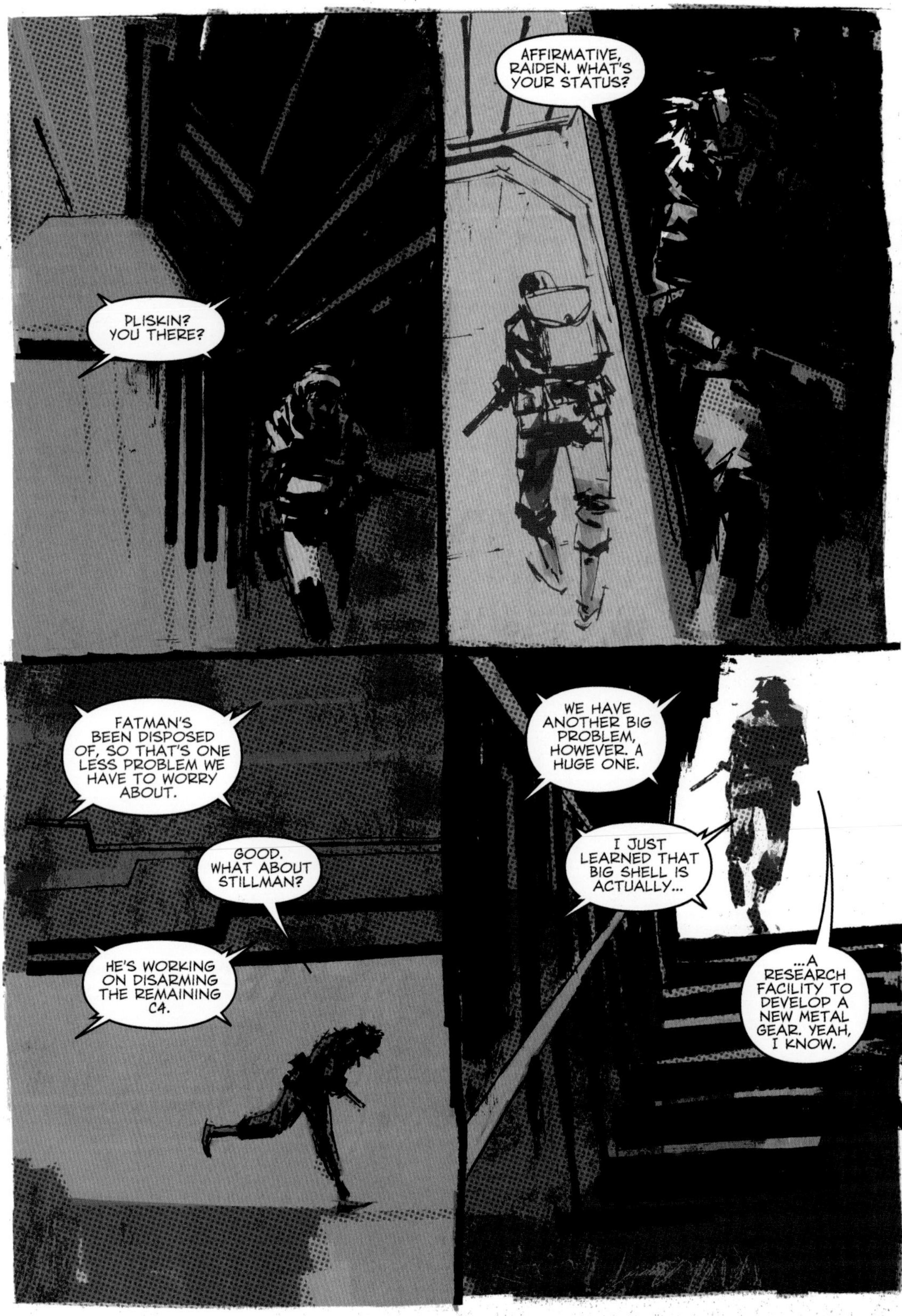
PLISKIN? YOU THERE?
AFFIRMATIVE, RAIDEN. WHAT'S YOUR STATUS?
FATMAN'S BEEN DISPOSED OF, SO THAT'S ONE LESS PROBLEM WE HAVE TO WORRY ABOUT.
GOOD. WHAT ABOUT STILLMAN?
HE'S WORKING ON DISARMING THE REMAINING C4.
WE HAVE ANOTHER BIG PROBLEM, HOWEVER. A HUGE ONE.
I JUST LEARNED THAT BIG SHELL IS ACTUALLY...
...A RESEARCH FACILITY TO DEVELOP A NEW METAL GEAR. YEAH, I KNOW.

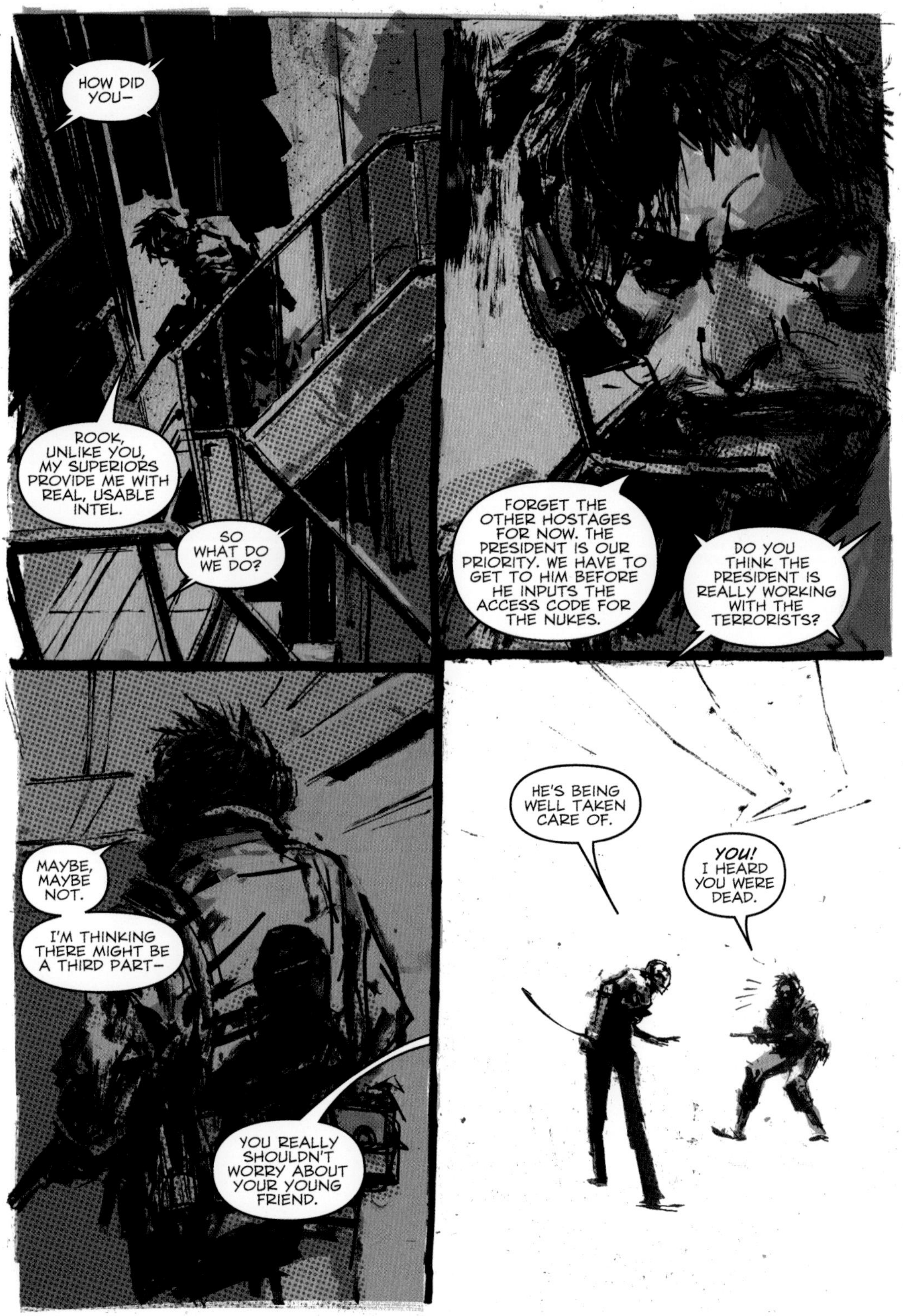
HOW DID YOU–
ROOK, UNLIKE YOU, MY SUPERIORS PROVIDE ME WITH REAL, USABLE INTEL.
SO WHAT DO WE DO?
FORGET THE OTHER HOSTAGES FOR NOW. THE PRESIDENT IS OUR PRIORITY. WE HAVE TO GET TO HIM BEFORE HE INPUTS THE ACCESS CODE FOR THE NUKES.
DO YOU THINK THE PRESIDENT IS REALLY WORKING WITH THE TERRORISTS?
MAYBE, MAYBE NOT.
I'M THINKING THERE MIGHT BE A THIRD PART–
YOU REALLY SHOULDN'T WORRY ABOUT YOUR YOUNG FRIEND.
HE'S BEING WELL TAKEN CARE OF.
YOU! I HEARD YOU WERE DEAD.

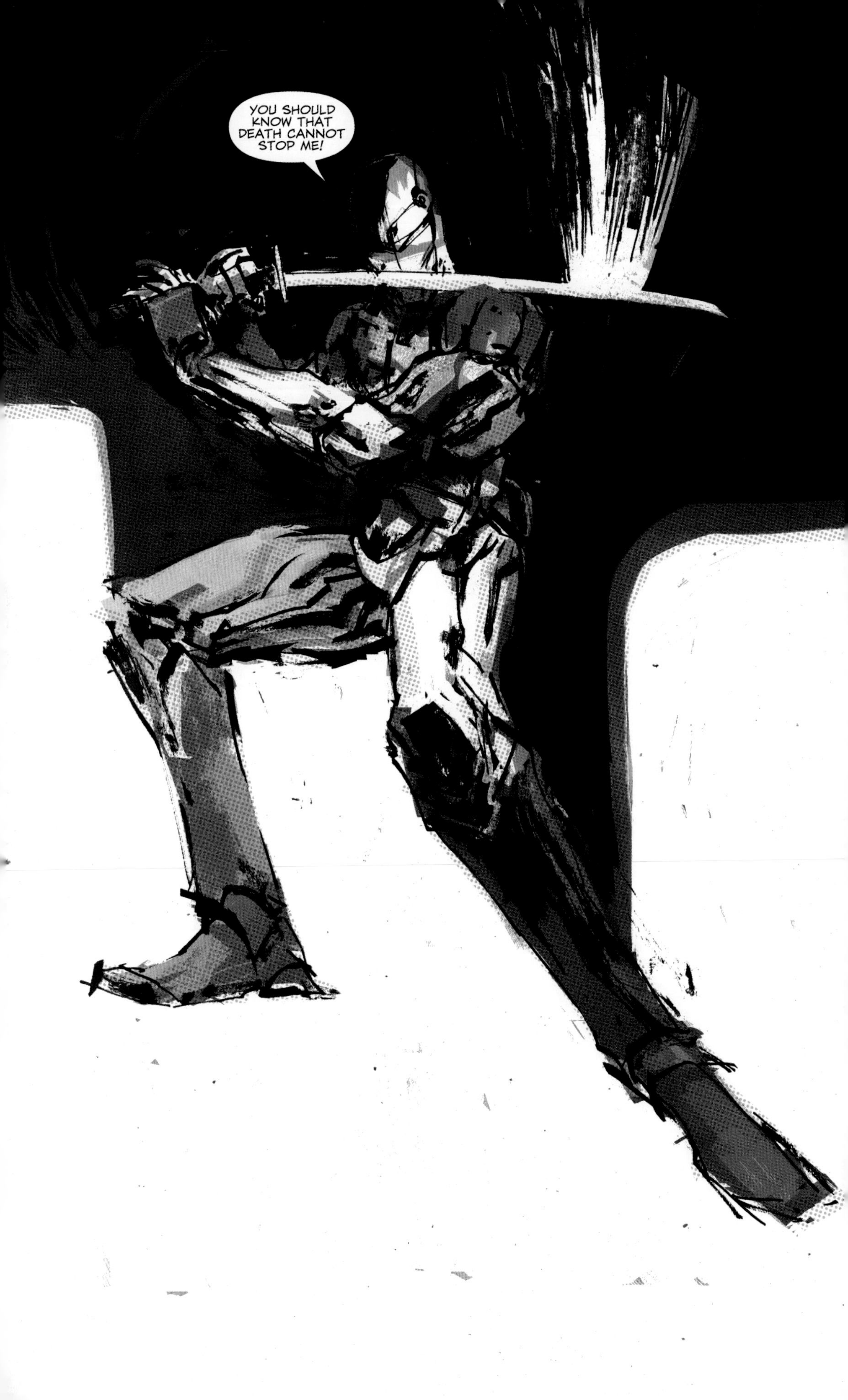
YOU SHOULD KNOW THAT DEATH CANNOT STOP ME!

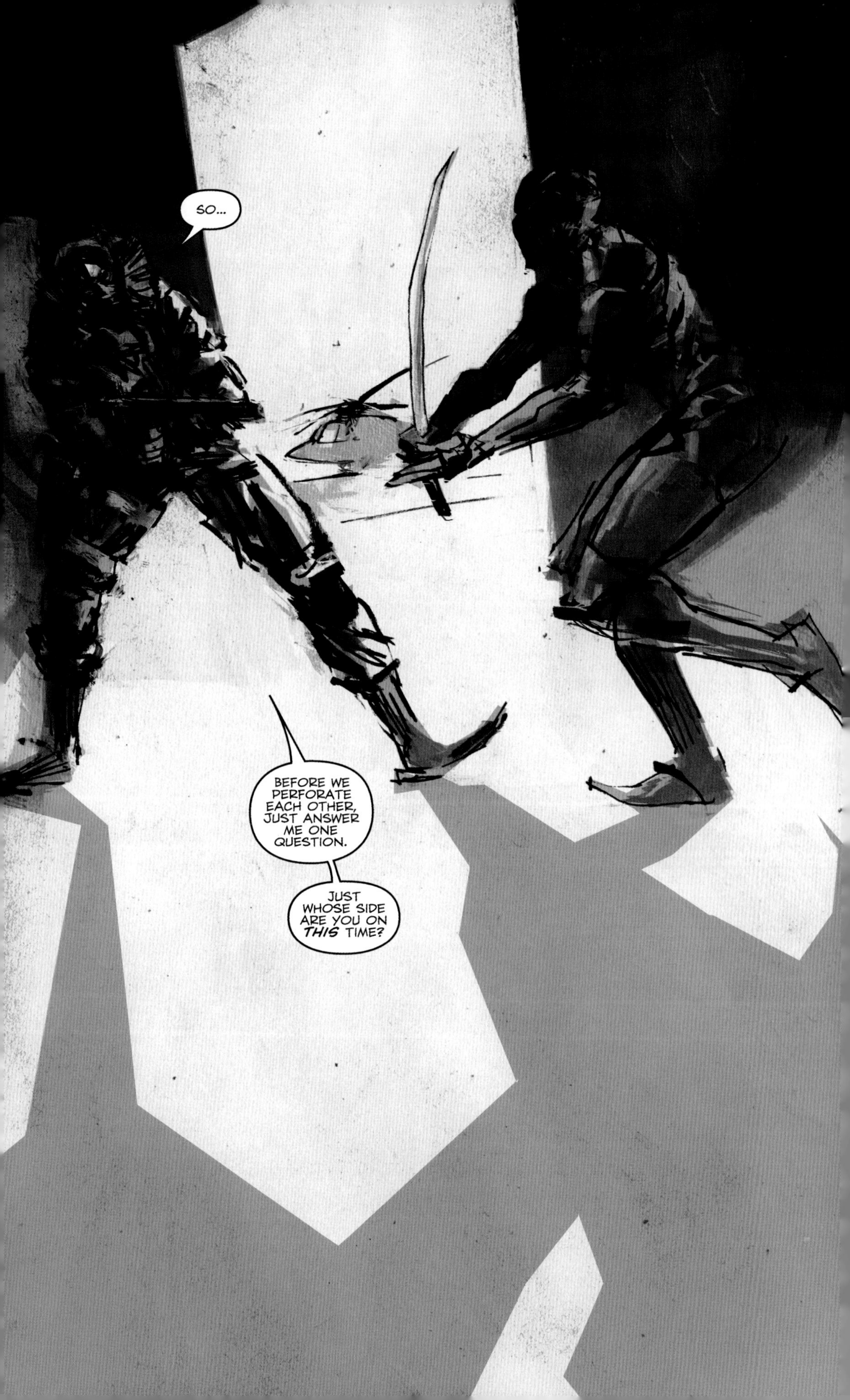
SO...
BEFORE WE PERFORATE EACH OTHER, JUST ANSWER ME ONE QUESTION.
JUST WHOSE SIDE ARE YOU ON *THIS* TIME?

THE SAME SIDE I'VE ALWAYS BEEN ON.
MINE.
UH-HUH. BUT THERE'S DEFINITELY SOMEONE ELSE PULLING YOUR STRINGS.
SO, PARDON ME IF I'M JUST A TAD SKEPTICAL AT THIS POINT IN TIME.
YOU DIDN'T HAVE TO RESPOND TO MY COMMUNIQUE.
YOU DIDN'T HAVE TO COME TO BIG SHELL.
YEAH, BUT I'VE BEEN KNOWN TO PUT MYSELF INTO REALLY STUPID SITUATIONS, SO DON'T START PATTING YOURSELF ON THE BACK YET.
TRUST IS SOMETHING YOU EARN. CAPICE?

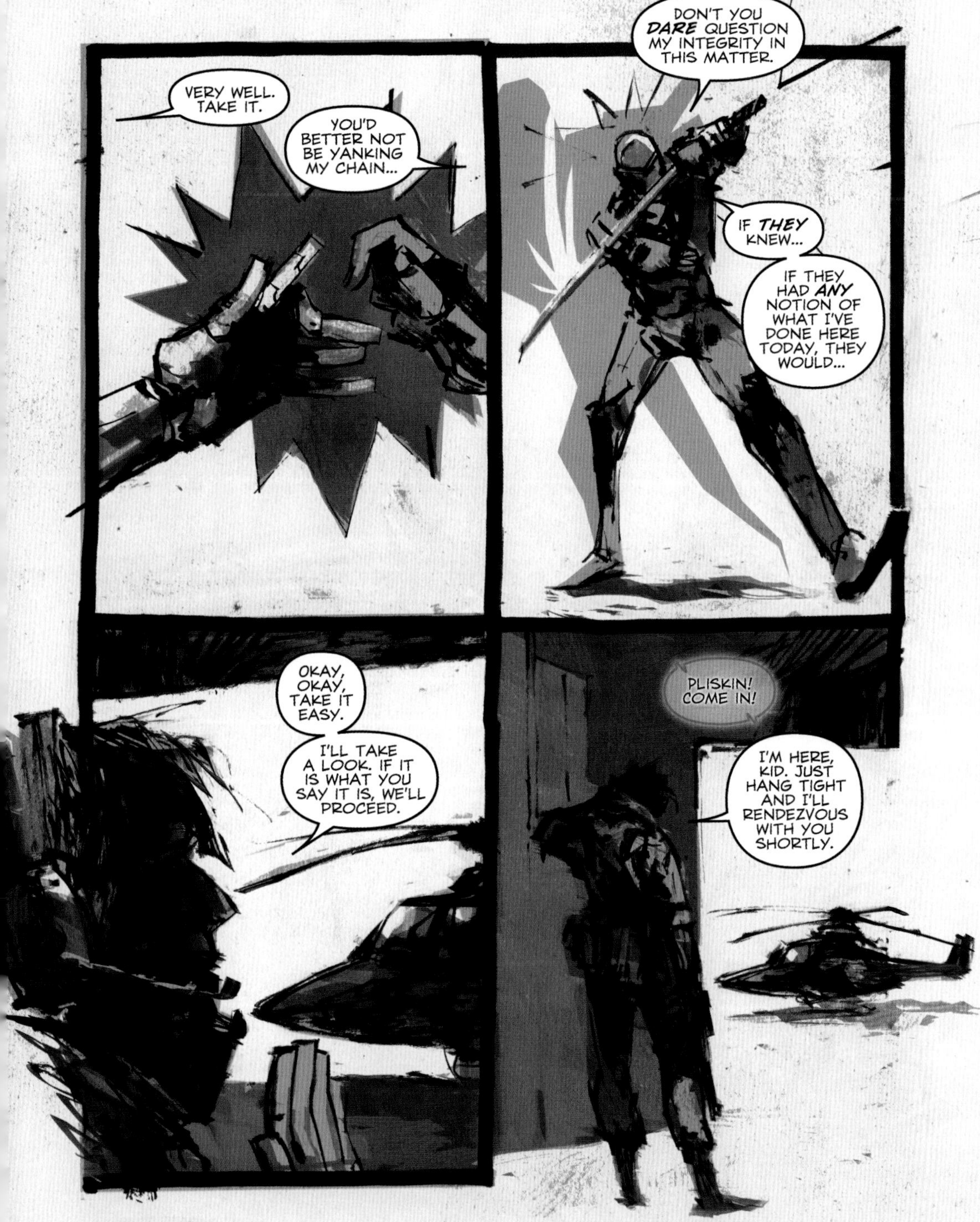
VERY WELL. TAKE IT.
YOU'D BETTER NOT BE YANKING MY CHAIN...
DON'T YOU DARE QUESTION MY INTEGRITY IN THIS MATTER.
IF THEY KNEW...
IF THEY HAD ANY NOTION OF WHAT I'VE DONE HERE TODAY, THEY WOULD...
OKAY, OKAY, TAKE IT EASY.
I'LL TAKE A LOOK. IF IT IS WHAT YOU SAY IT IS, WE'LL PROCEED.
PLISKIN! COME IN!
I'M HERE, KID. JUST HANG TIGHT AND I'LL RENDEZVOUS WITH YOU SHORTLY.

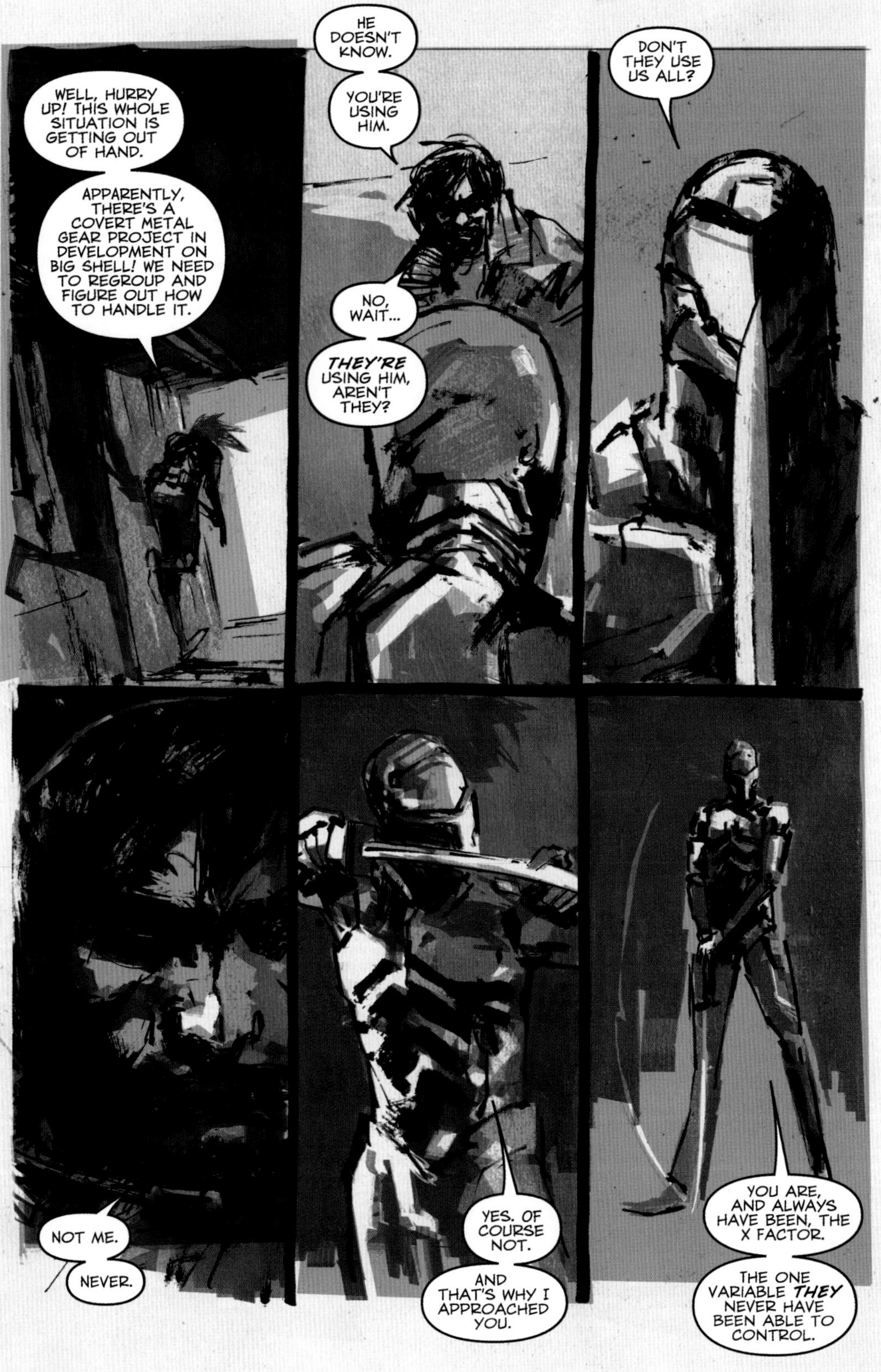
WELL, HURRY UP! THIS WHOLE SITUATION IS GETTING OUT OF HAND.
APPARENTLY, THERE'S A COVERT METAL GEAR PROJECT IN DEVELOPMENT ON BIG SHELL! WE NEED TO REGROUP AND FIGURE OUT HOW TO HANDLE IT.
HE DOESN'T KNOW.
YOU'RE USING HIM.
NO, WAIT...
THEY'RE USING HIM, AREN'T THEY?
DON'T THEY USE US ALL?
NOT ME.
NEVER.
YES. OF COURSE NOT.
AND THAT'S WHY I APPROACHED YOU.
YOU ARE, AND ALWAYS HAVE BEEN, THE X FACTOR.
THE ONE VARIABLE THEY NEVER HAVE BEEN ABLE TO CONTROL.

"RAIDEN, HOWEVER, IS ANOTHER MATTER ENTIRELY..."
MR. STILLMAN, IT'S RAIDEN. WHERE ARE YOU?
THE CORE B1 FILTRATION CHAMBER.
IS IT GOING WELL?
BETTER THAN EXPECTED. NO GUARDS ARE POSTED HERE, SO I'VE GOT FREE REIGN TO DISARM FATMAN'S REMAINING C4.
PRETTY BASIC BOMB ASSEMBLY. NOTHING I CAN'T HAND-
EEEEEEEEE
AAAH!
TSK, TSK. NOW YOU'VE DONE IT.
NO WAY...
I AM *FATMAN,* AND THIS IS A RECORDING FOR THE WITLESS WONDER WHO'S FOOLISHLY ATTEMPTING TO DEFILE MY WORKS OF ART.
WHAT THE HELL?
YOU HAVE JUST TRIGGERED A MICROWAVE PROXIMITY EXPLOSIVE WITH A 7 FOOT RANGE AND A THIRTY SECOND TIMER.
IN OTHER WORDS, YOU'RE ALREADY *DEAD,* AND THERE'S *NOTHING* YOU CAN DO ABOUT IT.

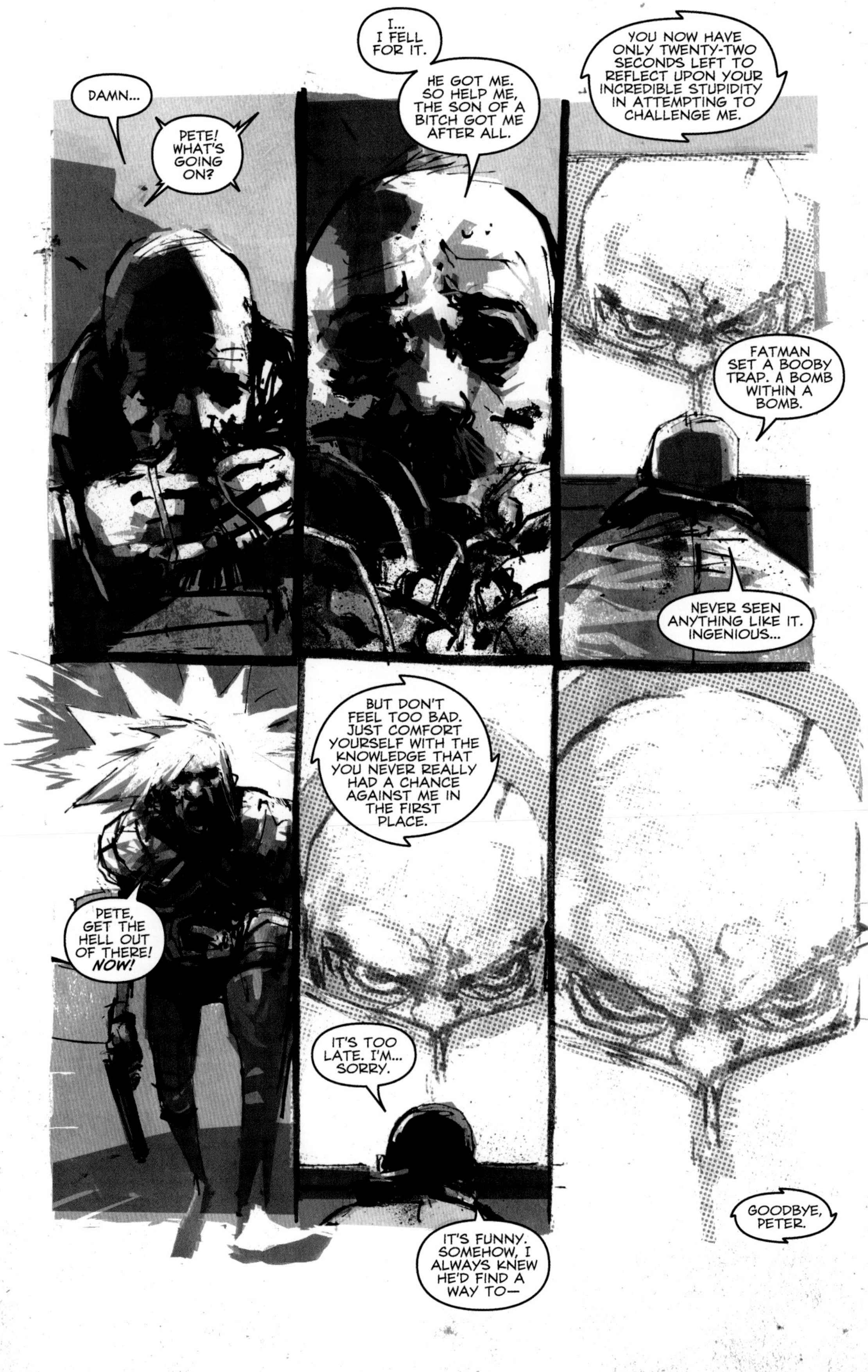
DAMN...
PETE! WHAT'S GOING ON?
I... I FELL FOR IT.
HE GOT ME. SO HELP ME, THE SON OF A BITCH GOT ME AFTER ALL.
YOU NOW HAVE ONLY TWENTY-TWO SECONDS LEFT TO REFLECT UPON YOUR INCREDIBLE STUPIDITY IN ATTEMPTING TO CHALLENGE ME.
FATMAN SET A BOOBY TRAP. A BOMB WITHIN A BOMB.
NEVER SEEN ANYTHING LIKE IT. INGENIOUS...
PETE, GET THE HELL OUT OF THERE! NOW!
BUT DON'T FEEL TOO BAD. JUST COMFORT YOURSELF WITH THE KNOWLEDGE THAT YOU NEVER REALLY HAD A CHANCE AGAINST ME IN THE FIRST PLACE.
IT'S TOO LATE. I'M... SORRY.
IT'S FUNNY. SOMEHOW, I ALWAYS KNEW HE'D FIND A WAY TO—
GOODBYE, PETER.

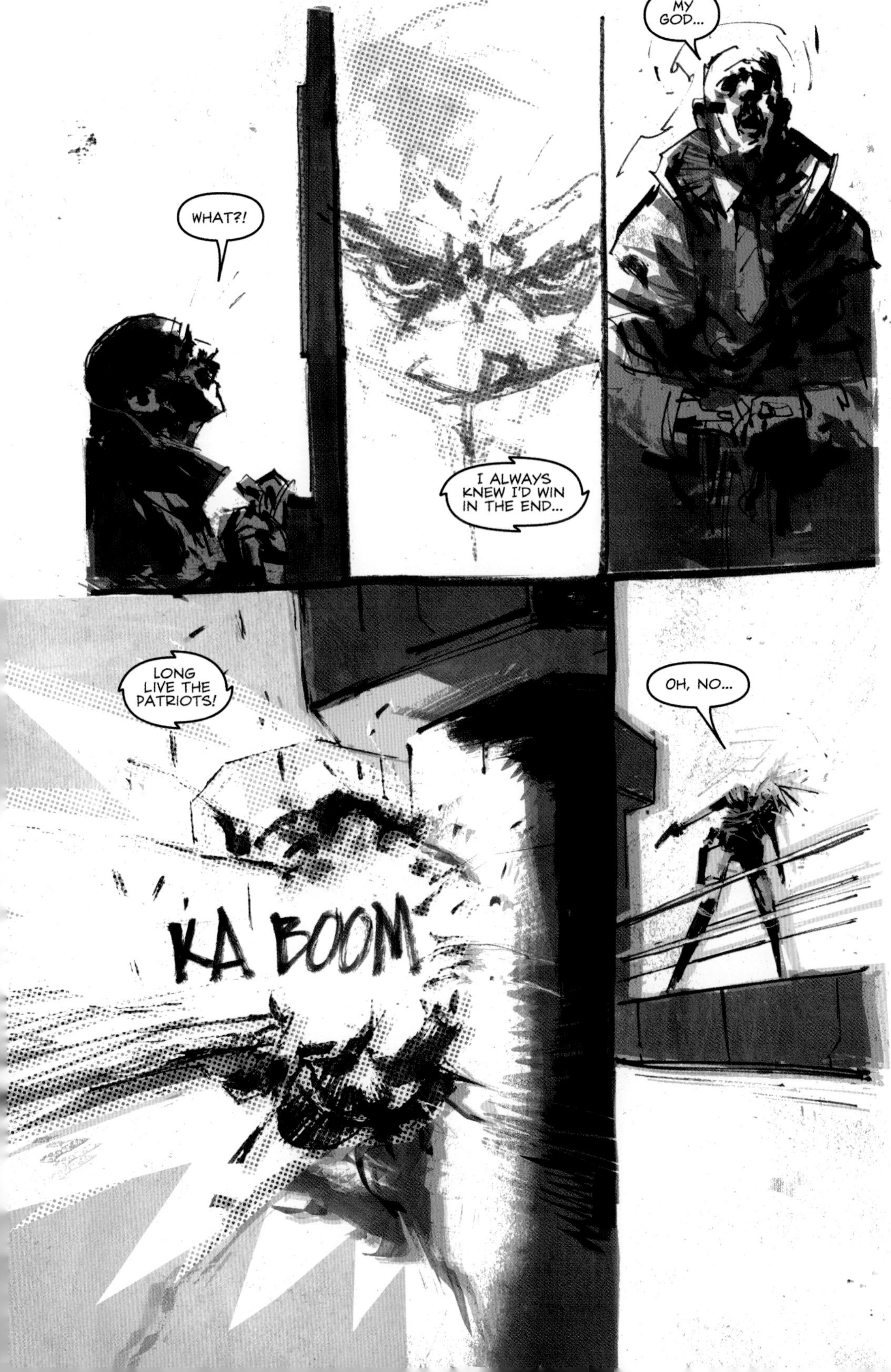
WHAT?!
I ALWAYS KNEW I'D WIN IN THE END...
MY GOD...
LONG LIVE THE PATRIOTS!
KA BOOM
OH, NO...

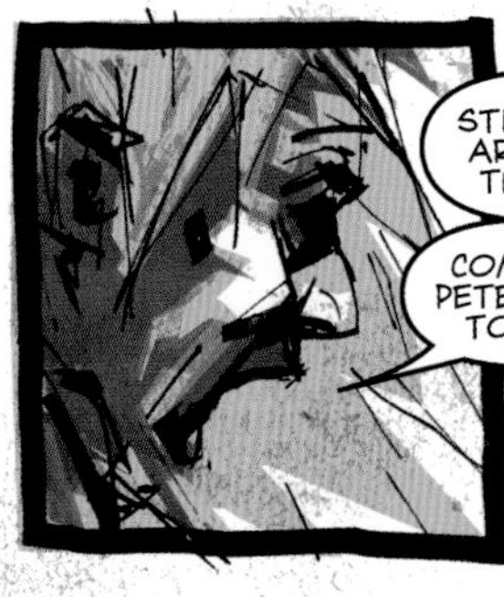
STILLMAN, ARE YOU THERE?
COME ON, PETE! *TALK* TO ME!

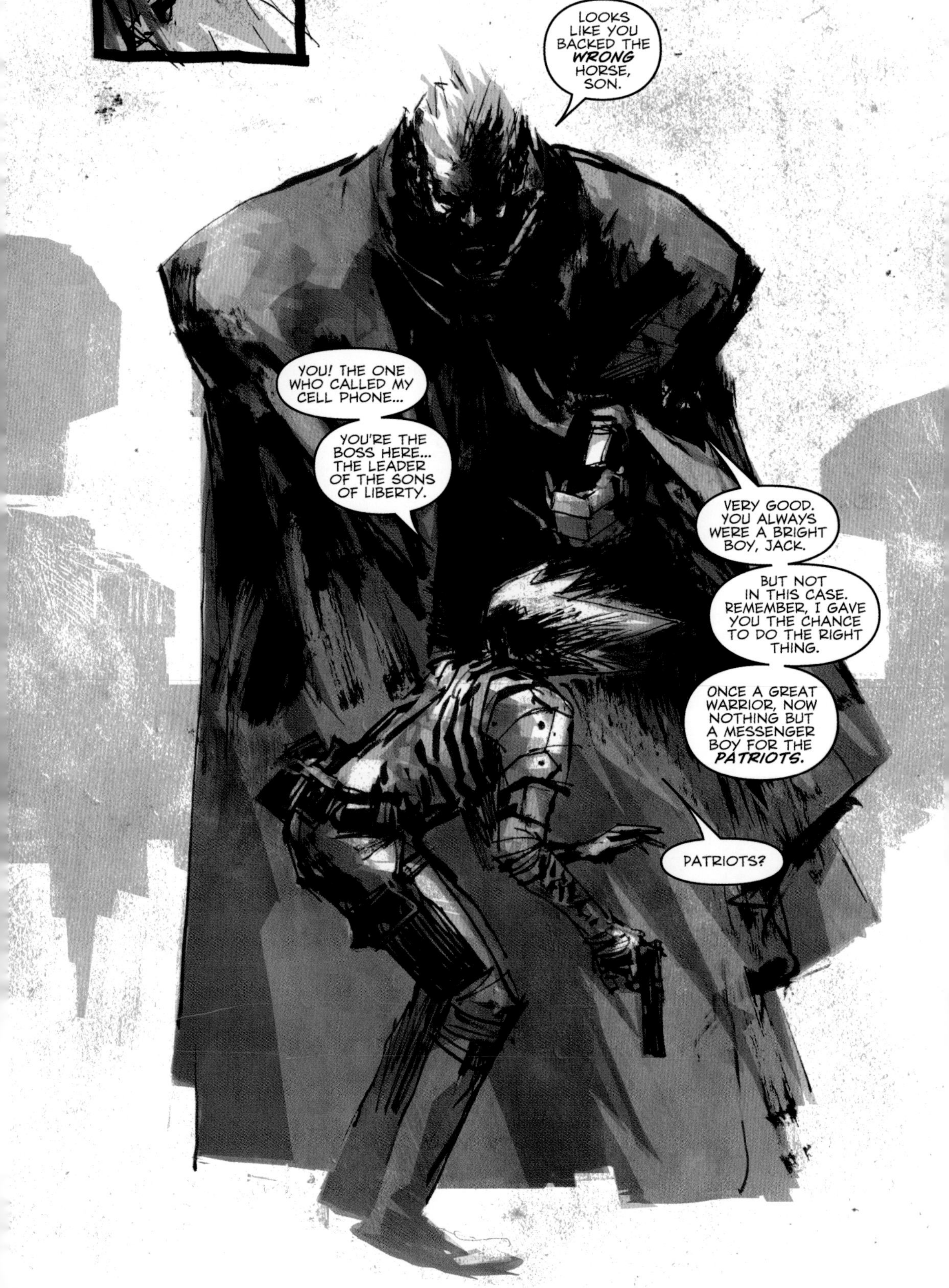
LOOKS LIKE YOU BACKED THE ***WRONG*** HORSE, SON.
YOU! THE ONE WHO CALLED MY CELL PHONE...
YOU'RE THE BOSS HERE... THE LEADER OF THE SONS OF LIBERTY.
VERY GOOD. YOU ALWAYS WERE A BRIGHT BOY, JACK.
BUT NOT IN THIS CASE. REMEMBER, I GAVE YOU THE CHANCE TO DO THE RIGHT THING.
ONCE A GREAT WARRIOR, NOW NOTHING BUT A MESSENGER BOY FOR THE ***PATRIOTS.***
PATRIOTS?

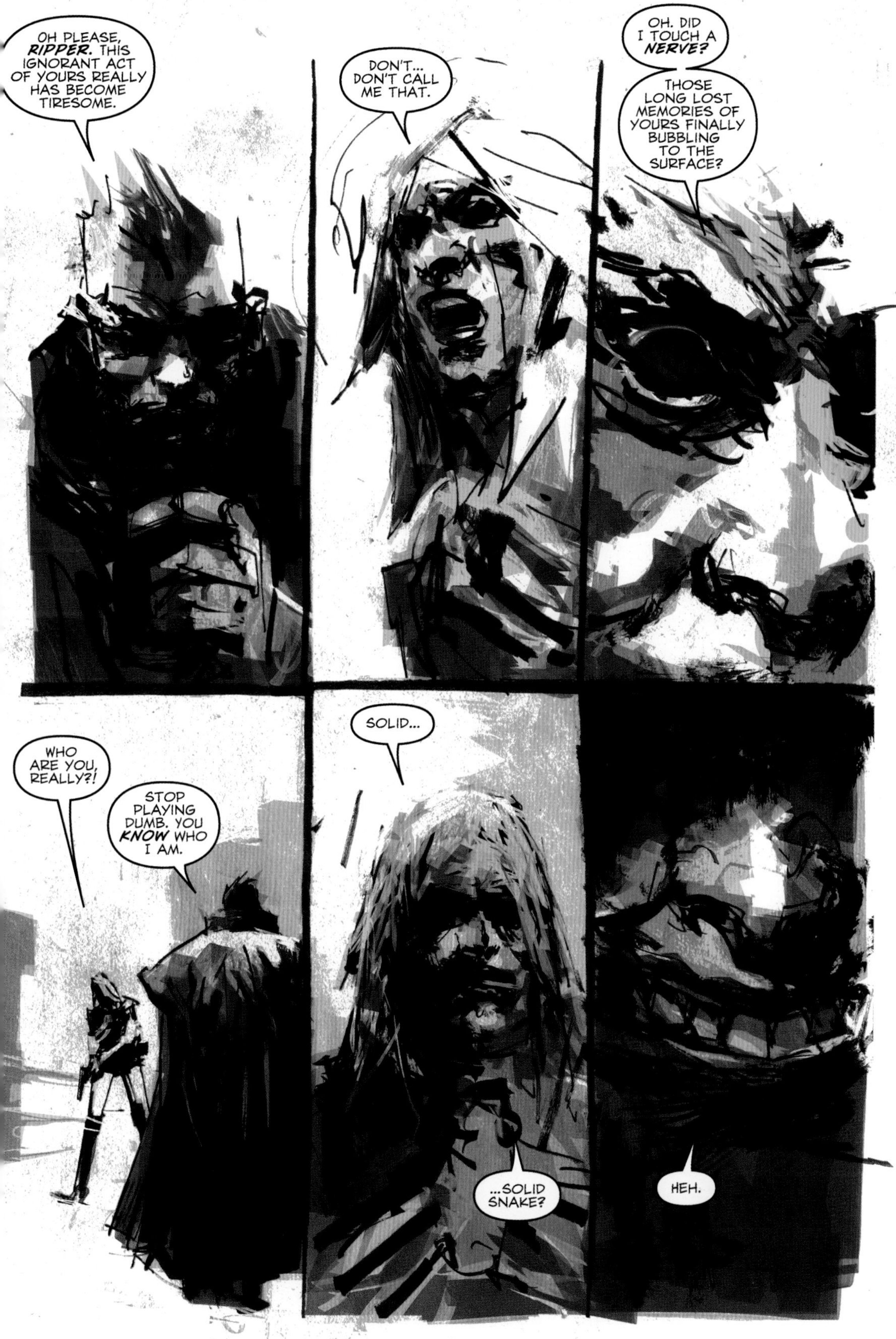
OH PLEASE, **RIPPER.** THIS IGNORANT ACT OF YOURS REALLY HAS BECOME TIRESOME.
DON'T... DON'T CALL ME THAT.
OH. DID I TOUCH A ***NERVE?***
THOSE LONG LOST MEMORIES OF YOURS FINALLY BUBBLING TO THE SURFACE?
WHO ARE YOU, REALLY?!
STOP PLAYING DUMB. YOU ***KNOW*** WHO I AM.
SOLID...
...SOLID SNAKE?
HEH.

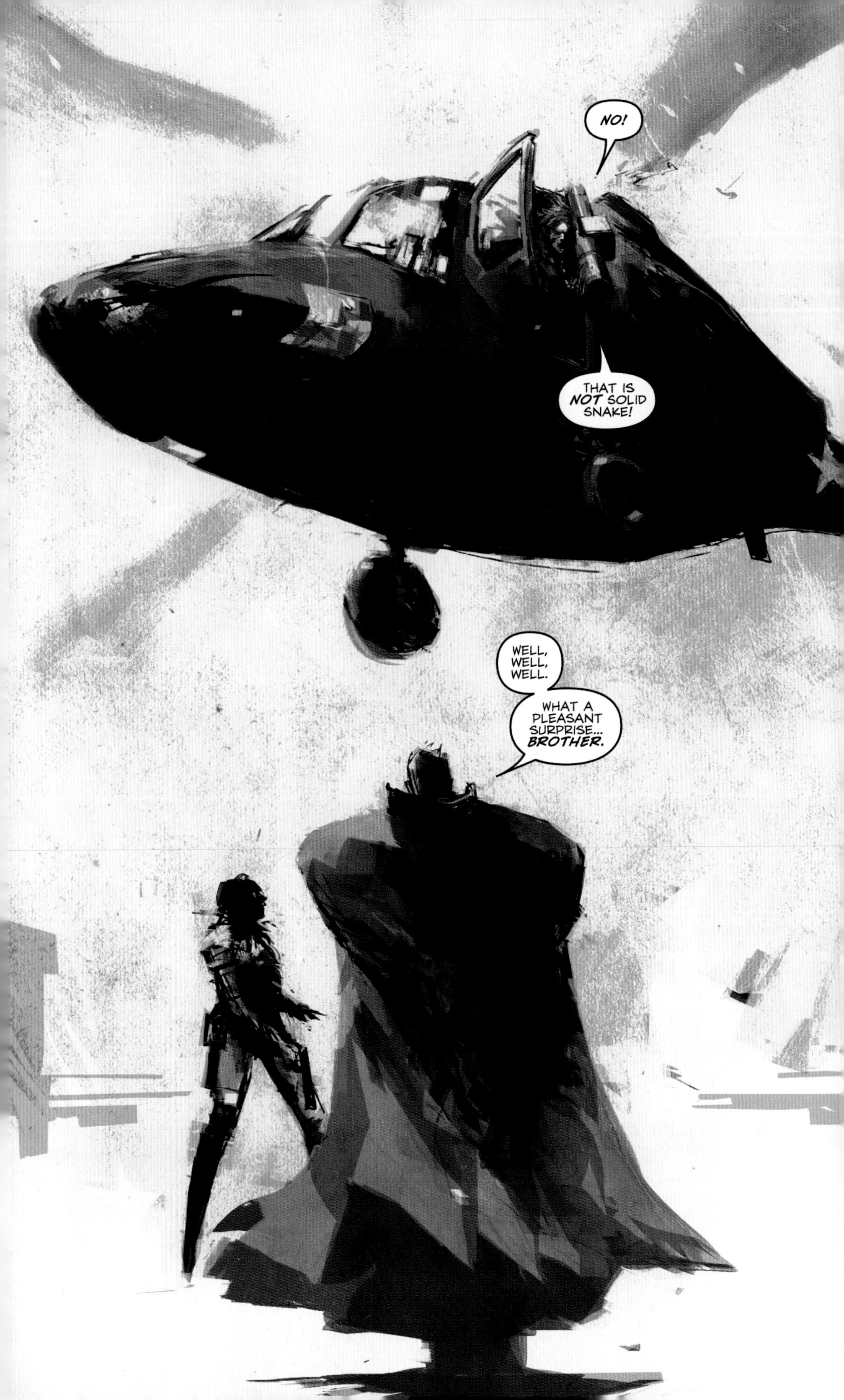
NO!
THAT IS NOT SOLID SNAKE!
WELL, WELL, WELL.
WHAT A PLEASANT SURPRISE... BROTHER.

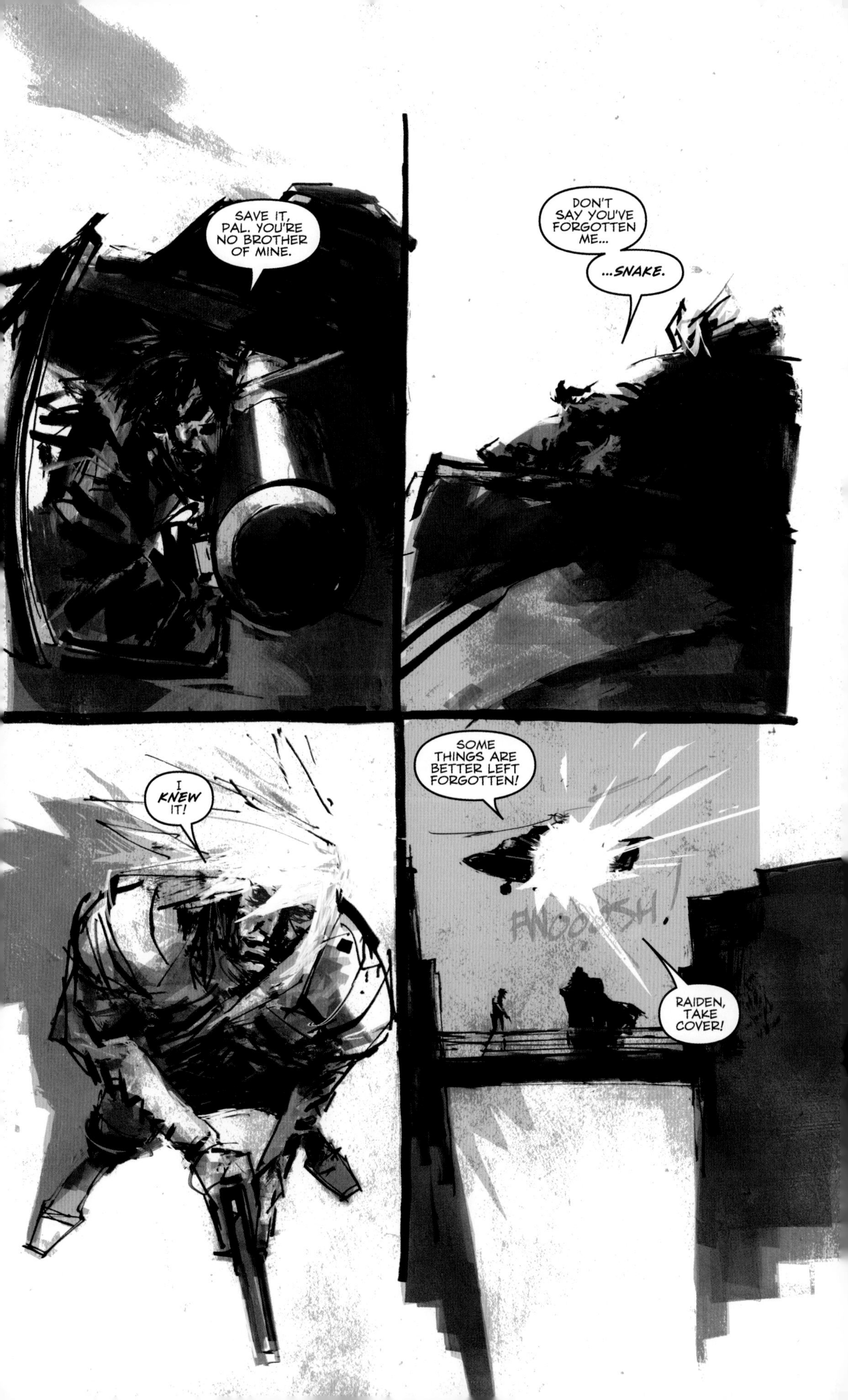
SAVE IT, PAL. YOU'RE NO BROTHER OF MINE.
DON'T SAY YOU'VE FORGOTTEN ME...
...SNAKE.
I KNEW IT!
SOME THINGS ARE BETTER LEFT FORGOTTEN!
RAIDEN, TAKE COVER!

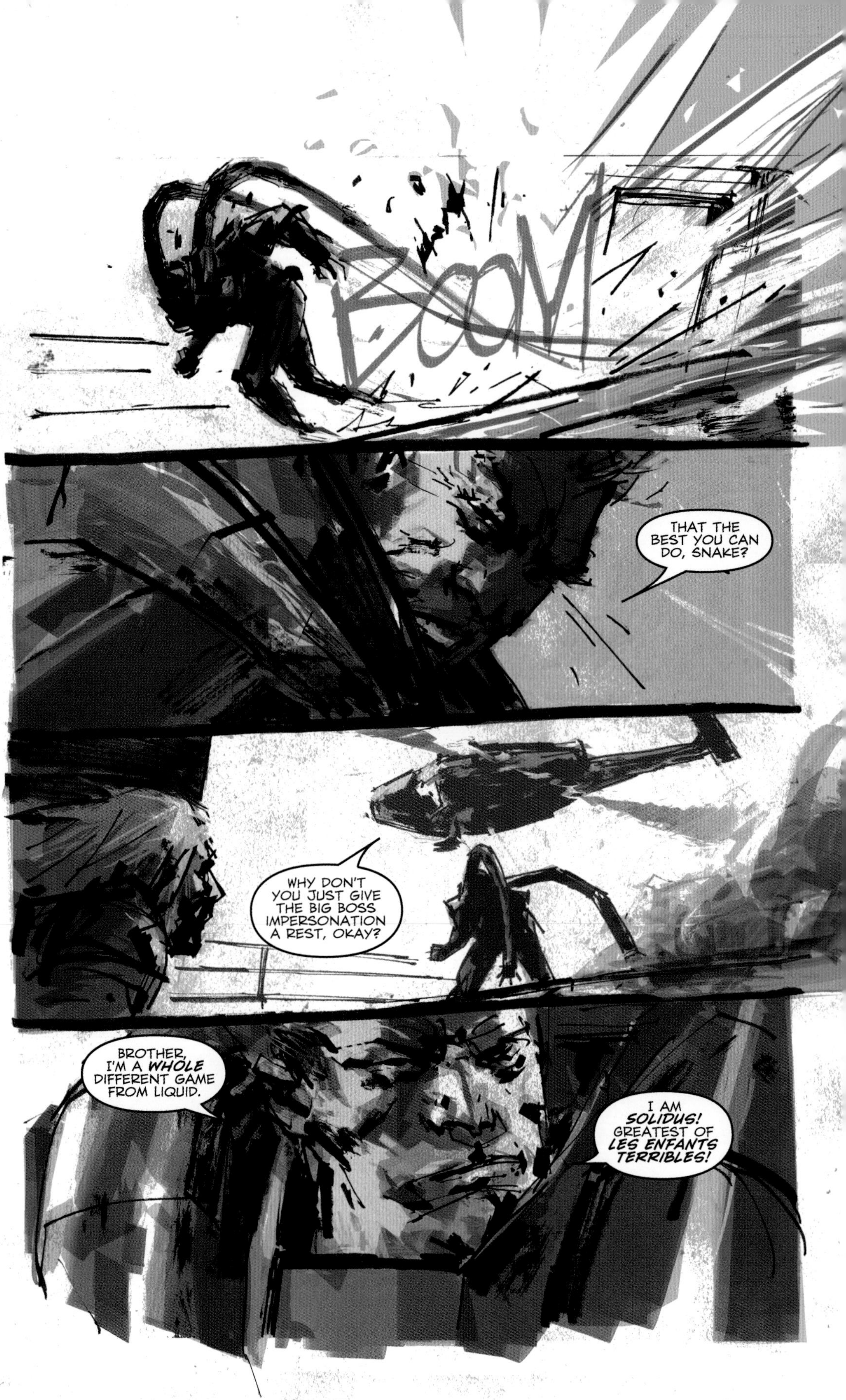
BOOM!
THAT THE BEST YOU CAN DO, SNAKE?
WHY DON'T YOU JUST GIVE THE BIG BOSS IMPERSONATION A REST, OKAY?
BROTHER, I'M A *WHOLE* DIFFERENT GAME FROM LIQUID.
I AM *SOLIDUS!* GREATEST OF *LES ENFANTS TERRIBLES!*

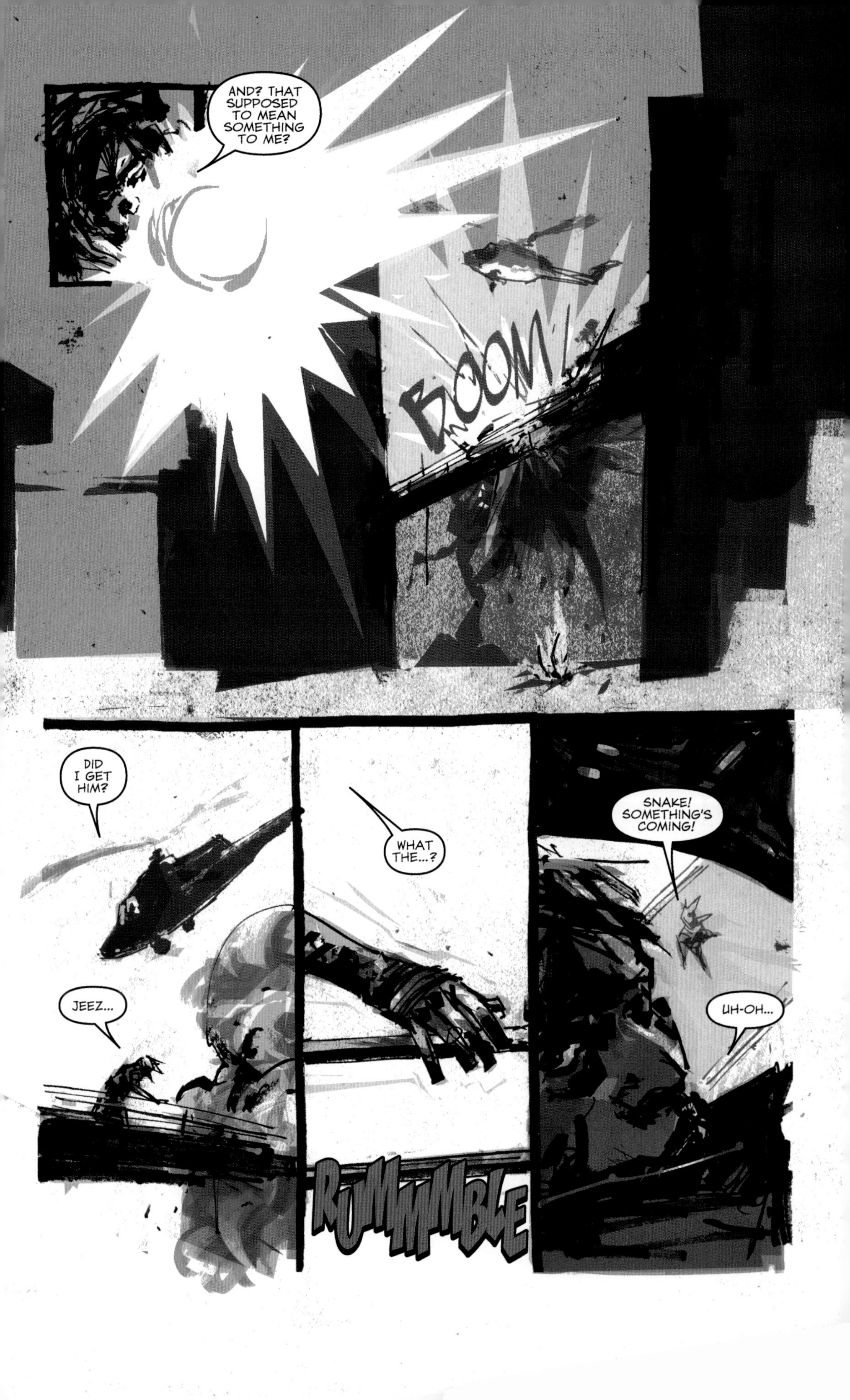
AND? THAT SUPPOSED TO MEAN SOMETHING TO ME?
BOOM
DID I GET HIM?
JEEZ...
WHAT THE...?
RUMMMBLE
SNAKE! SOMETHING'S COMING!
UH-OH...

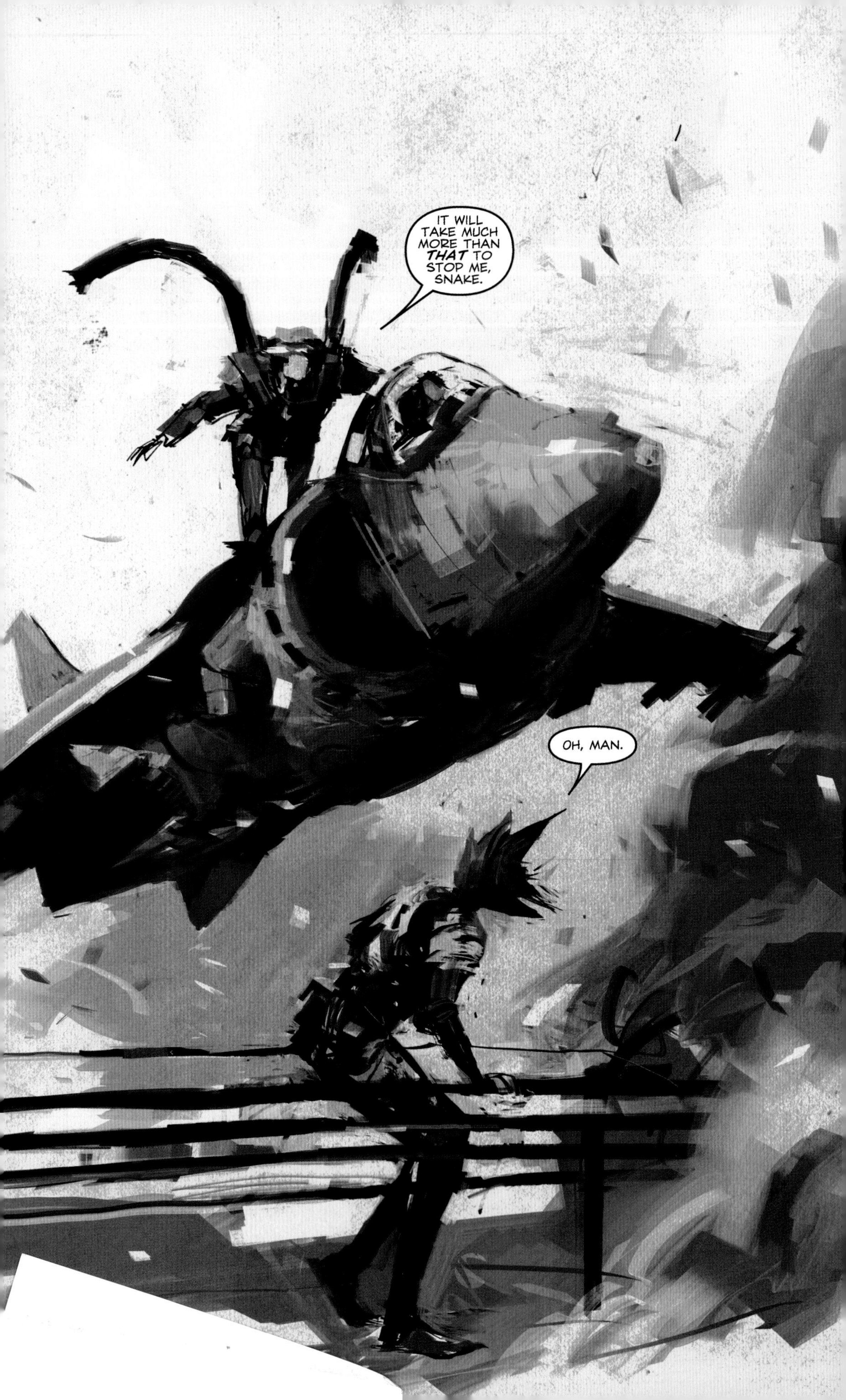
IT WILL TAKE MUCH MORE THAN *THAT* TO STOP ME, SNAKE.
OH, MAN.

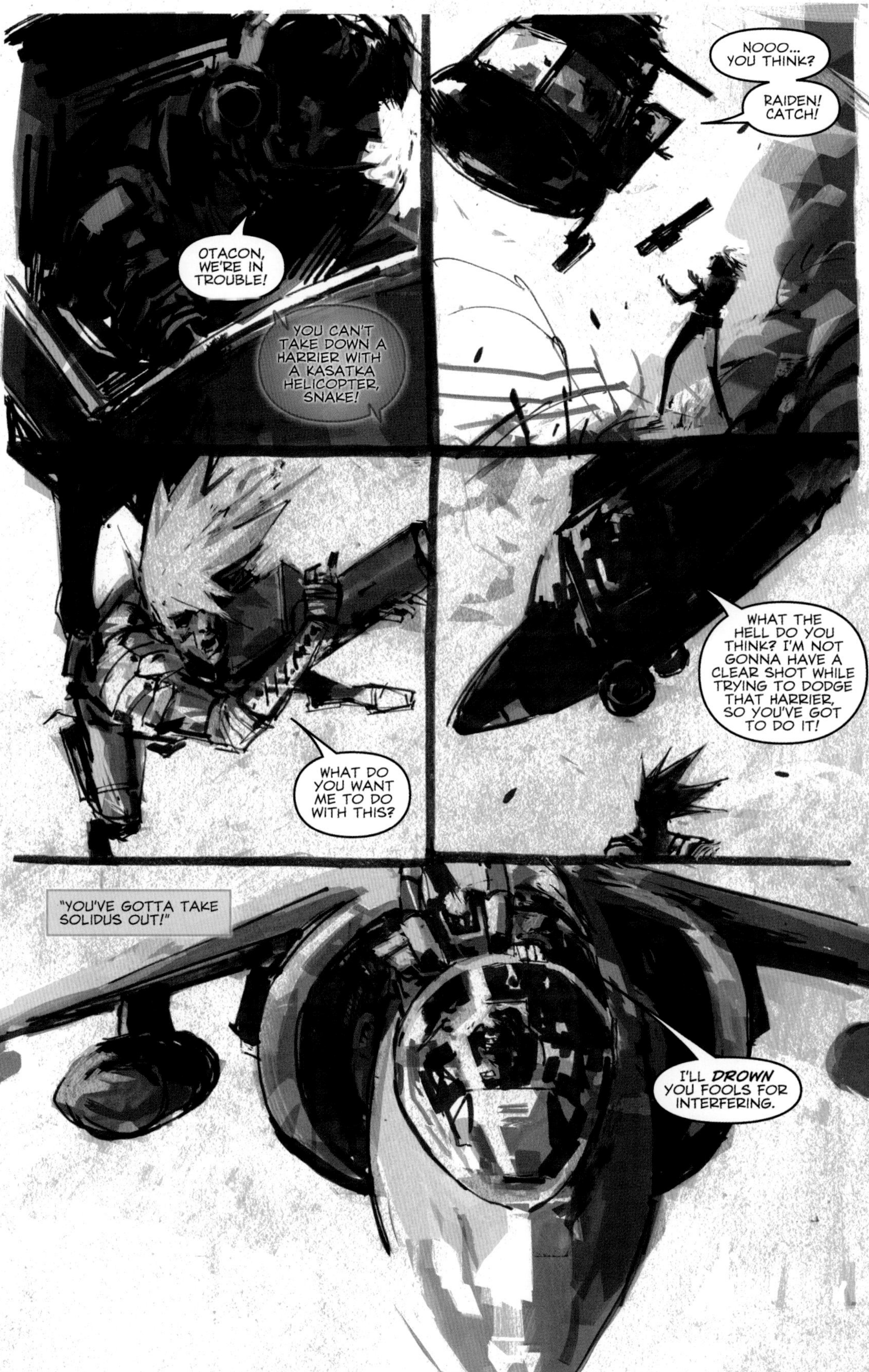
OTACON, WE'RE IN TROUBLE!
YOU CAN'T TAKE DOWN A HARRIER WITH A KASATKA HELICOPTER, SNAKE!
NOOO... YOU THINK?
RAIDEN! CATCH!
WHAT DO YOU WANT ME TO DO WITH THIS?
WHAT THE HELL DO YOU THINK? I'M NOT GONNA HAVE A CLEAR SHOT WHILE TRYING TO DODGE THAT HARRIER, SO YOU'VE GOT TO DO IT!
"YOU'VE GOTTA TAKE SOLIDUS OUT!"
I'LL DROWN YOU FOOLS FOR INTERFERING.

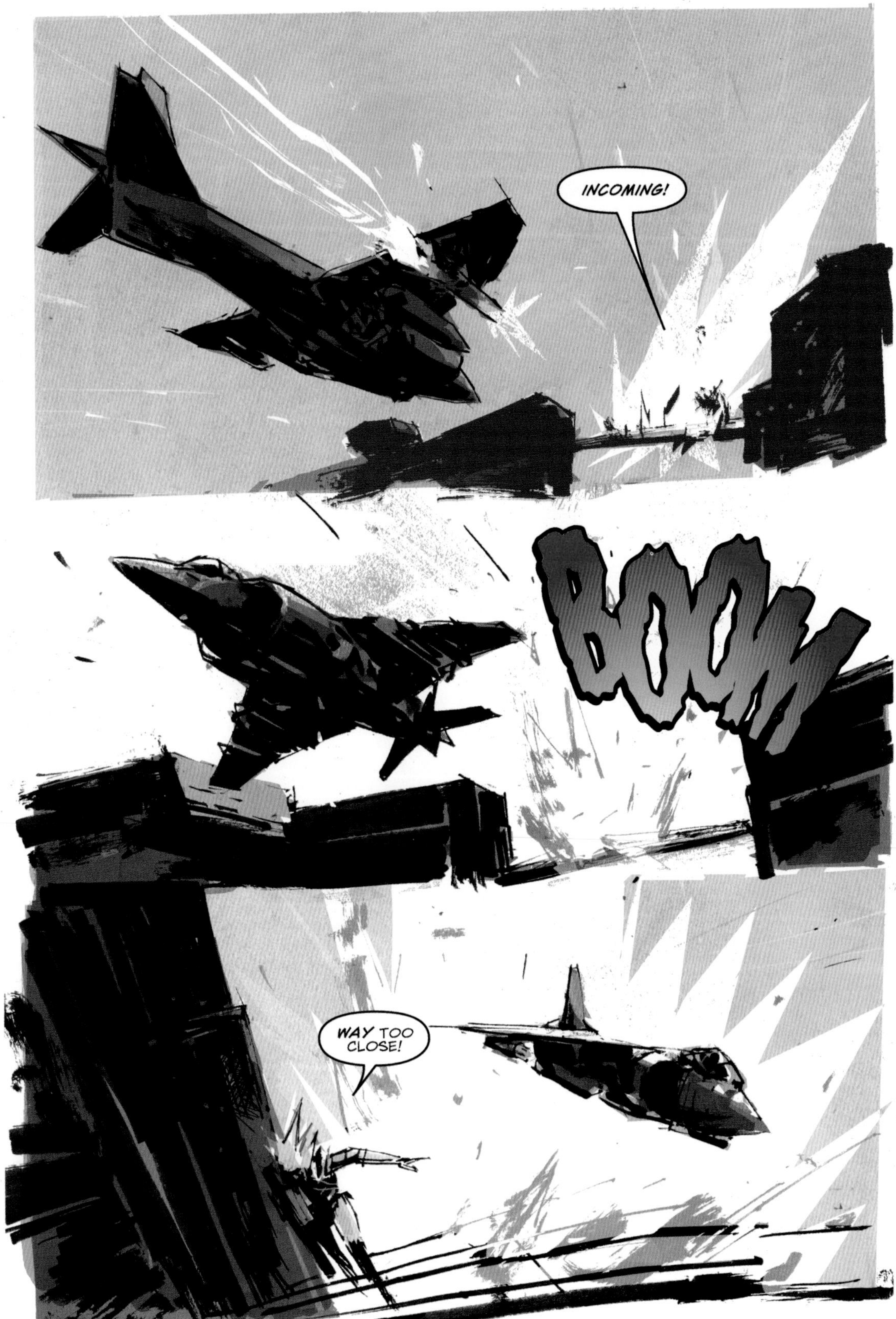
INCOMING!
BOOM
WAY TOO CLOSE!

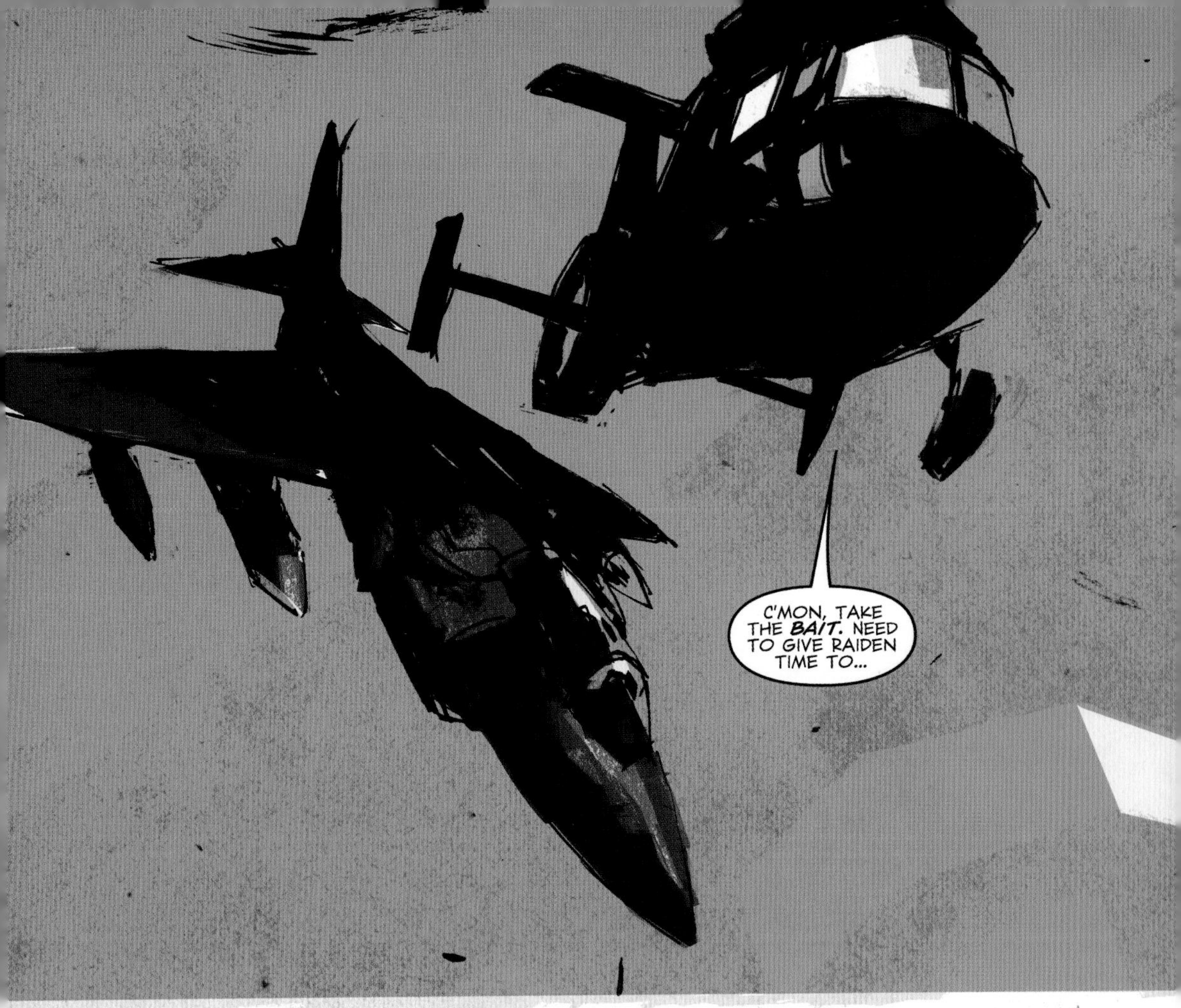
C'MON, TAKE THE BAIT. NEED TO GIVE RAIDEN TIME TO...

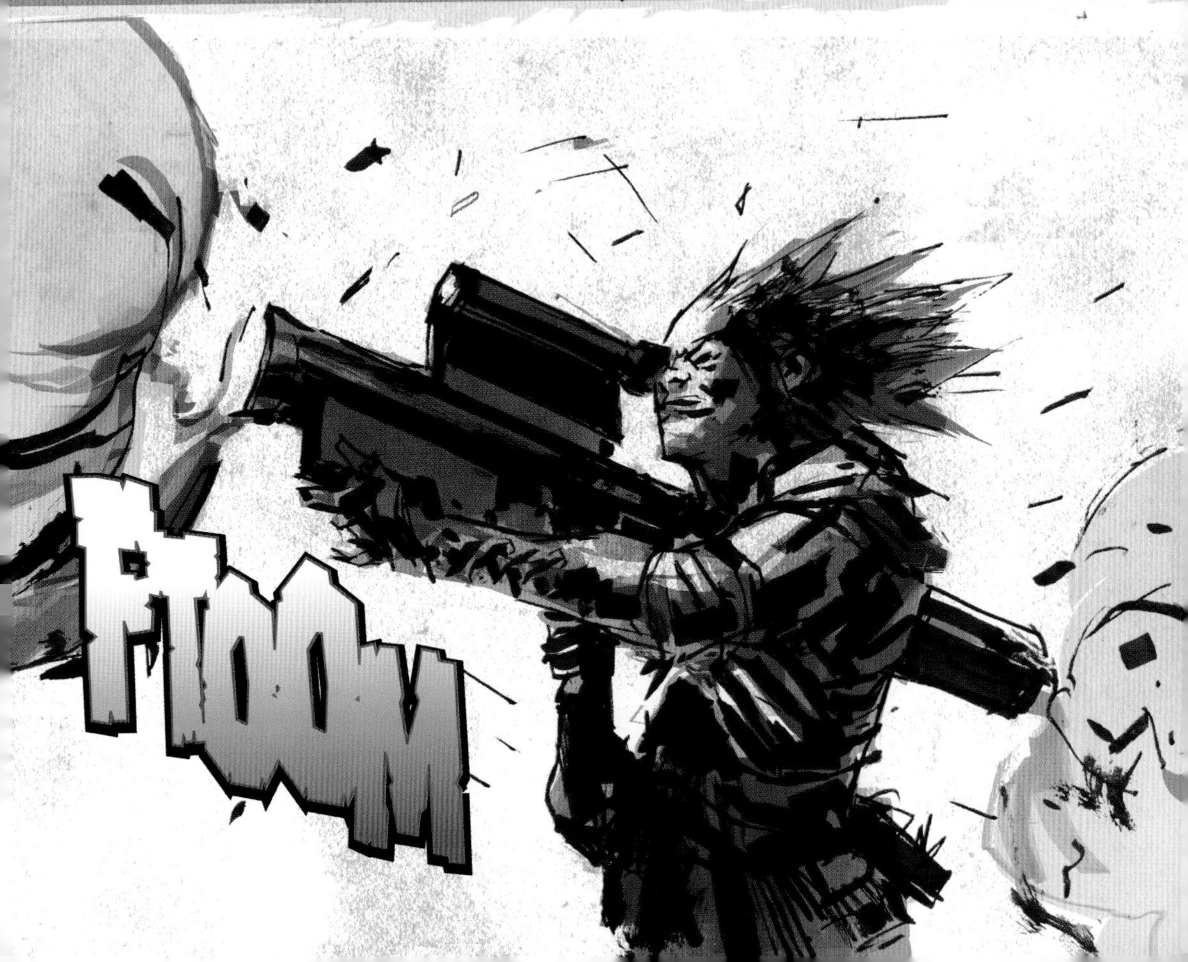
FTOOM

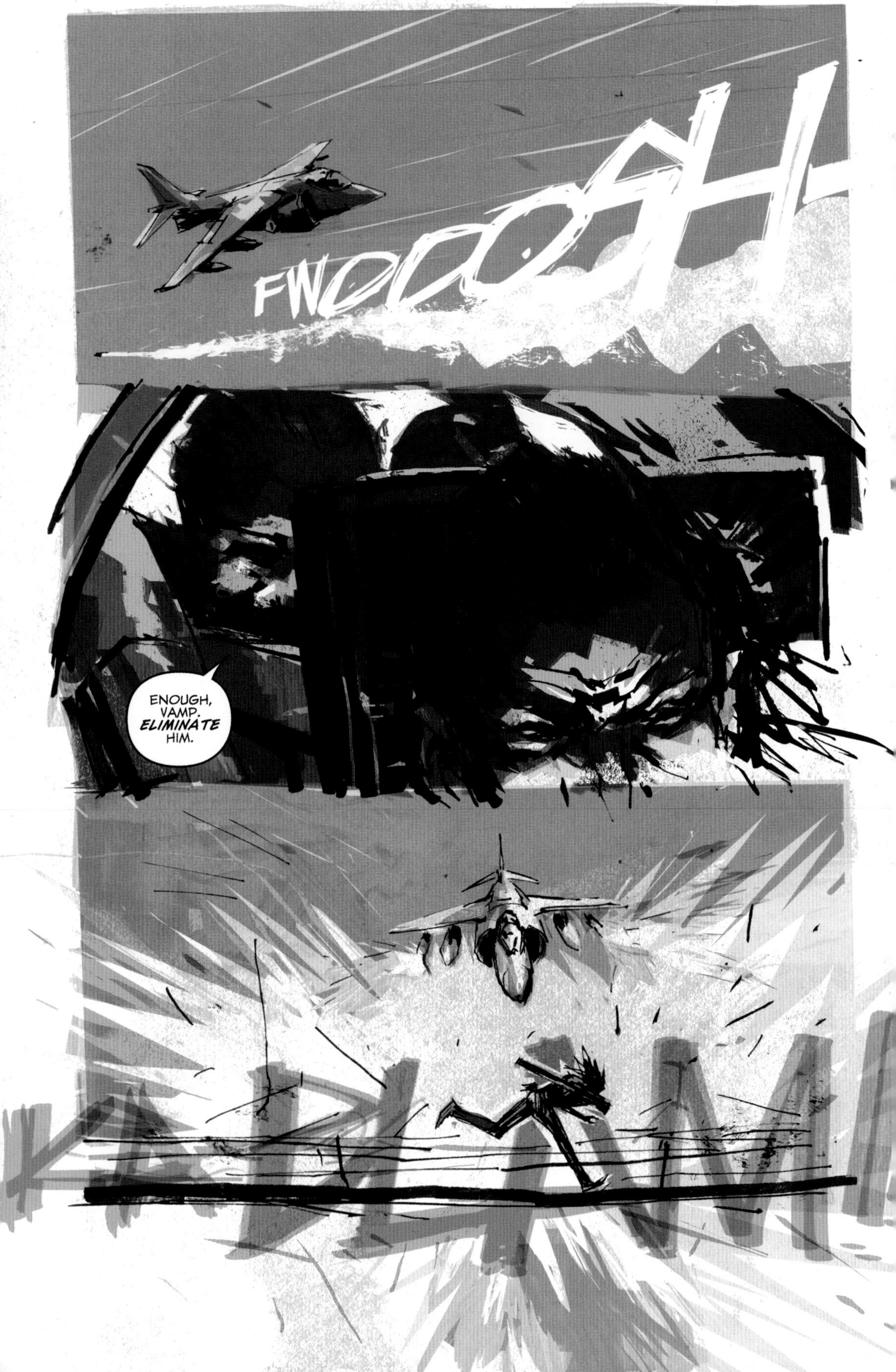
FWOOOSH
ENOUGH, VAMP. *ELIMINATE* HIM.

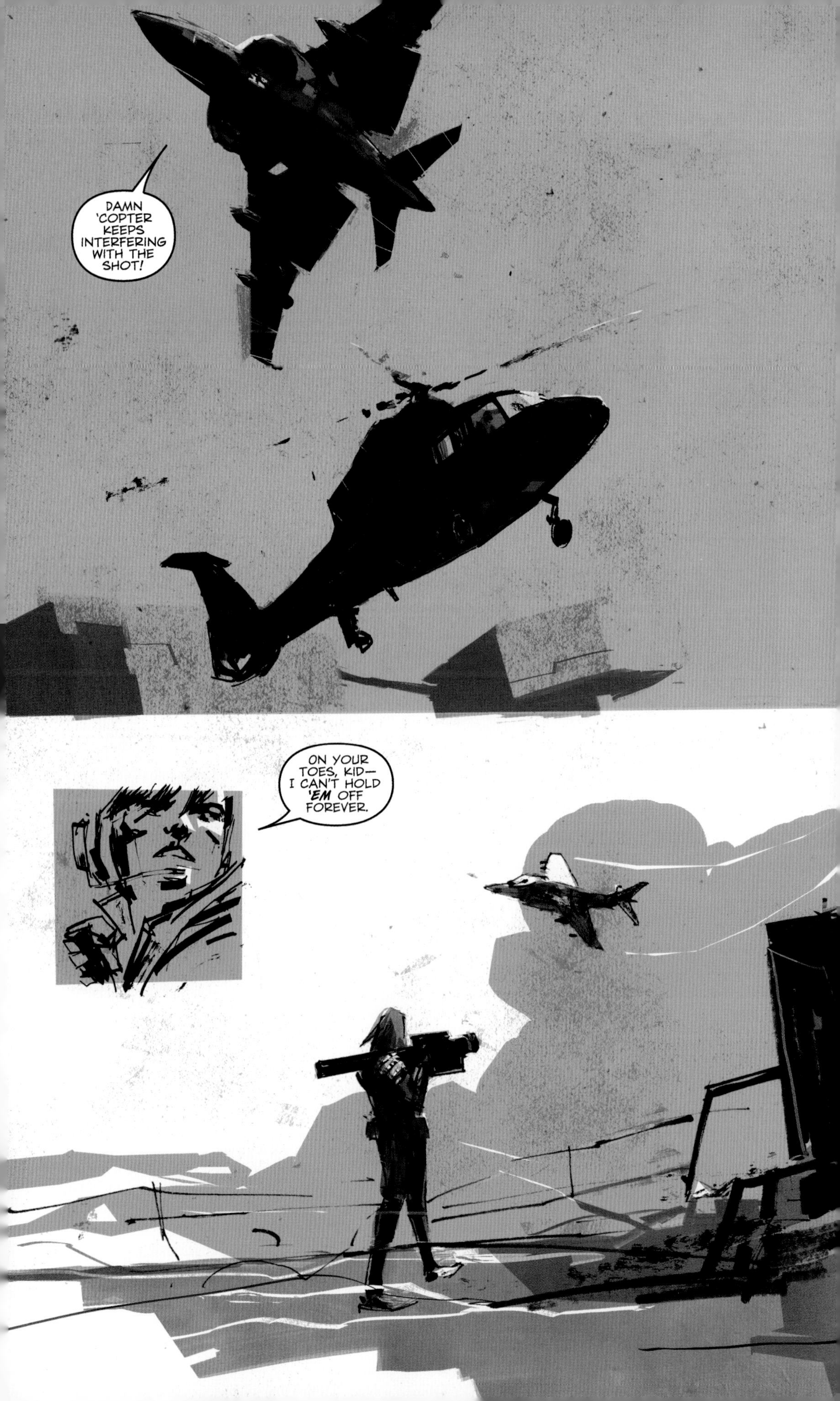
DAMN 'COPTER KEEPS INTERFERING WITH THE SHOT!
ON YOUR TOES, KID— I CAN'T HOLD 'EM OFF FOREVER.

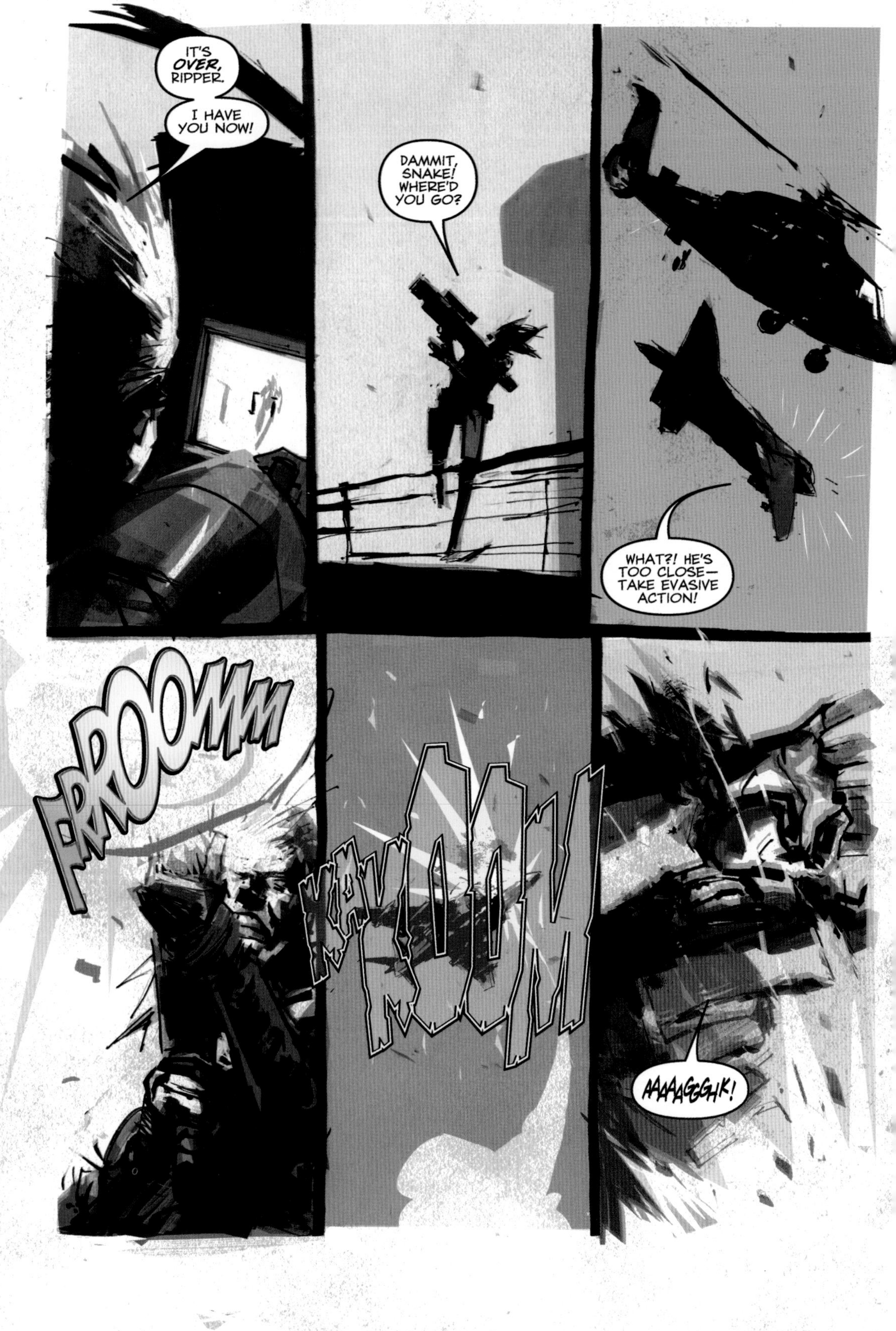
IT'S *OVER,* RIPPER.
I HAVE YOU NOW!
DAMMIT, SNAKE! WHERE'D YOU GO?
WHAT?! HE'S TOO CLOSE— TAKE EVASIVE ACTION!
FRROOMM
KA-BOOM
AAAAAGGHK!

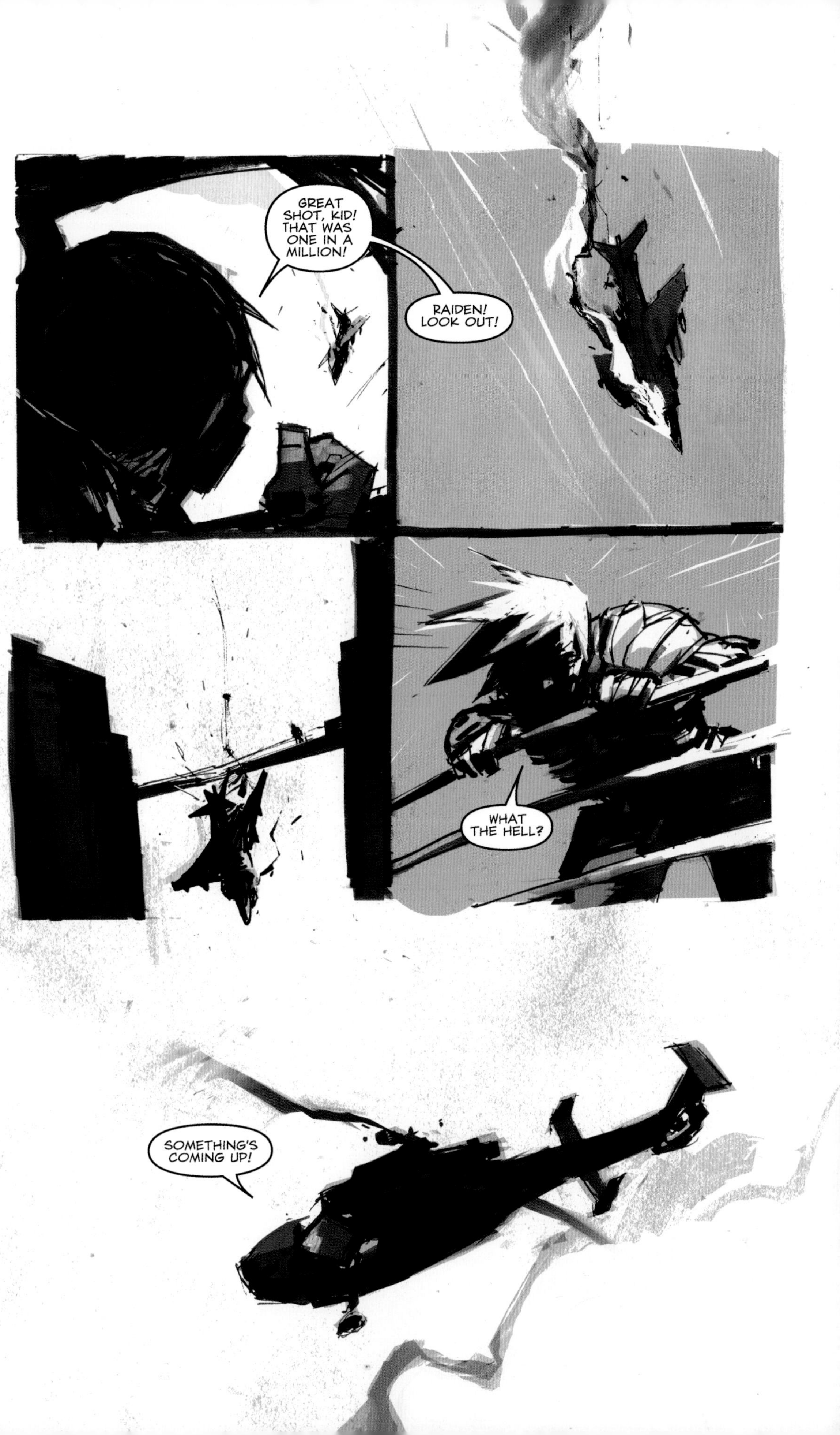
GREAT SHOT, KID! THAT WAS ONE IN A MILLION!
RAIDEN! LOOK OUT!
WHAT THE HELL?
SOMETHING'S COMING UP!

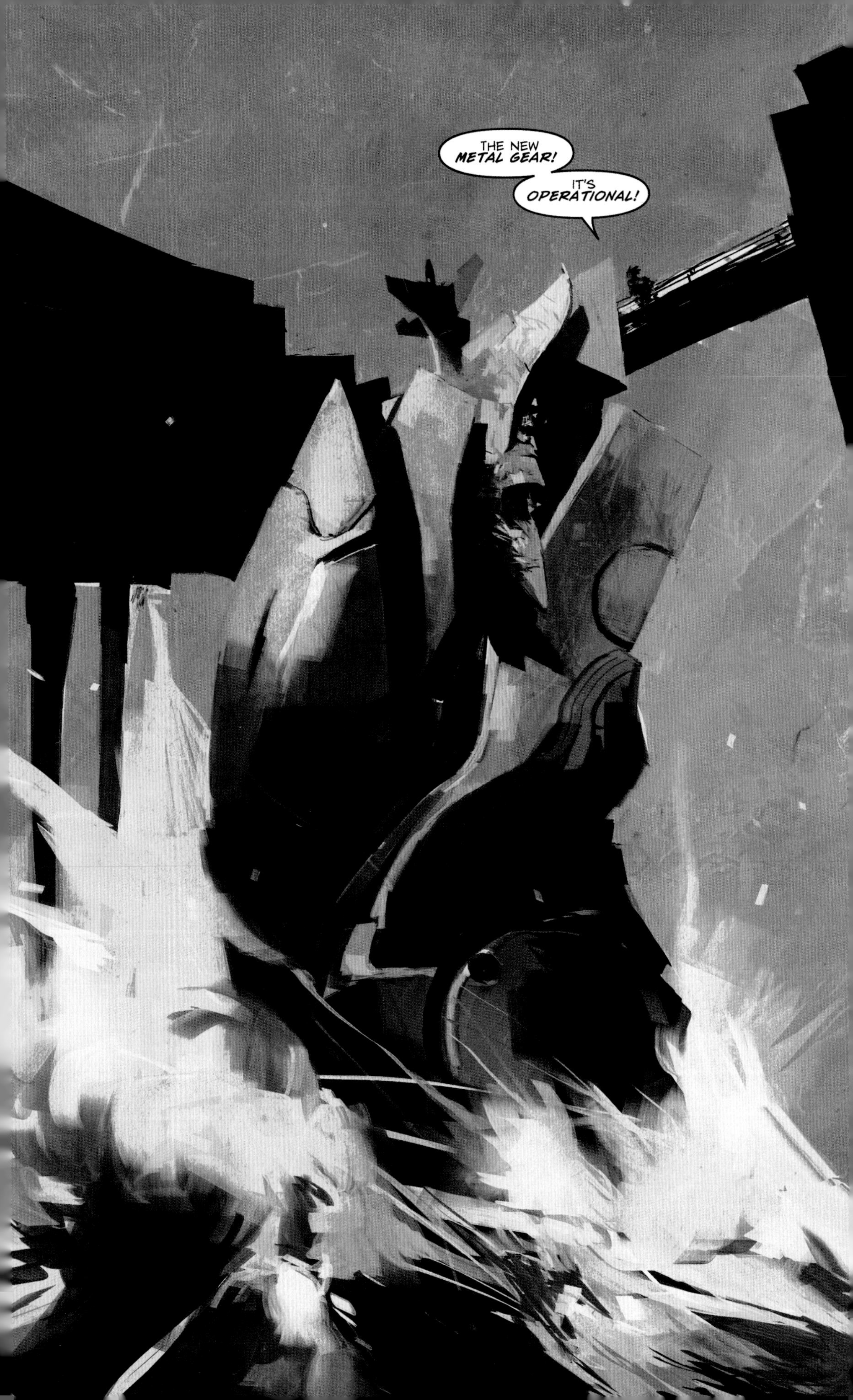
THE NEW *METAL GEAR!*
IT'S *OPERATIONAL!*

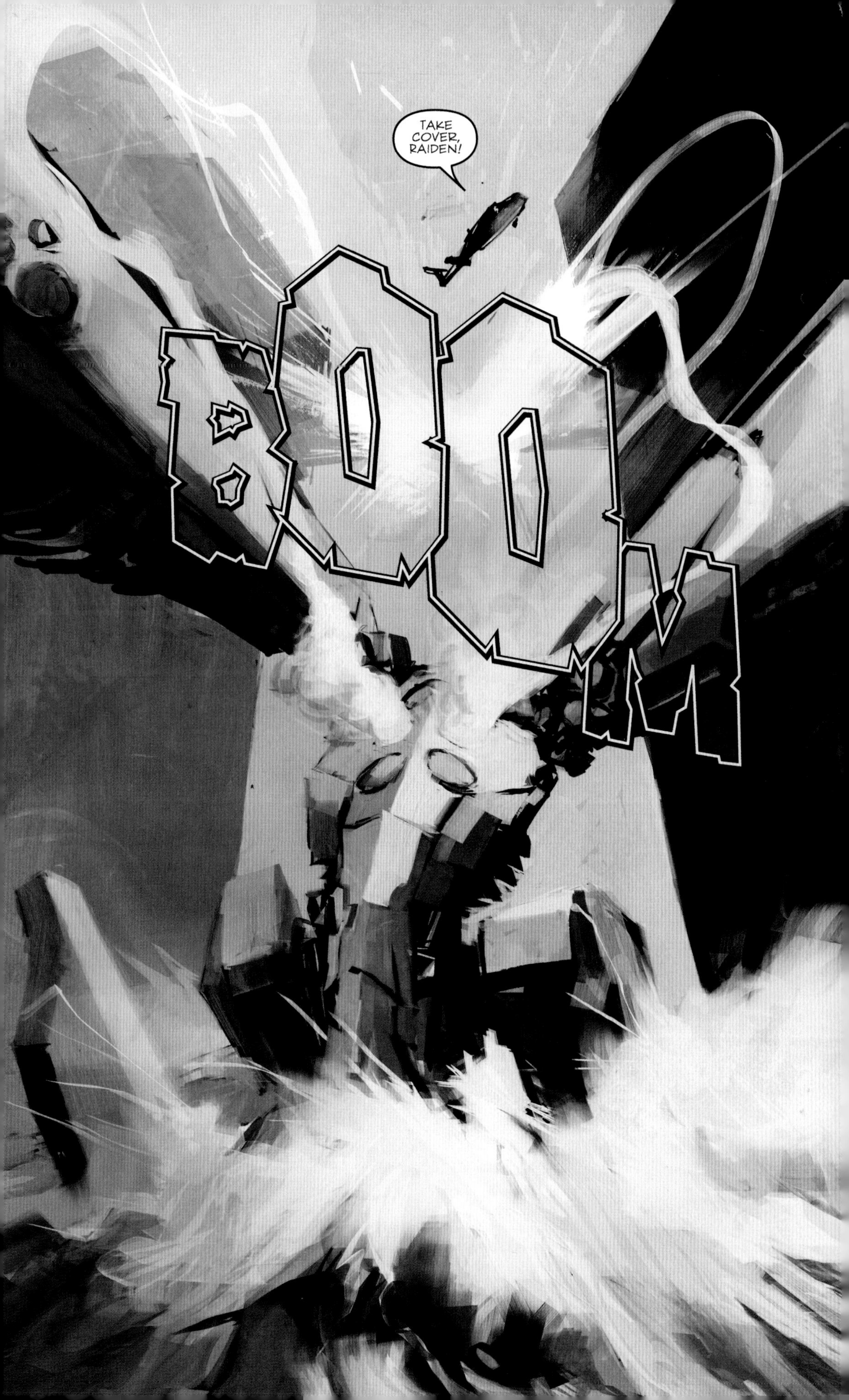
TAKE COVER, RAIDEN!
BOOOM

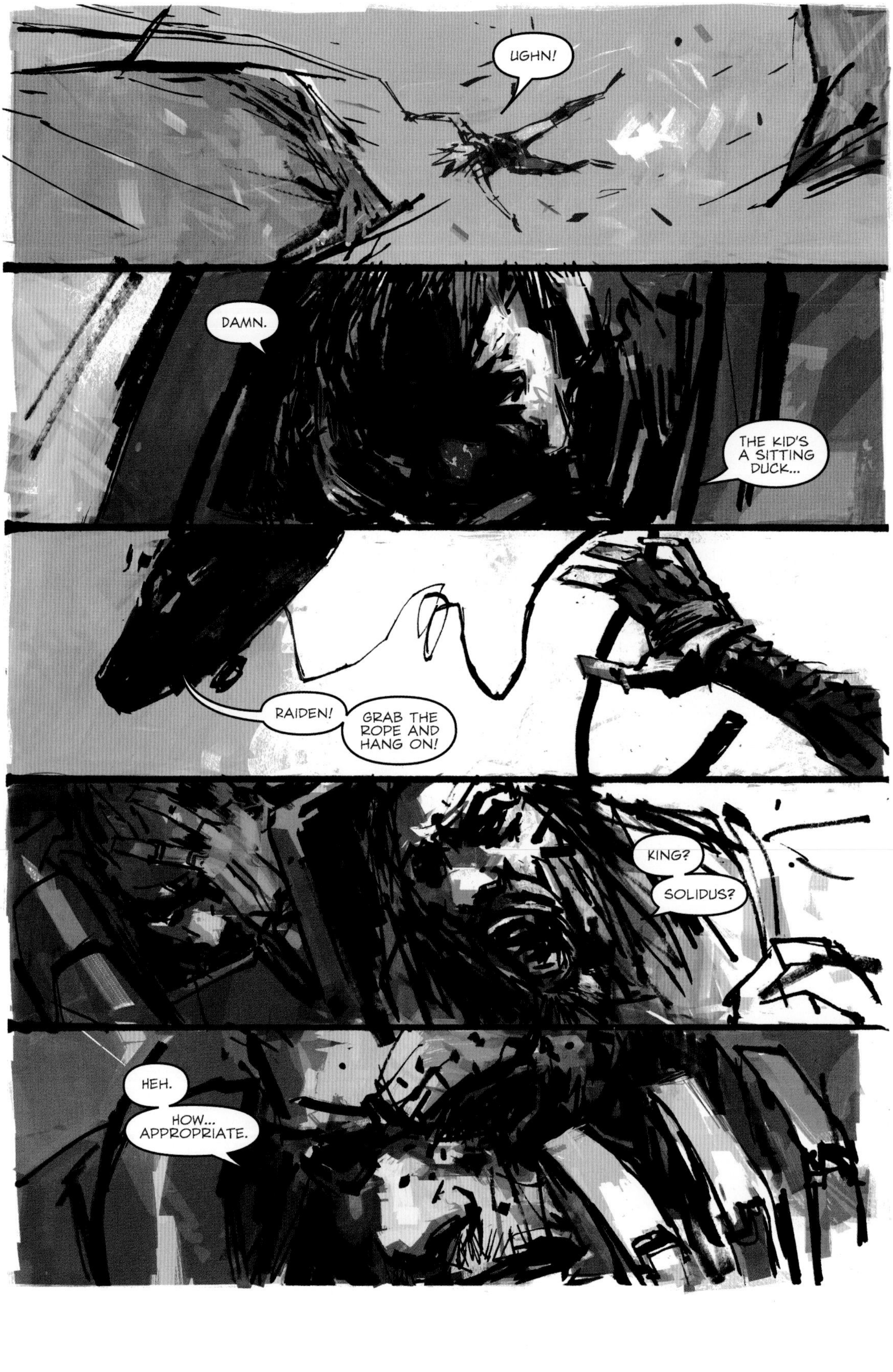
UGHN!
DAMN.
THE KID'S A SITTING DUCK...
RAIDEN!
GRAB THE ROPE AND HANG ON!
KING?
SOLIDUS?
HEH.
HOW... APPROPRIATE.

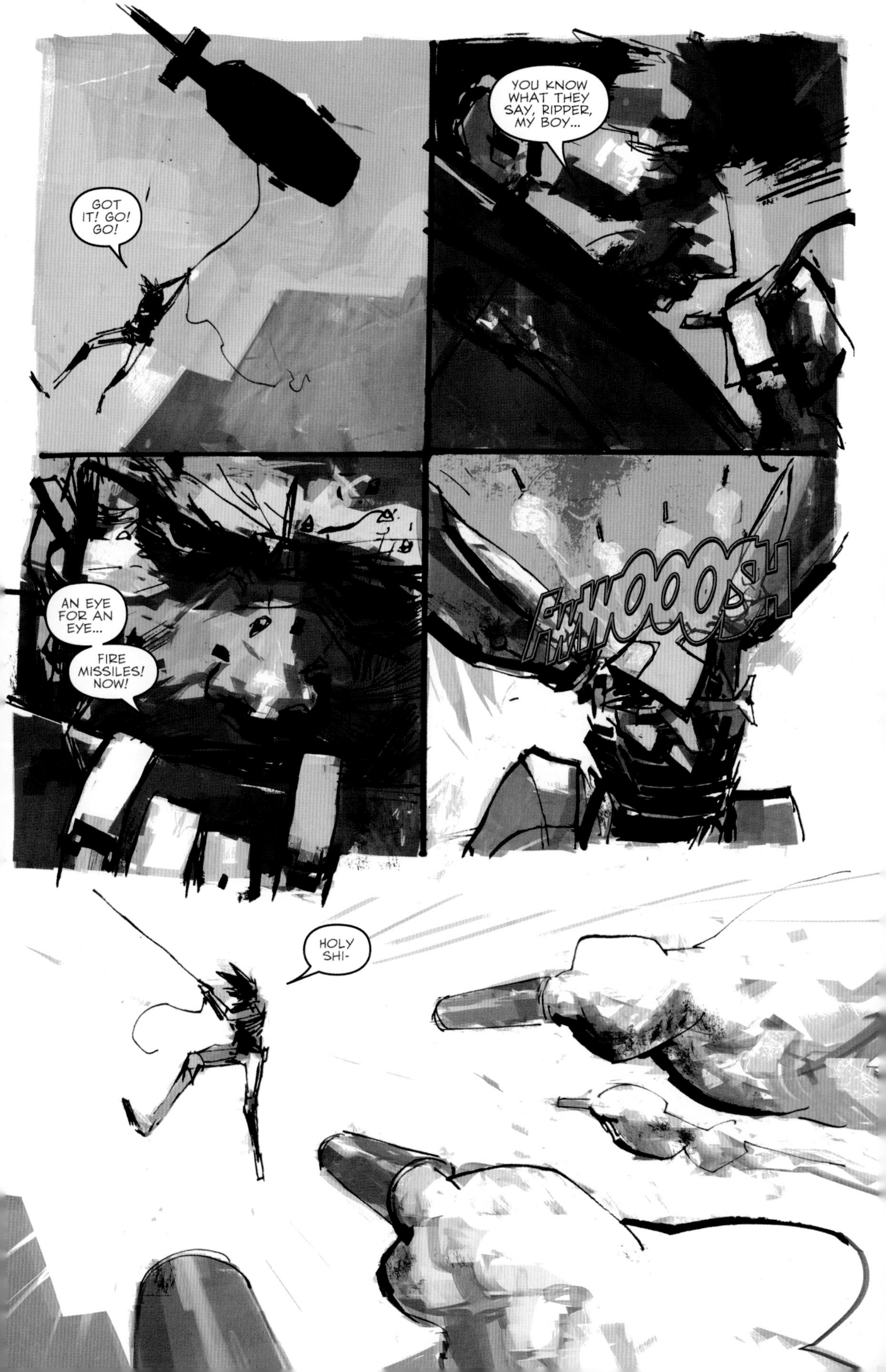
GOT IT! GO! GO!
YOU KNOW WHAT THEY SAY, RIPPER, MY BOY...
AN EYE FOR AN EYE...
FIRE MISSILES! NOW!
FWWOOOSH
HOLY SHI-

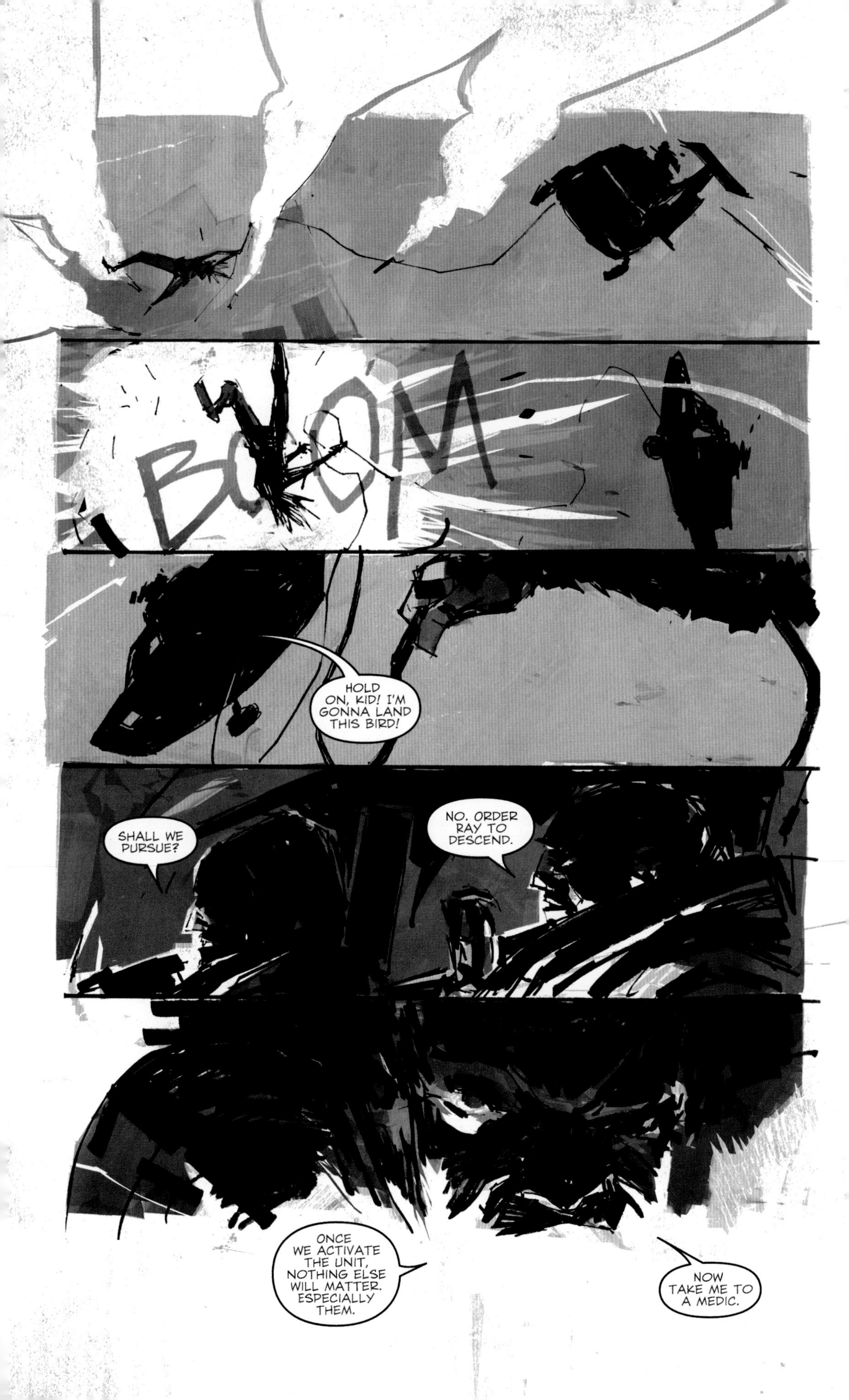
BOOM
HOLD ON, KID! I'M GONNA LAND THIS BIRD!
SHALL WE PURSUE?
NO. ORDER RAY TO DESCEND.
ONCE WE ACTIVATE THE UNIT, NOTHING ELSE WILL MATTER. ESPECIALLY THEM.
NOW TAKE ME TO A MEDIC.

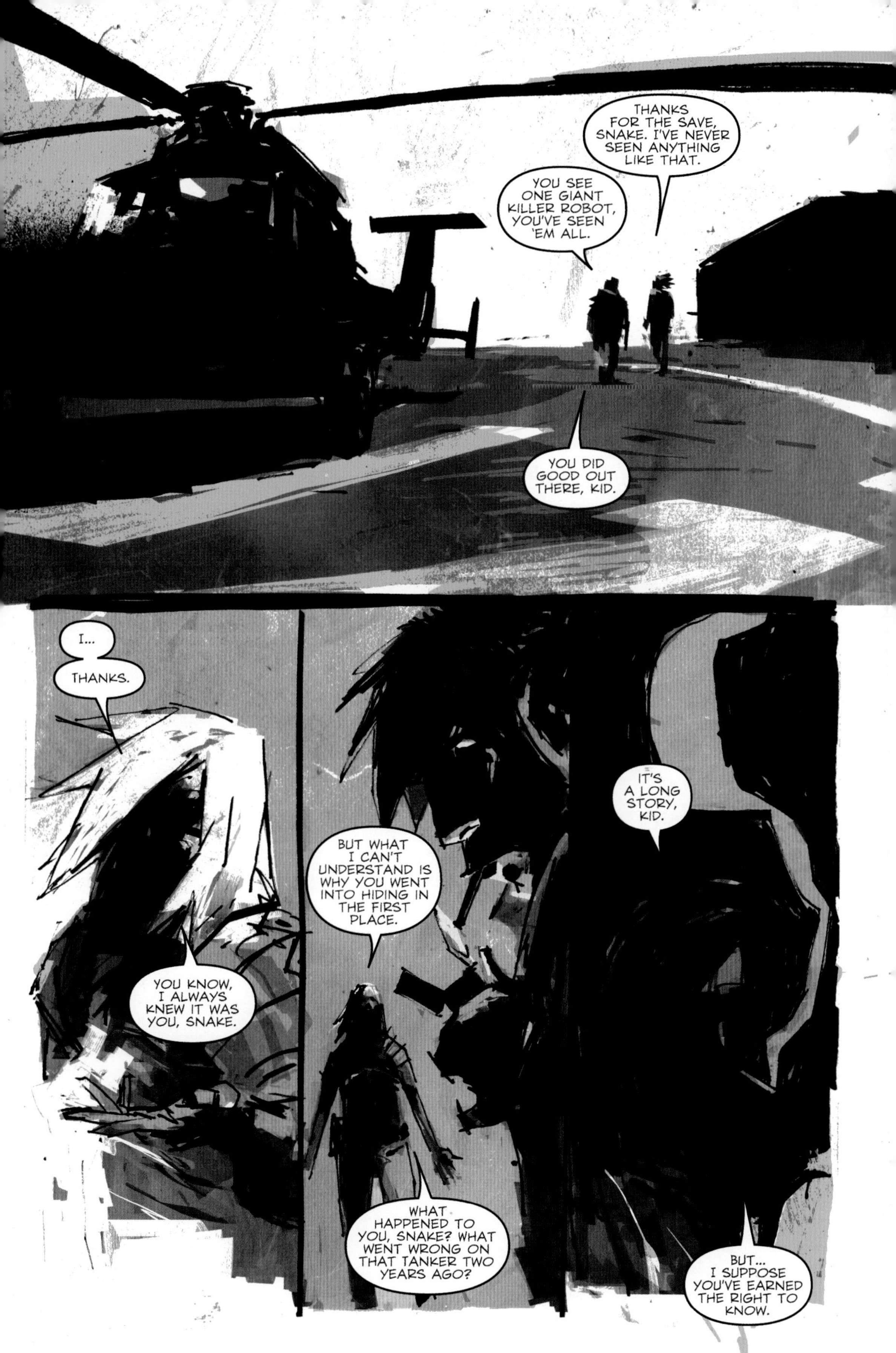
THANKS FOR THE SAVE, SNAKE. I'VE NEVER SEEN ANYTHING LIKE THAT.
YOU SEE ONE GIANT KILLER ROBOT, YOU'VE SEEN 'EM ALL.
YOU DID GOOD OUT THERE, KID.
I...
THANKS.
YOU KNOW, I ALWAYS KNEW IT WAS YOU, SNAKE.
BUT WHAT I CAN'T UNDERSTAND IS WHY YOU WENT INTO HIDING IN THE FIRST PLACE.
WHAT HAPPENED TO YOU, SNAKE? WHAT WENT WRONG ON THAT TANKER TWO YEARS AGO?
IT'S A LONG STORY, KID.
BUT... I SUPPOSE YOU'VE EARNED THE RIGHT TO KNOW.

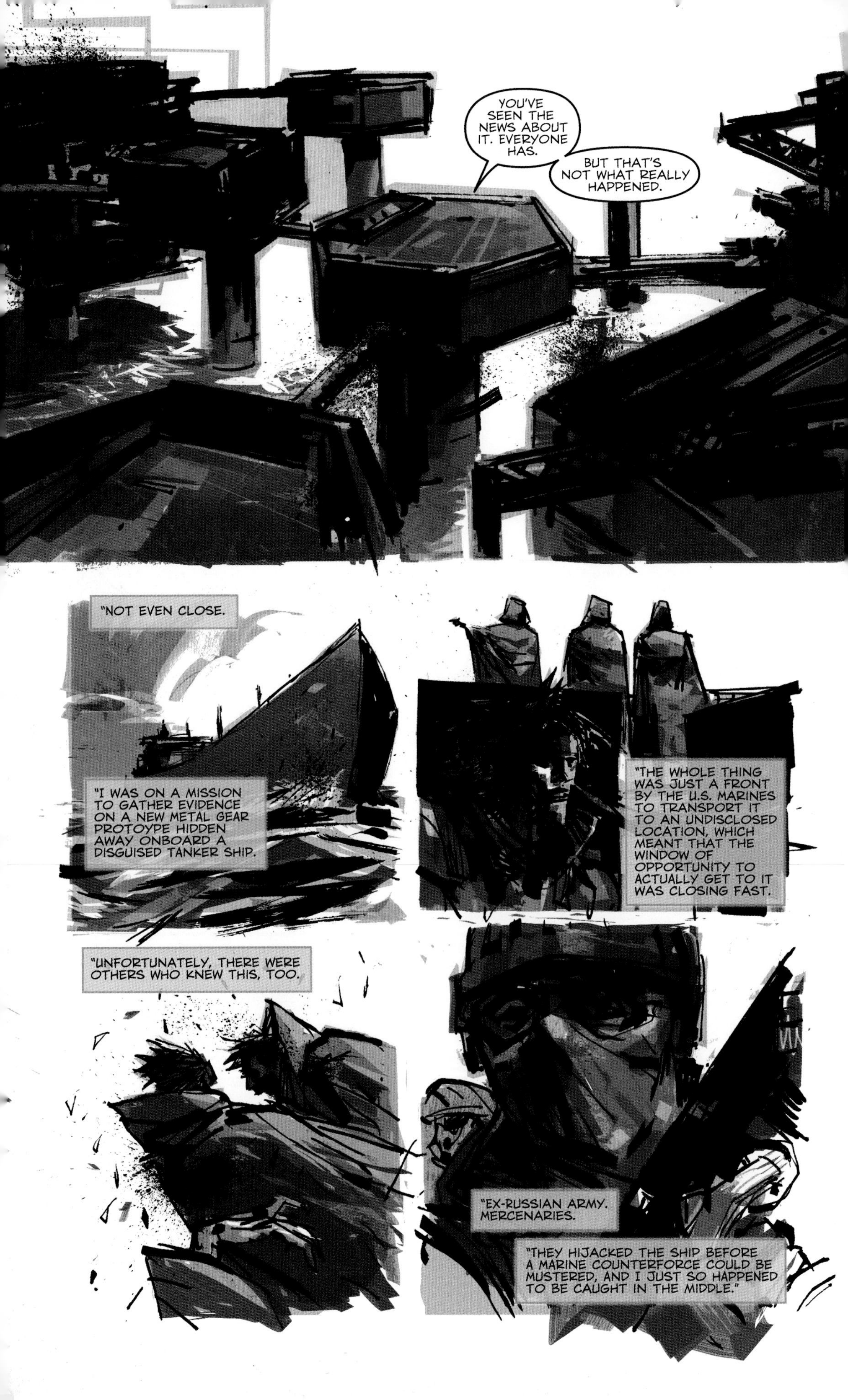
YOU'VE SEEN THE NEWS ABOUT IT. EVERYONE HAS.
BUT THAT'S NOT WHAT REALLY HAPPENED.
"NOT EVEN CLOSE.
"I WAS ON A MISSION TO GATHER EVIDENCE ON A NEW METAL GEAR PROTOYPE HIDDEN AWAY ONBOARD A DISGUISED TANKER SHIP.
"THE WHOLE THING WAS JUST A FRONT BY THE U.S. MARINES TO TRANSPORT IT TO AN UNDISCLOSED LOCATION, WHICH MEANT THAT THE WINDOW OF OPPORTUNITY TO ACTUALLY GET TO IT WAS CLOSING FAST.
"UNFORTUNATELY, THERE WERE OTHERS WHO KNEW THIS, TOO.
"EX-RUSSIAN ARMY. MERCENARIES.
"THEY HIJACKED THE SHIP BEFORE A MARINE COUNTERFORCE COULD BE MUSTERED, AND I JUST SO HAPPENED TO BE CAUGHT IN THE MIDDLE."

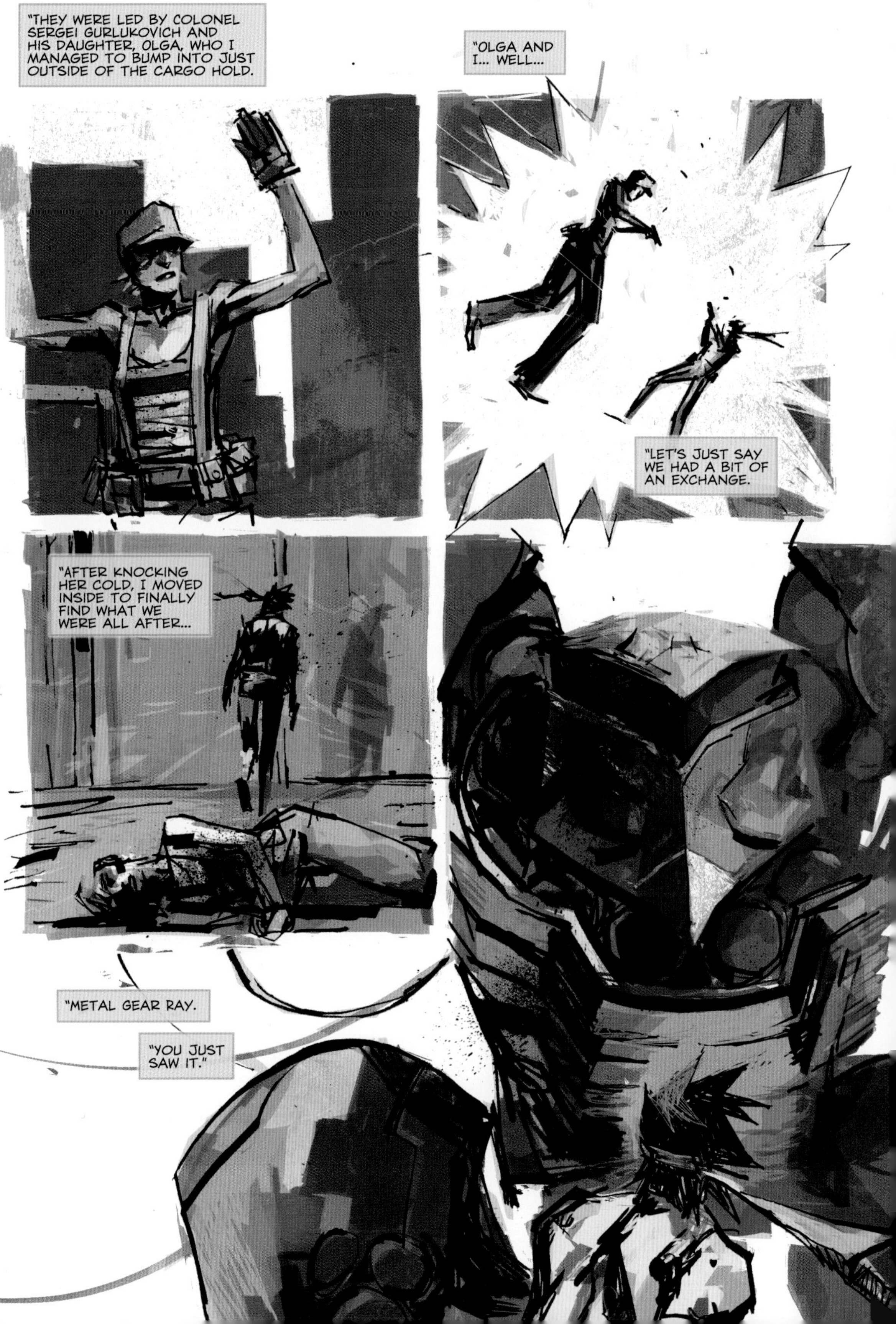
"THEY WERE LED BY COLONEL SERGEI GURLUKOVICH AND HIS DAUGHTER, OLGA, WHO I MANAGED TO BUMP INTO JUST OUTSIDE OF THE CARGO HOLD.
"OLGA AND I... WELL...
"LET'S JUST SAY WE HAD A BIT OF AN EXCHANGE.
"AFTER KNOCKING HER COLD, I MOVED INSIDE TO FINALLY FIND WHAT WE WERE ALL AFTER...
"METAL GEAR RAY.
"YOU JUST SAW IT."

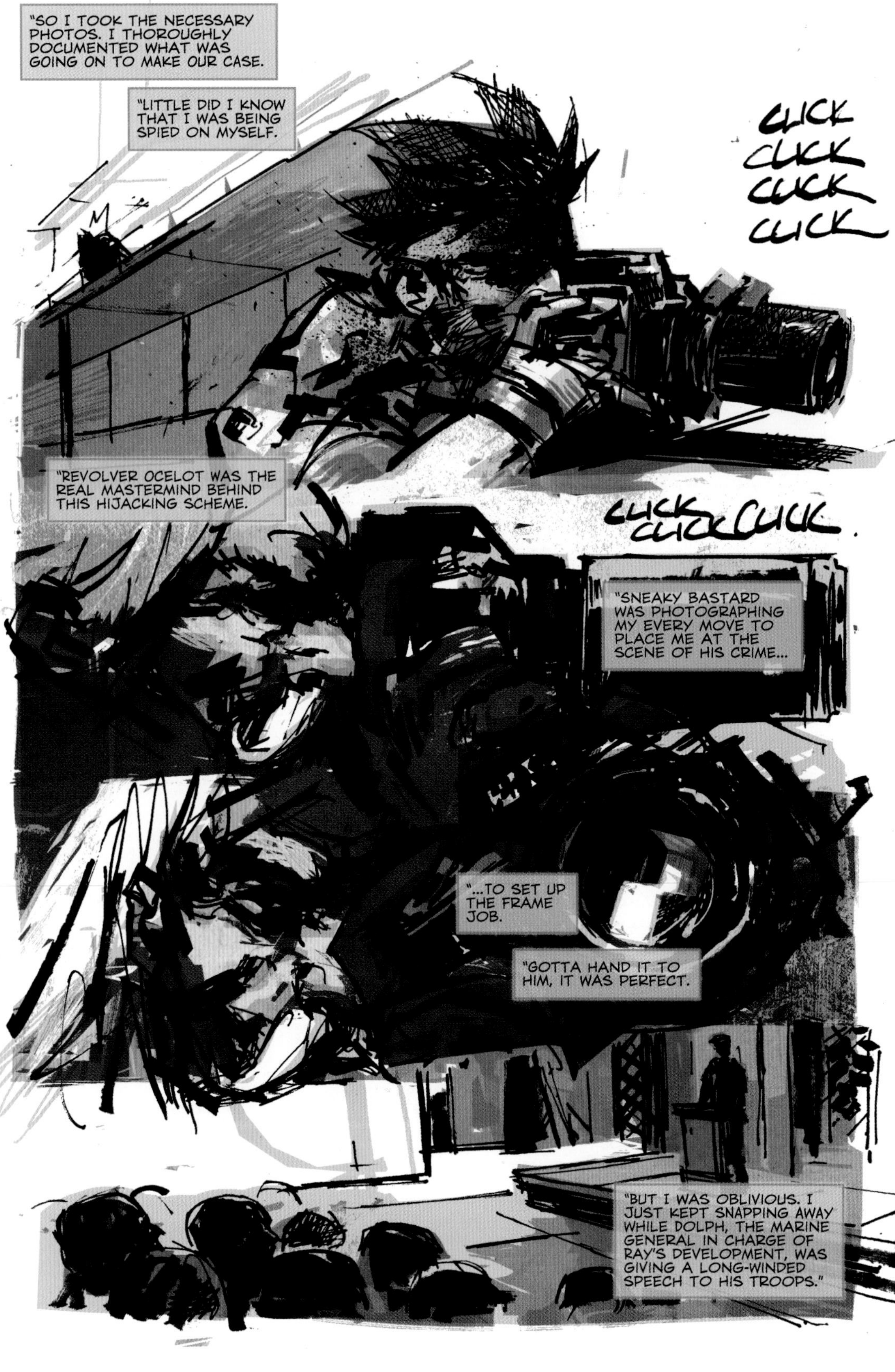
"SO I TOOK THE NECESSARY PHOTOS. I THOROUGHLY DOCUMENTED WHAT WAS GOING ON TO MAKE OUR CASE.
"LITTLE DID I KNOW THAT I WAS BEING SPIED ON MYSELF.
CLICK
CLICK
CLICK
CLICK
"REVOLVER OCELOT WAS THE REAL MASTERMIND BEHIND THIS HIJACKING SCHEME.
CLICK
CLICK CLICK
"SNEAKY BASTARD WAS PHOTOGRAPHING MY EVERY MOVE TO PLACE ME AT THE SCENE OF HIS CRIME...
"...TO SET UP THE FRAME JOB.
"GOTTA HAND IT TO HIM, IT WAS PERFECT.
"BUT I WAS OBLIVIOUS. I JUST KEPT SNAPPING AWAY WHILE DOLPH, THE MARINE GENERAL IN CHARGE OF RAY'S DEVELOPMENT, WAS GIVING A LONG-WINDED SPEECH TO HIS TROOPS."

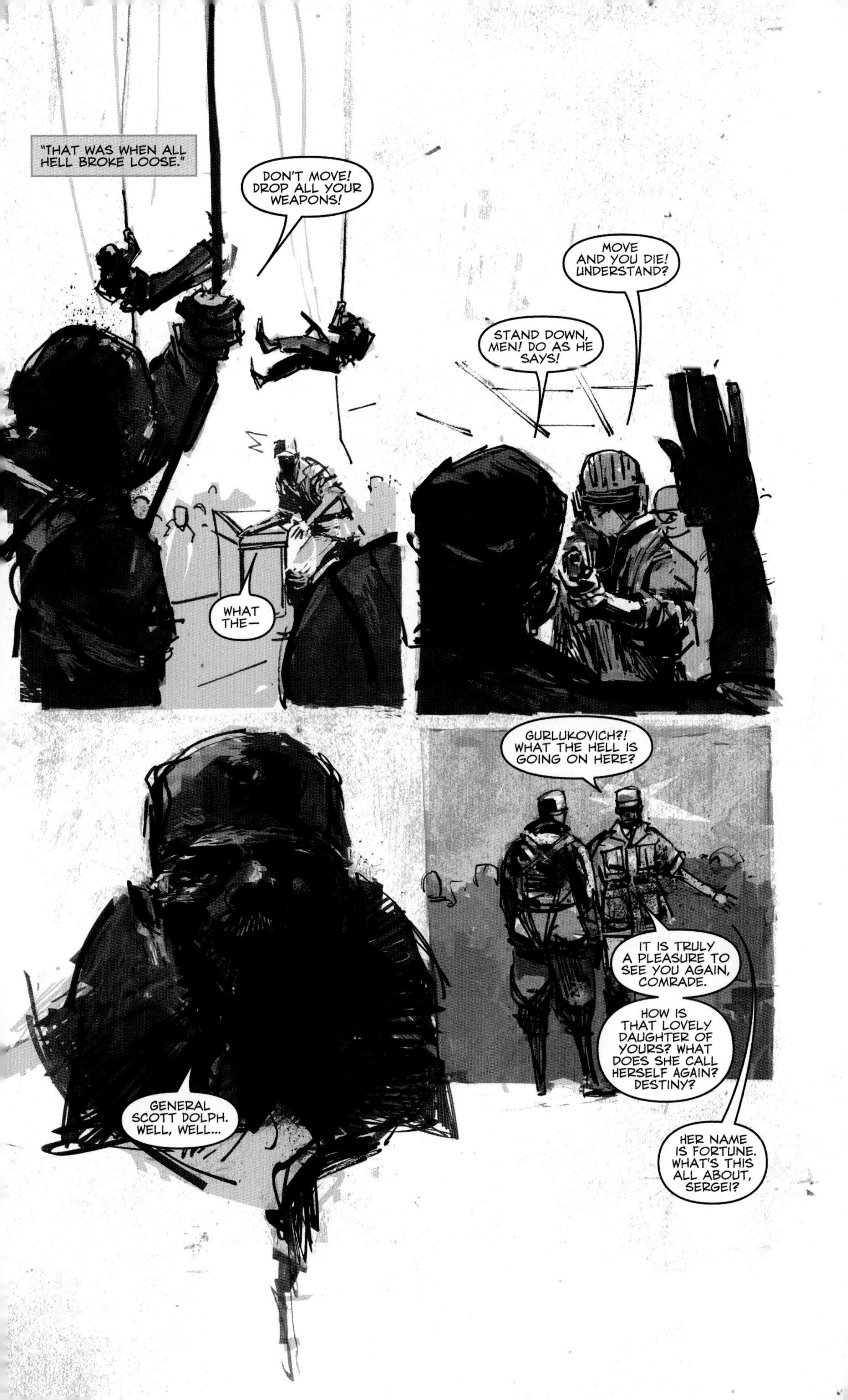
"THAT WAS WHEN ALL HELL BROKE LOOSE."
DON'T MOVE! DROP ALL YOUR WEAPONS!
WHAT THE—
MOVE AND YOU DIE! UNDERSTAND?
STAND DOWN, MEN! DO AS HE SAYS!
GENERAL SCOTT DOLPH. WELL, WELL...
GURLUKOVICH?! WHAT THE HELL IS GOING ON HERE?
IT IS TRULY A PLEASURE TO SEE YOU AGAIN, COMRADE.
HOW IS THAT LOVELY DAUGHTER OF YOURS? WHAT DOES SHE CALL HERSELF AGAIN? DESTINY?
HER NAME IS FORTUNE. WHAT'S THIS ALL ABOUT, SERGEI?

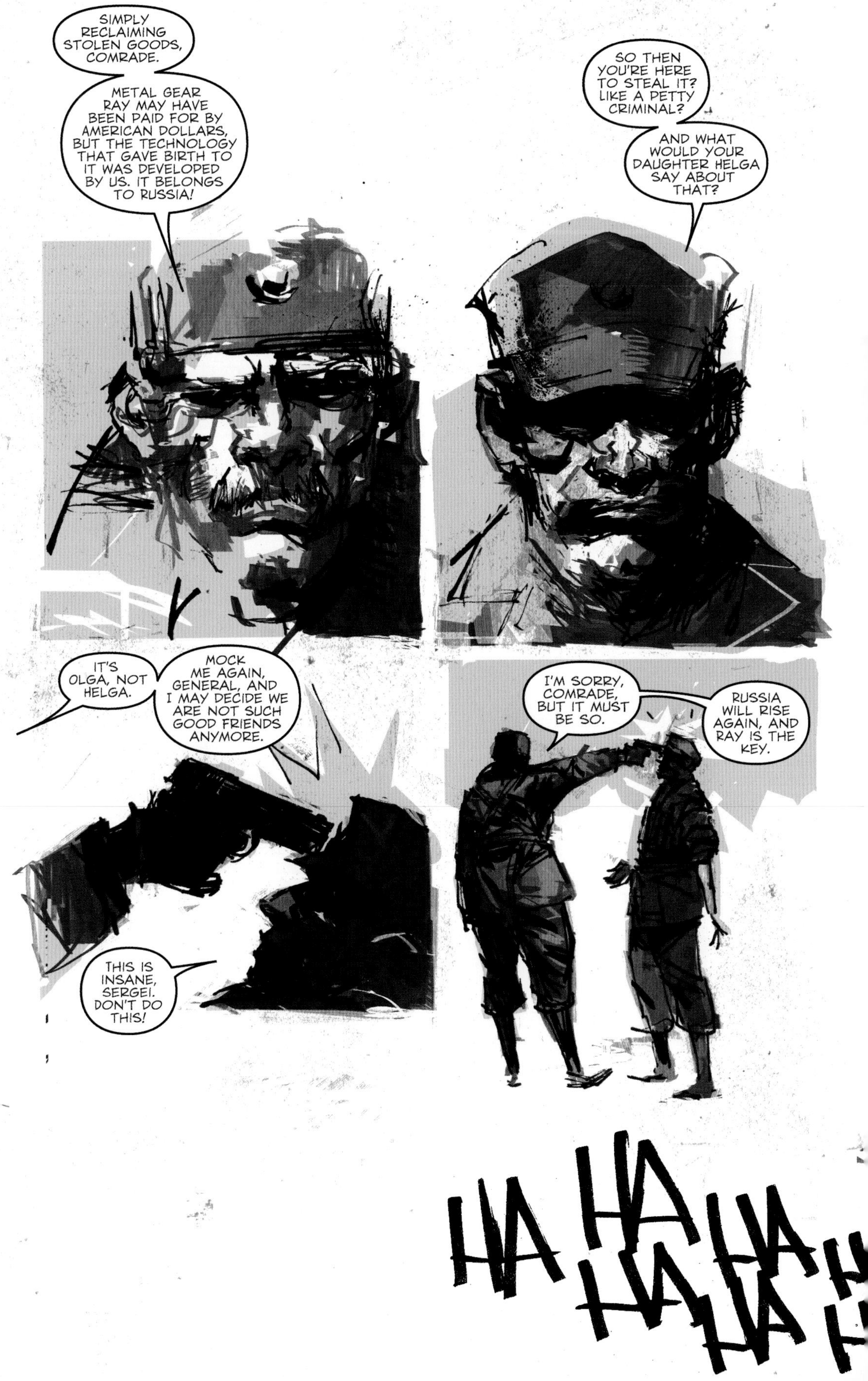
SIMPLY RECLAIMING STOLEN GOODS, COMRADE.
METAL GEAR RAY MAY HAVE BEEN PAID FOR BY AMERICAN DOLLARS, BUT THE TECHNOLOGY THAT GAVE BIRTH TO IT WAS DEVELOPED BY US. IT BELONGS TO RUSSIA!
SO THEN YOU'RE HERE TO STEAL IT? LIKE A PETTY CRIMINAL?
AND WHAT WOULD YOUR DAUGHTER HELGA SAY ABOUT THAT?
IT'S OLGA, NOT HELGA.
MOCK ME AGAIN, GENERAL, AND I MAY DECIDE WE ARE NOT SUCH GOOD FRIENDS ANYMORE.
THIS IS INSANE, SERGEI. DON'T DO THIS!
I'M SORRY, COMRADE, BUT IT MUST BE SO.
RUSSIA WILL RISE AGAIN, AND RAY IS THE KEY.
HA HA HA HA HA HA HA

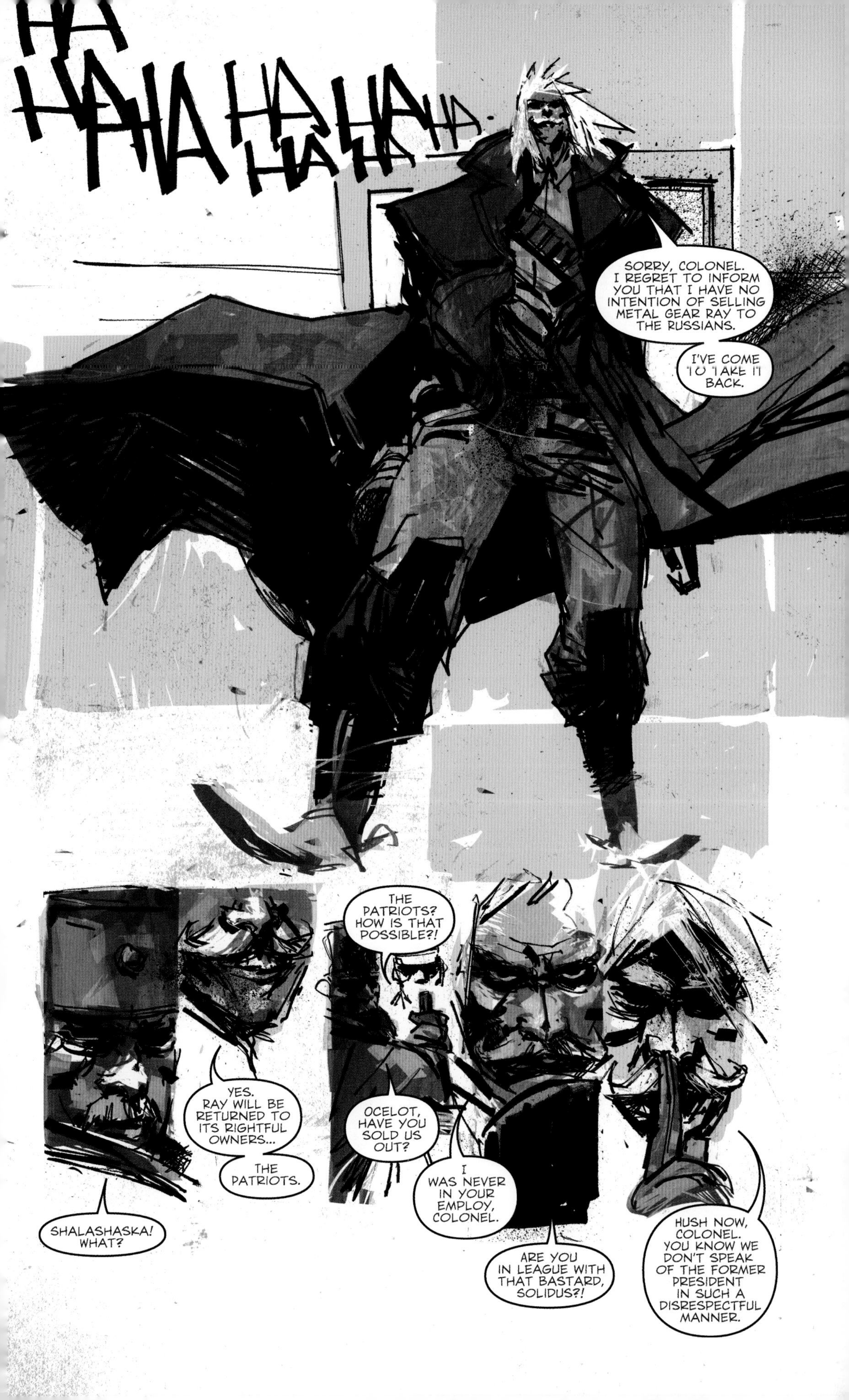
HA HA HA HA HA HA HA HA HA HA
SORRY, COLONEL. I REGRET TO INFORM YOU THAT I HAVE NO INTENTION OF SELLING METAL GEAR RAY TO THE RUSSIANS.
I'VE COME TO TAKE IT BACK.
SHALASHASKA! WHAT?
YES. RAY WILL BE RETURNED TO ITS RIGHTFUL OWNERS...
THE PATRIOTS.
THE PATRIOTS? HOW IS THAT POSSIBLE?!
OCELOT, HAVE YOU SOLD US OUT?
I WAS NEVER IN YOUR EMPLOY, COLONEL.
ARE YOU IN LEAGUE WITH THAT BASTARD, SOLIDUS?!
HUSH NOW, COLONEL. YOU KNOW WE DON'T SPEAK OF THE FORMER PRESIDENT IN SUCH A DISRESPECTFUL MANNER.

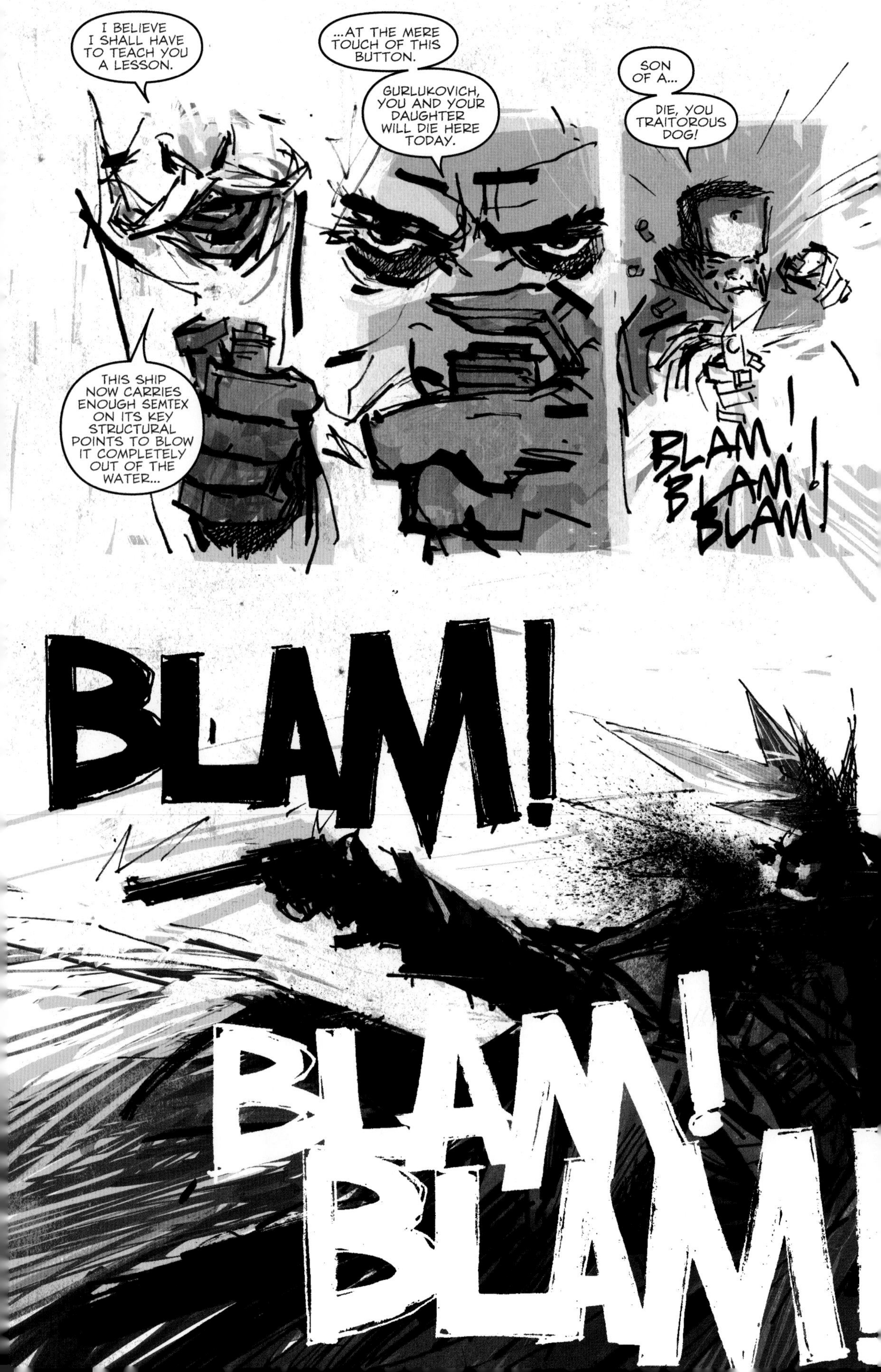
I BELIEVE I SHALL HAVE TO TEACH YOU A LESSON.
THIS SHIP NOW CARRIES ENOUGH SEMTEX ON ITS KEY STRUCTURAL POINTS TO BLOW IT COMPLETELY OUT OF THE WATER...
...AT THE MERE TOUCH OF THIS BUTTON.
GURLUKOVICH, YOU AND YOUR DAUGHTER WILL DIE HERE TODAY.
SON OF A...
DIE, YOU TRAITOROUS DOG!
BLAM! BLAM! BLAM!
BLAM!
BLAM!
BLAM!

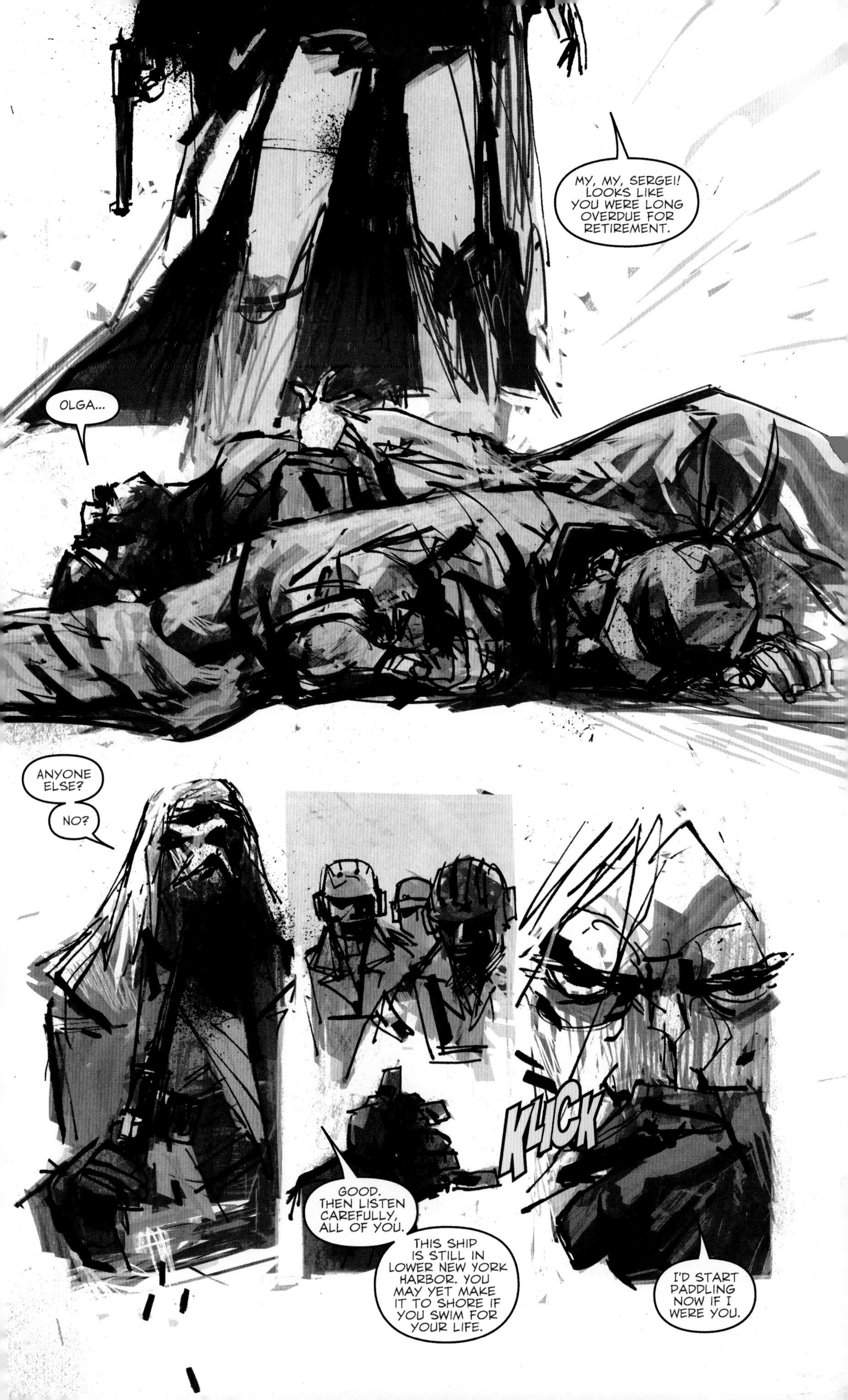
MY, MY, SERGEI! LOOKS LIKE YOU WERE LONG OVERDUE FOR RETIREMENT.
OLGA...
ANYONE ELSE?
NO?
GOOD. THEN LISTEN CAREFULLY, ALL OF YOU.
THIS SHIP IS STILL IN LOWER NEW YORK HARBOR. YOU MAY YET MAKE IT TO SHORE IF YOU SWIM FOR YOUR LIFE.
KLICK
I'D START PADDLING NOW IF I WERE YOU.

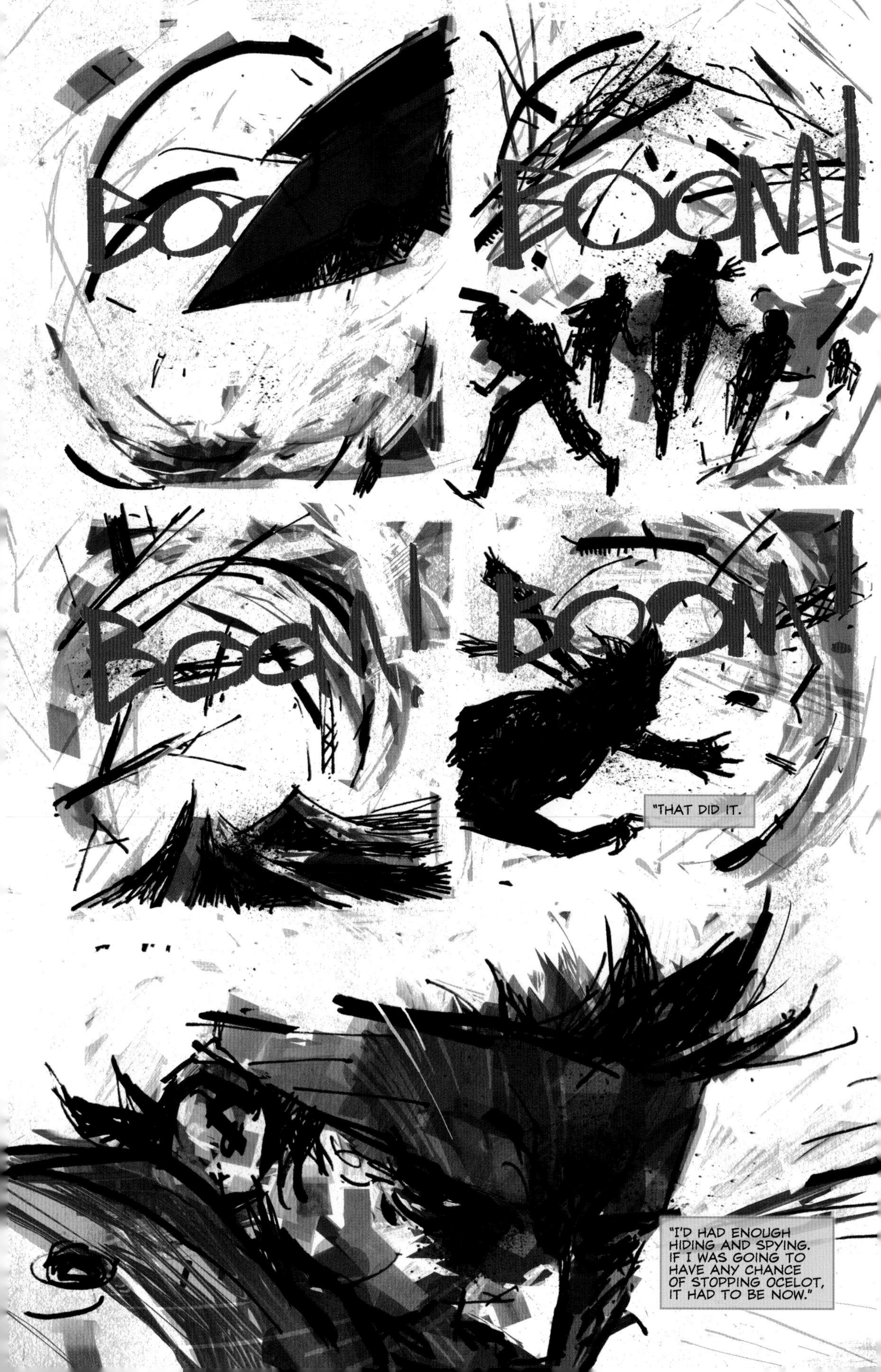
BOOM!
BOOM!
BOOM!
"THAT DID IT.
"I'D HAD ENOUGH HIDING AND SPYING. IF I WAS GOING TO HAVE ANY CHANCE OF STOPPING OCELOT, IT HAD TO BE NOW."

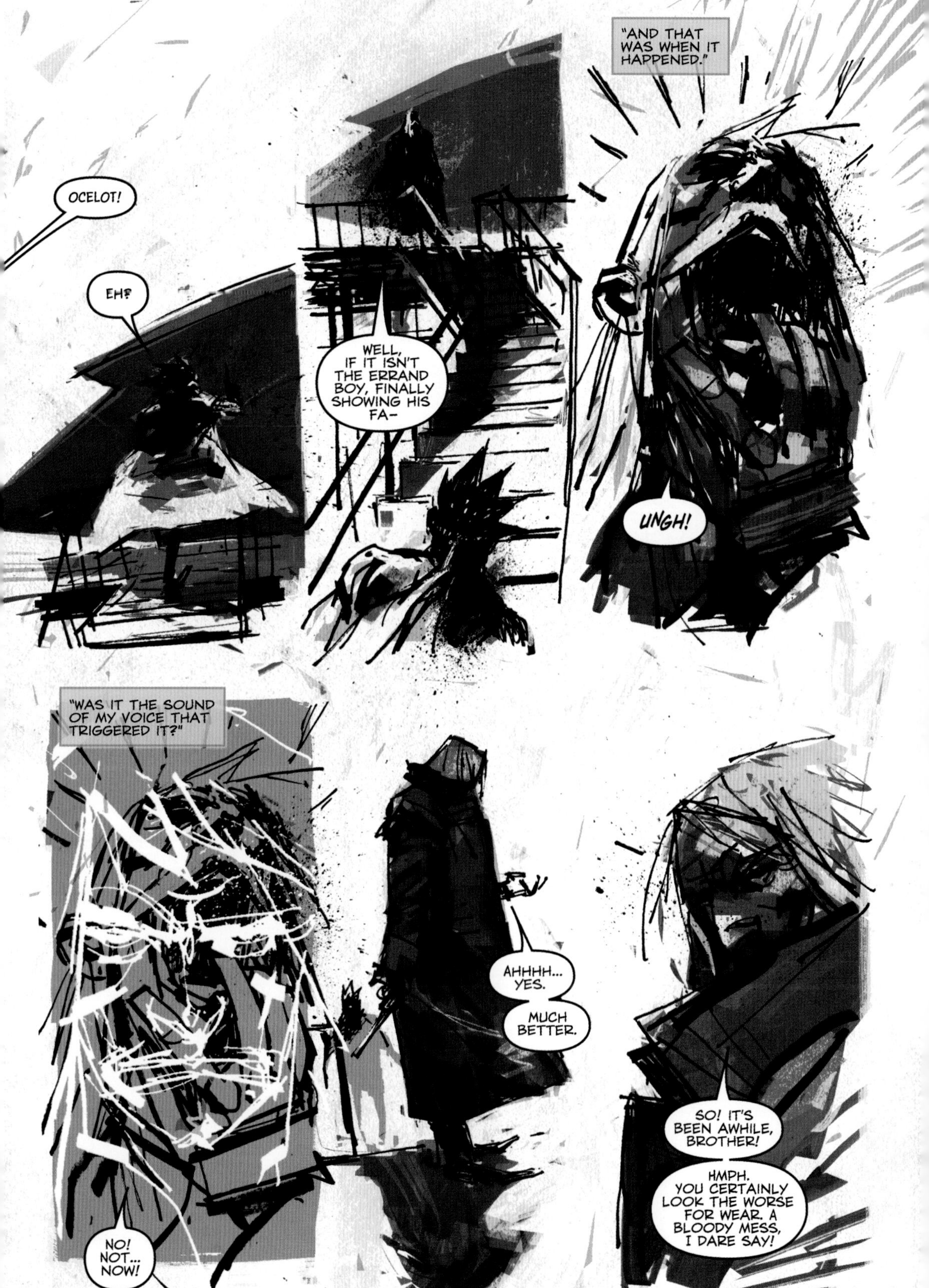
OCELOT!
EH?
WELL, IF IT ISN'T THE ERRAND BOY, FINALLY SHOWING HIS FA-
"AND THAT WAS WHEN IT HAPPENED."
UNGH!
"WAS IT THE SOUND OF MY VOICE THAT TRIGGERED IT?"
NO! NOT... NOW!
AHHHH... YES.
MUCH BETTER.
SO! IT'S BEEN AWHILE, BROTHER!
HMPH. YOU CERTAINLY LOOK THE WORSE FOR WEAR. A BLOODY MESS, I DARE SAY!

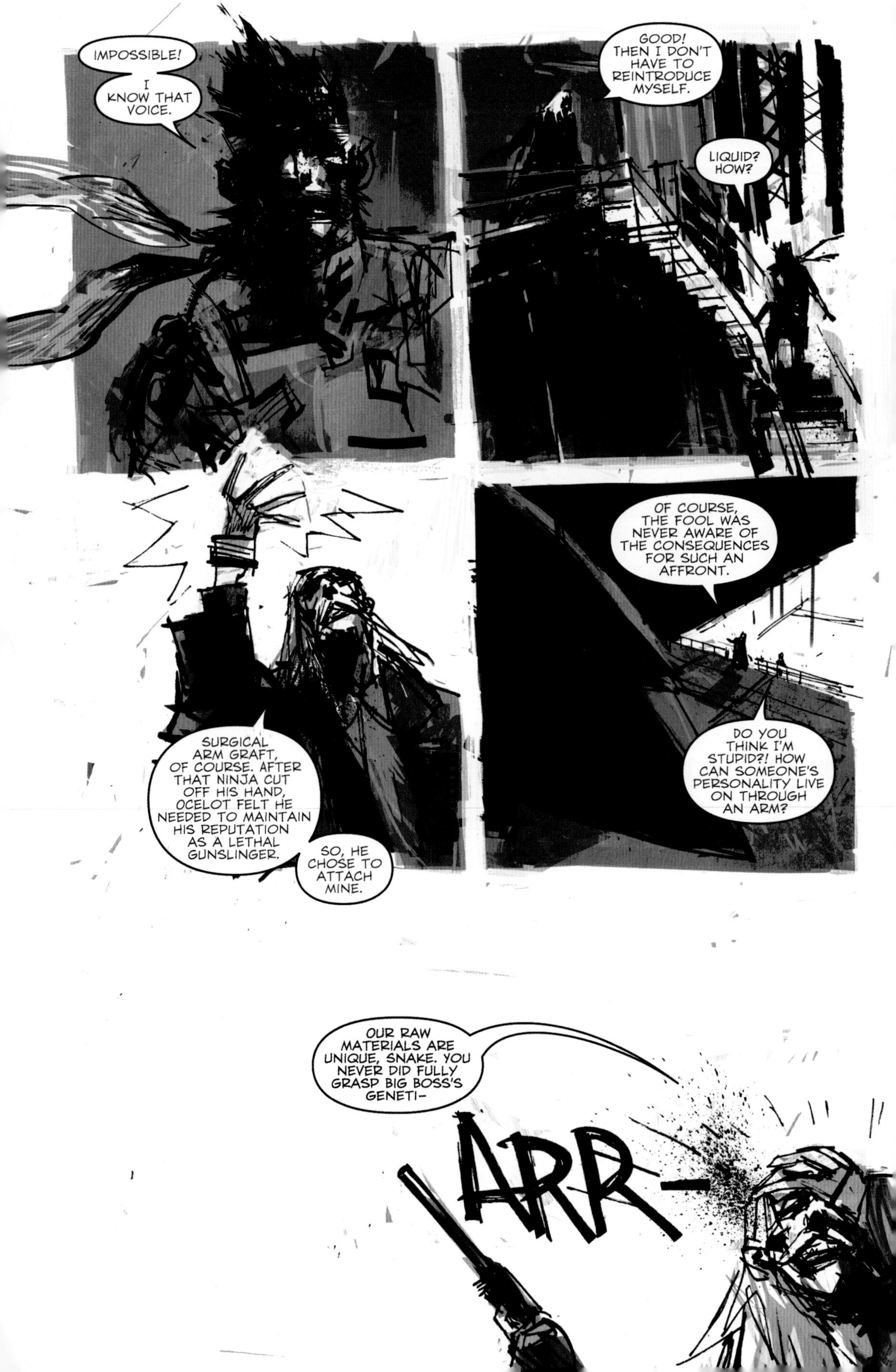
IMPOSSIBLE!
I KNOW THAT VOICE.
GOOD! THEN I DON'T HAVE TO REINTRODUCE MYSELF.
LIQUID? HOW?
SURGICAL ARM GRAFT, OF COURSE. AFTER THAT NINJA CUT OFF HIS HAND, OCELOT FELT HE NEEDED TO MAINTAIN HIS REPUTATION AS A LETHAL GUNSLINGER.
SO, HE CHOSE TO ATTACH MINE.
OF COURSE, THE FOOL WAS NEVER AWARE OF THE CONSEQUENCES FOR SUCH AN AFFRONT.
DO YOU THINK I'M STUPID?! HOW CAN SOMEONE'S PERSONALITY LIVE ON THROUGH AN ARM?
OUR RAW MATERIALS ARE UNIQUE, SNAKE. YOU NEVER DID FULLY GRASP BIG BOSS'S GENETI-
ARR-

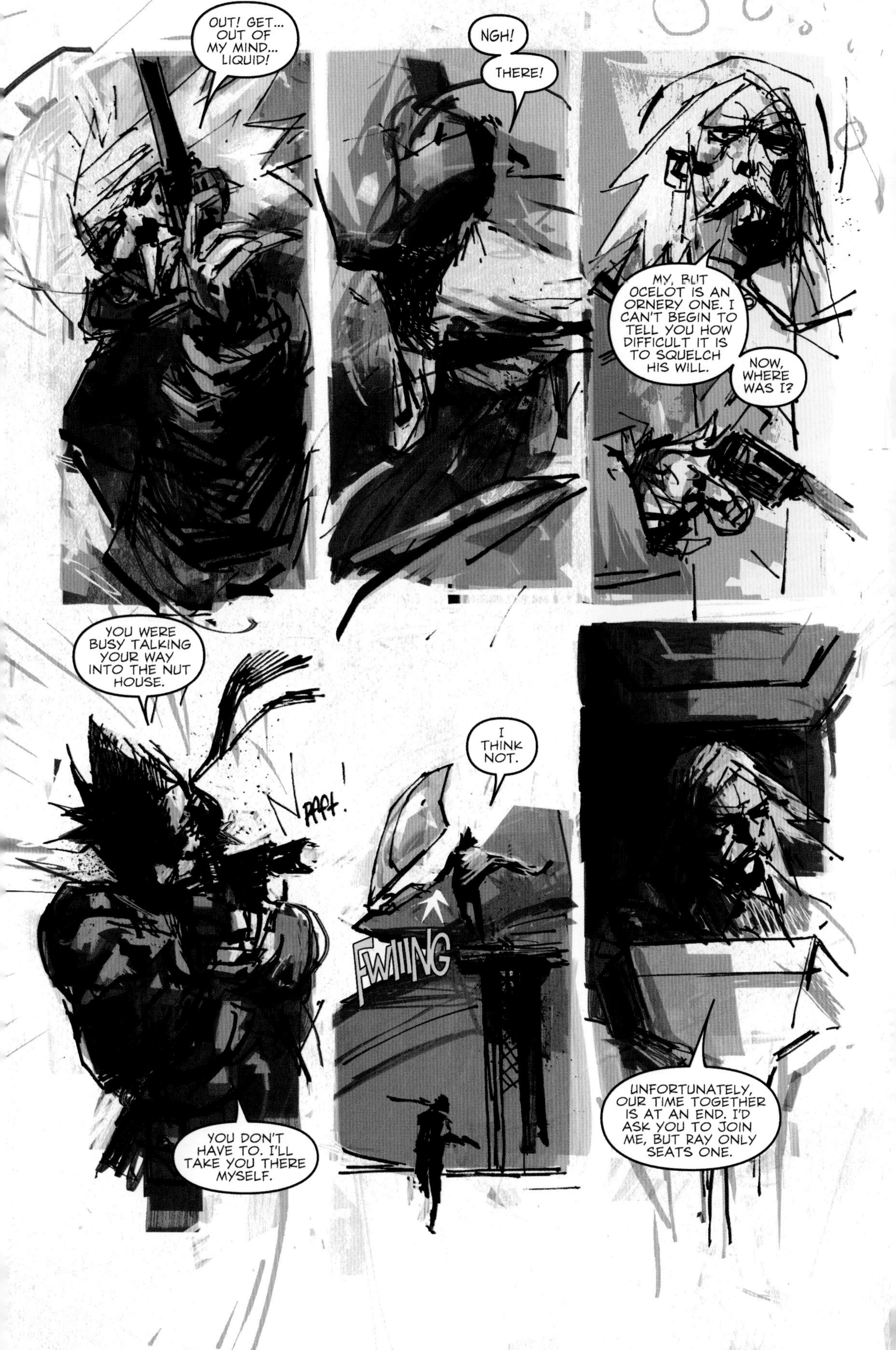
OUT! GET... OUT OF MY MIND... LIQUID!
NGH!
THERE!
MY, BUT OCELOT IS AN ORNERY ONE. I CAN'T BEGIN TO TELL YOU HOW DIFFICULT IT IS TO SQUELCH HIS WILL.
NOW, WHERE WAS I?
YOU WERE BUSY TALKING YOUR WAY INTO THE NUT HOUSE.
YOU DON'T HAVE TO. I'LL TAKE YOU THERE MYSELF.
I THINK NOT.
FWIIING
UNFORTUNATELY, OUR TIME TOGETHER IS AT AN END. I'D ASK YOU TO JOIN ME, BUT RAY ONLY SEATS ONE.

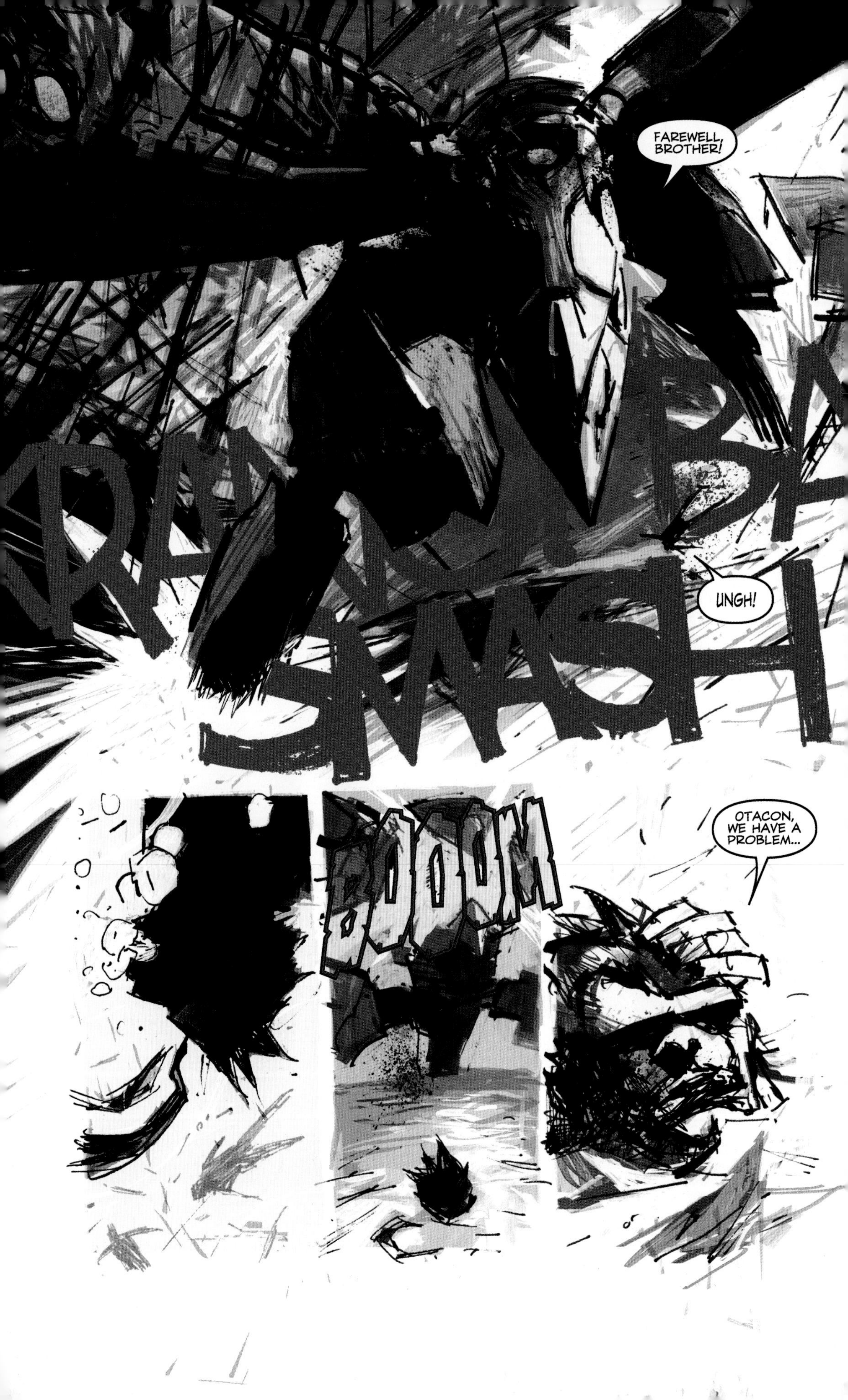
FAREWELL, BROTHER!
SMASH
UNGH!
BOOOM
OTACON, WE HAVE A PROBLEM...

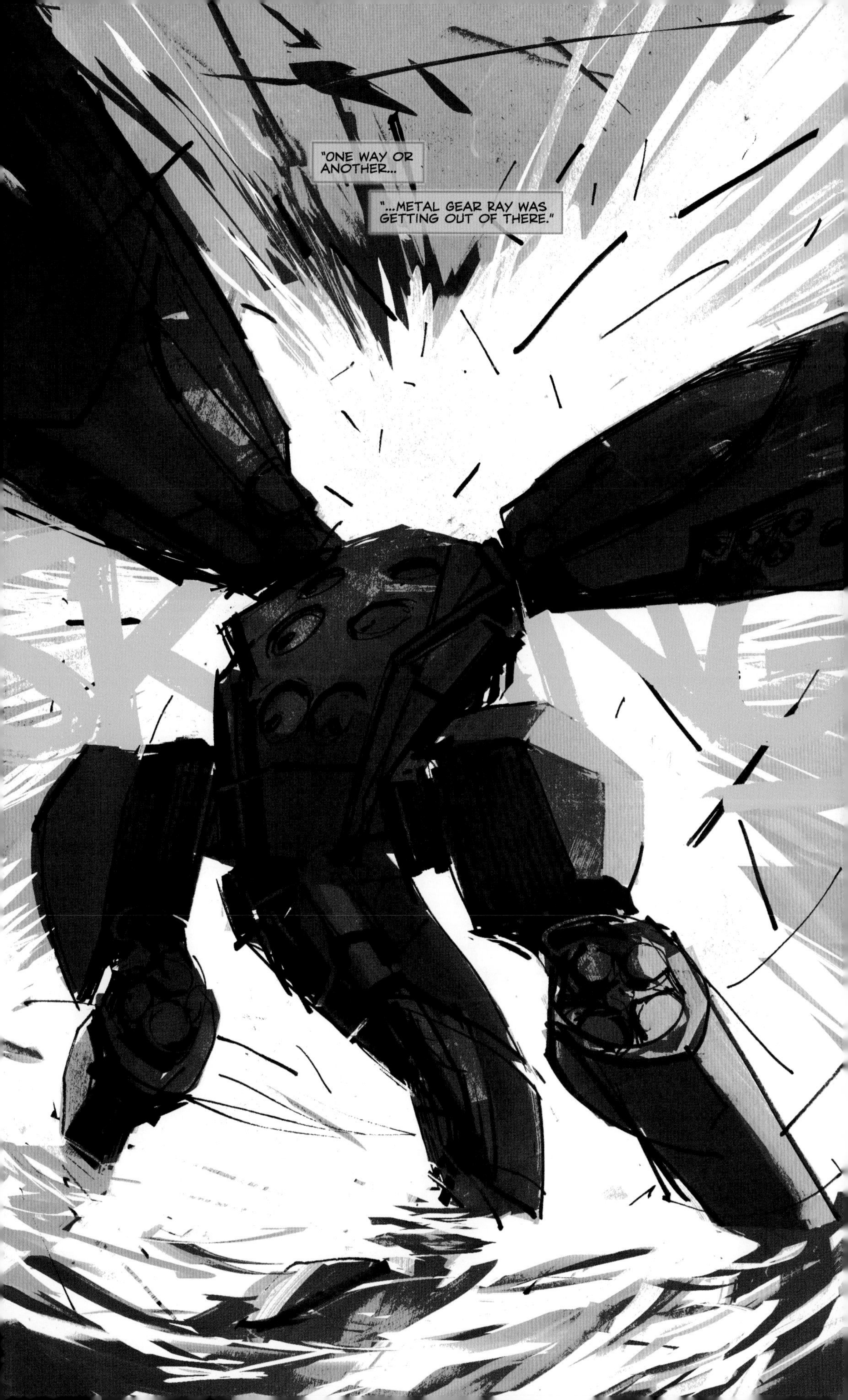
"ONE WAY OR ANOTHER...
"...METAL GEAR RAY WAS GETTING OUT OF THERE."

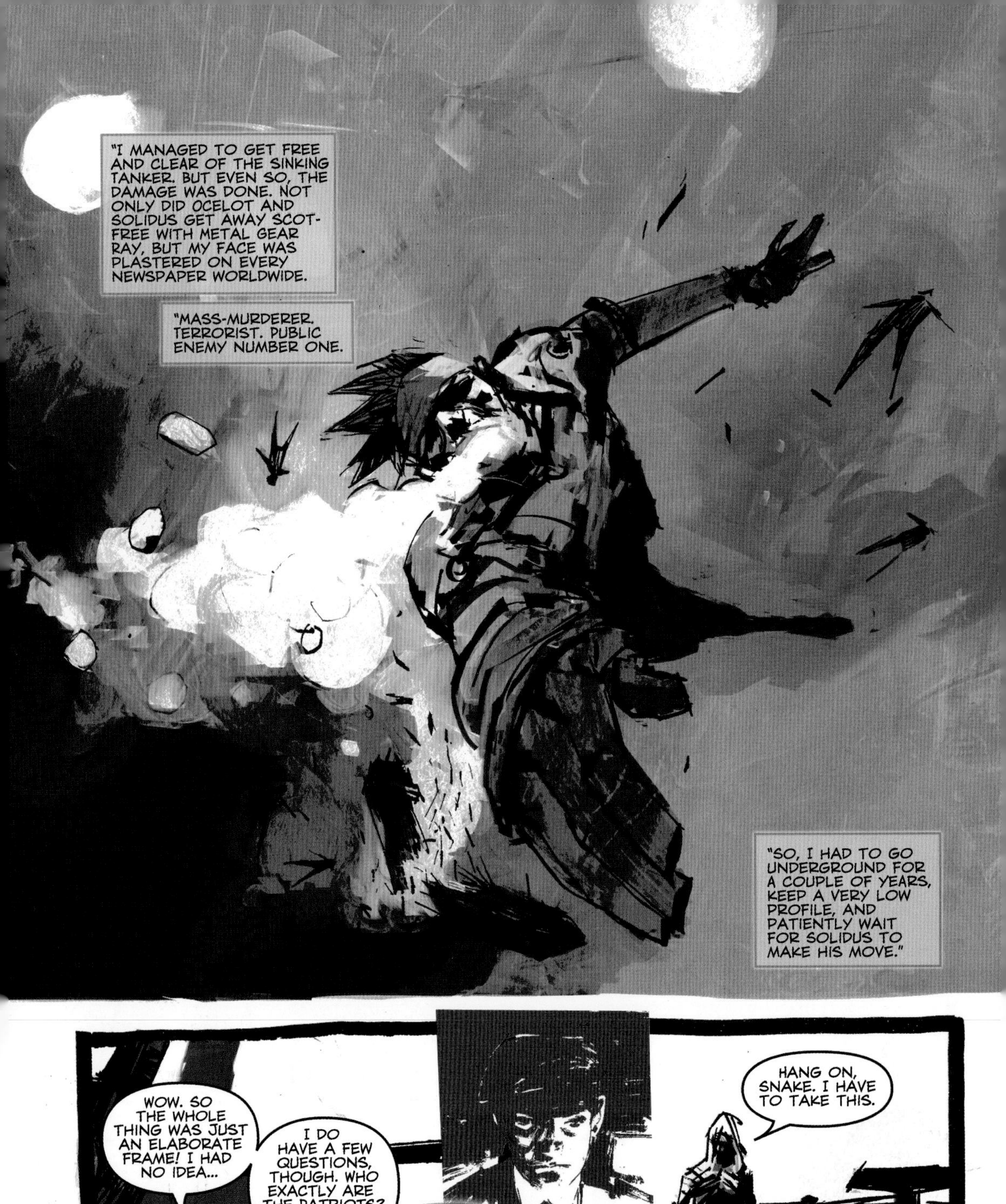
"I MANAGED TO GET FREE AND CLEAR OF THE SINKING TANKER. BUT EVEN SO, THE DAMAGE WAS DONE. NOT ONLY DID OCELOT AND SOLIDUS GET AWAY SCOT-FREE WITH METAL GEAR RAY, BUT MY FACE WAS PLASTERED ON EVERY NEWSPAPER WORLDWIDE.
"MASS-MURDERER. TERRORIST. PUBLIC ENEMY NUMBER ONE.
"SO, I HAD TO GO UNDERGROUND FOR A COUPLE OF YEARS, KEEP A VERY LOW PROFILE, AND PATIENTLY WAIT FOR SOLIDUS TO MAKE HIS MOVE."

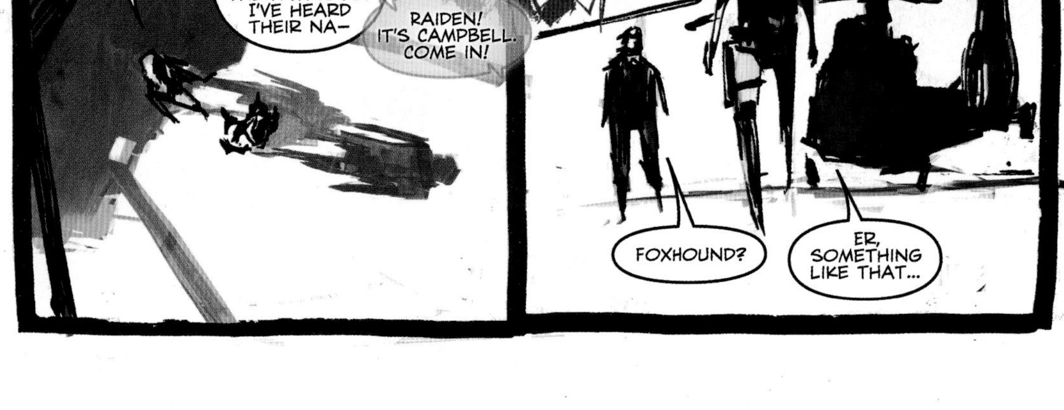
WOW. SO THE WHOLE THING WAS JUST AN ELABORATE FRAME! I HAD NO IDEA...
I DO HAVE A FEW QUESTIONS, THOUGH. WHO EXACTLY ARE THE PATRIOTS? I'VE HEARD THEIR NA–
RAIDEN! IT'S CAMPBELL. COME IN!
HANG ON, SNAKE. I HAVE TO TAKE THIS.
FOXHOUND?
ER, SOMETHING LIKE THAT...

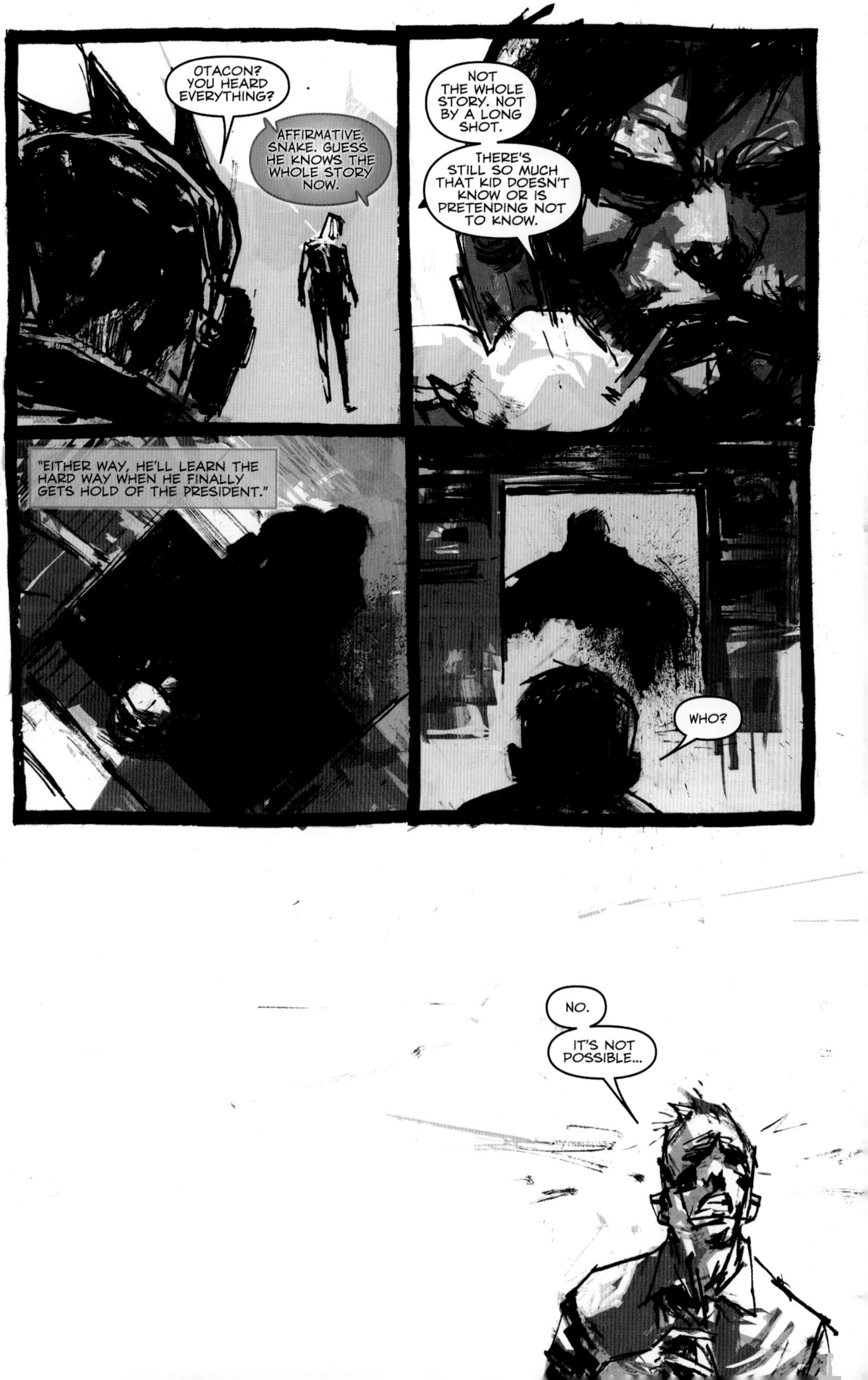
OTACON? YOU HEARD EVERYTHING?
AFFIRMATIVE, SNAKE. GUESS HE KNOWS THE WHOLE STORY NOW.
NOT THE WHOLE STORY. NOT BY A LONG SHOT.
THERE'S STILL SO MUCH THAT KID DOESN'T KNOW OR IS PRETENDING NOT TO KNOW.
"EITHER WAY, HE'LL LEARN THE HARD WAY WHEN HE FINALLY GETS HOLD OF THE PRESIDENT."
WHO?
NO.
IT'S NOT POSSIBLE...

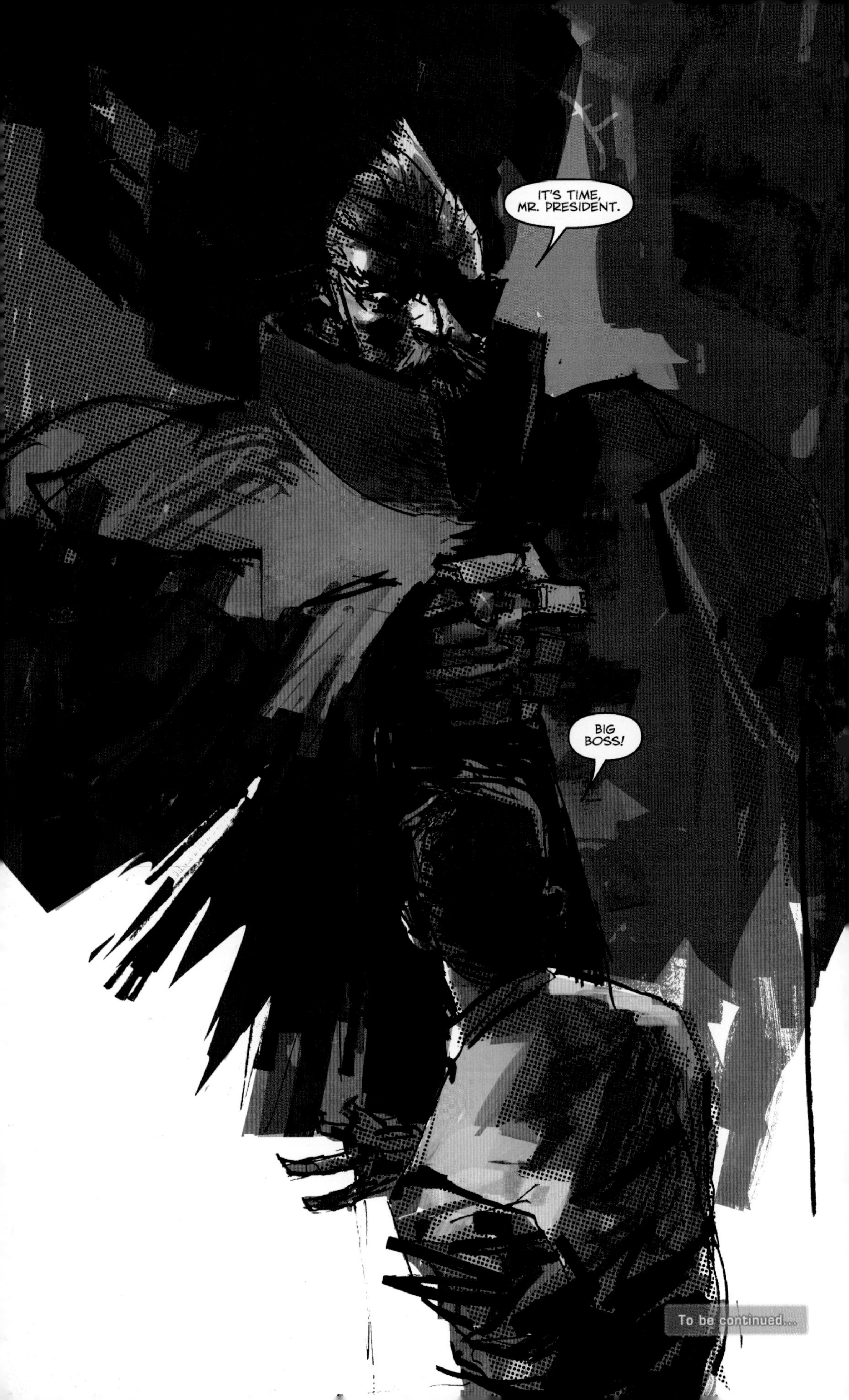
IT'S TIME, MR. PRESIDENT.
BIG BOSS!
To be continued...

>**Metal Gear Solid: Sons of Liberty**
>Cover Gallery : Art by **Ashley Wood**

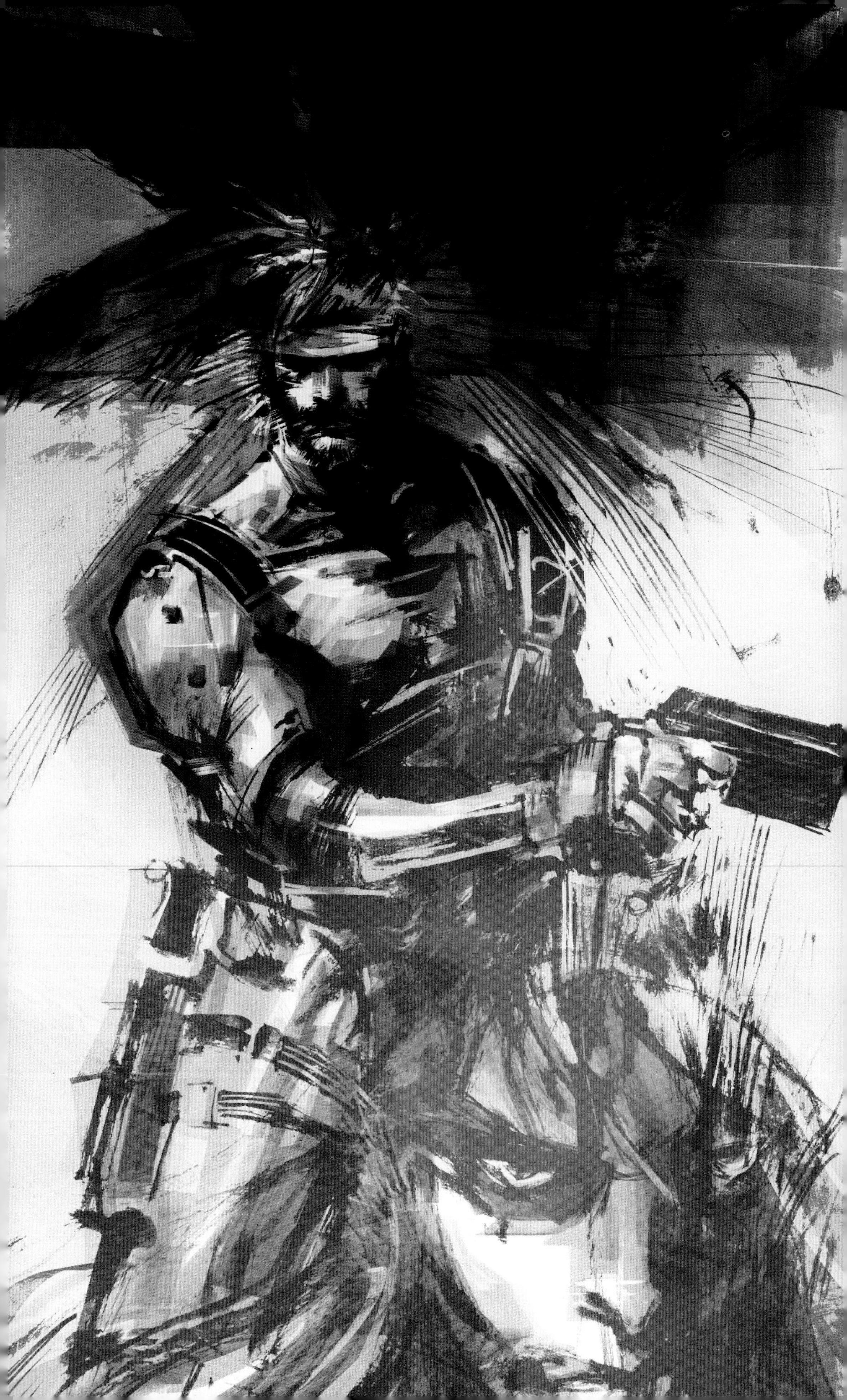

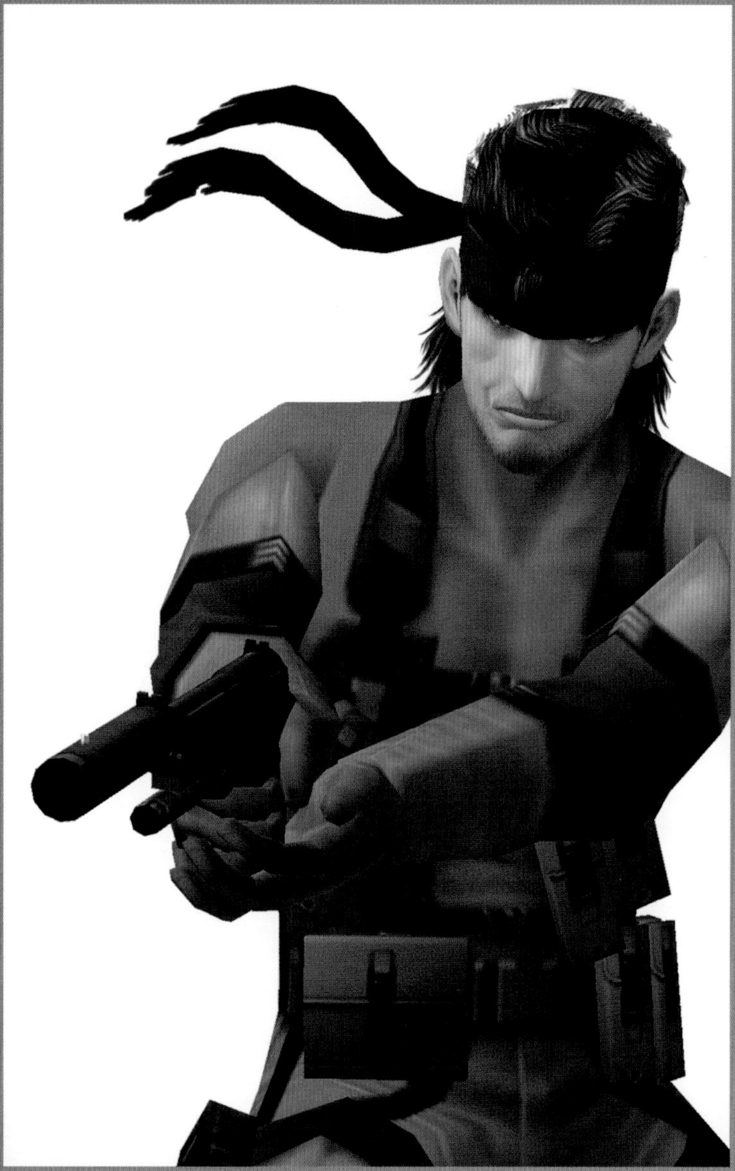

>Previous Page **: Number One Cover A**

>This Page **: Number One Cover :** Retailer Variant CGI Cover : Courtesy of Konami

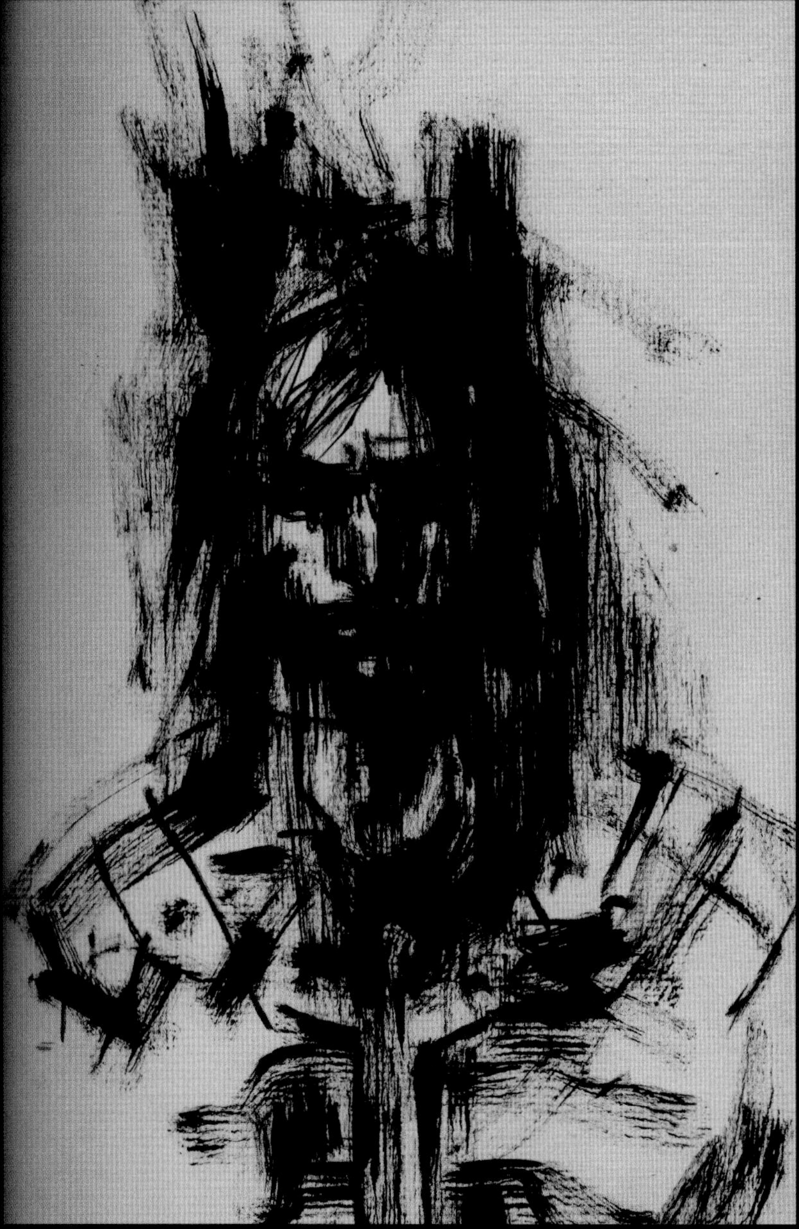

This Page **: Number One Cover :** Retailer Variant Sketch Cover

Opposite Page **: Number One Cover :** Variant Cover B by Alex Garner

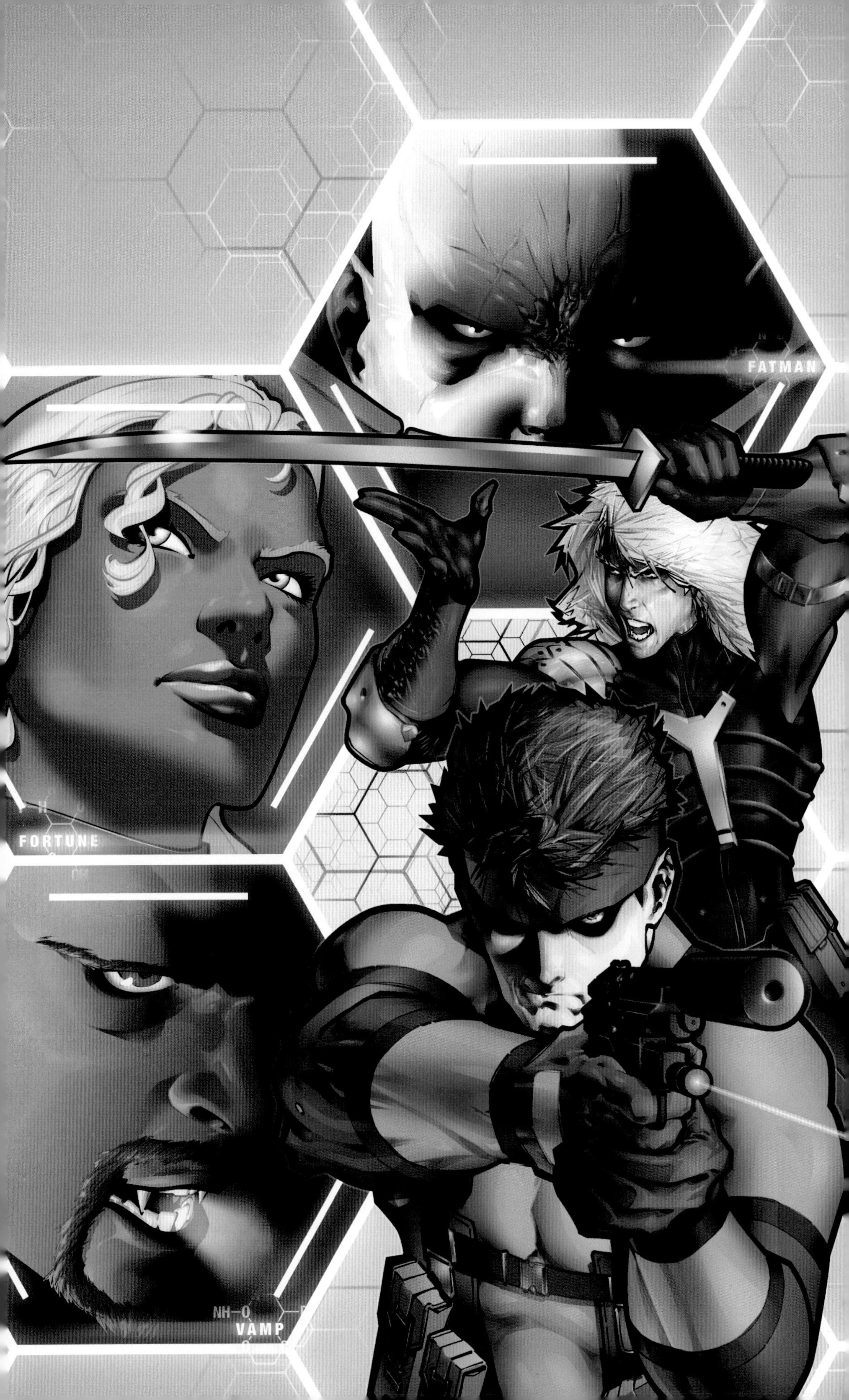
FATMAN
FORTUNE
NH–O
VAMP

>This Page : **Number Two Cover A**

>Next Page : **Number Two Cover B**

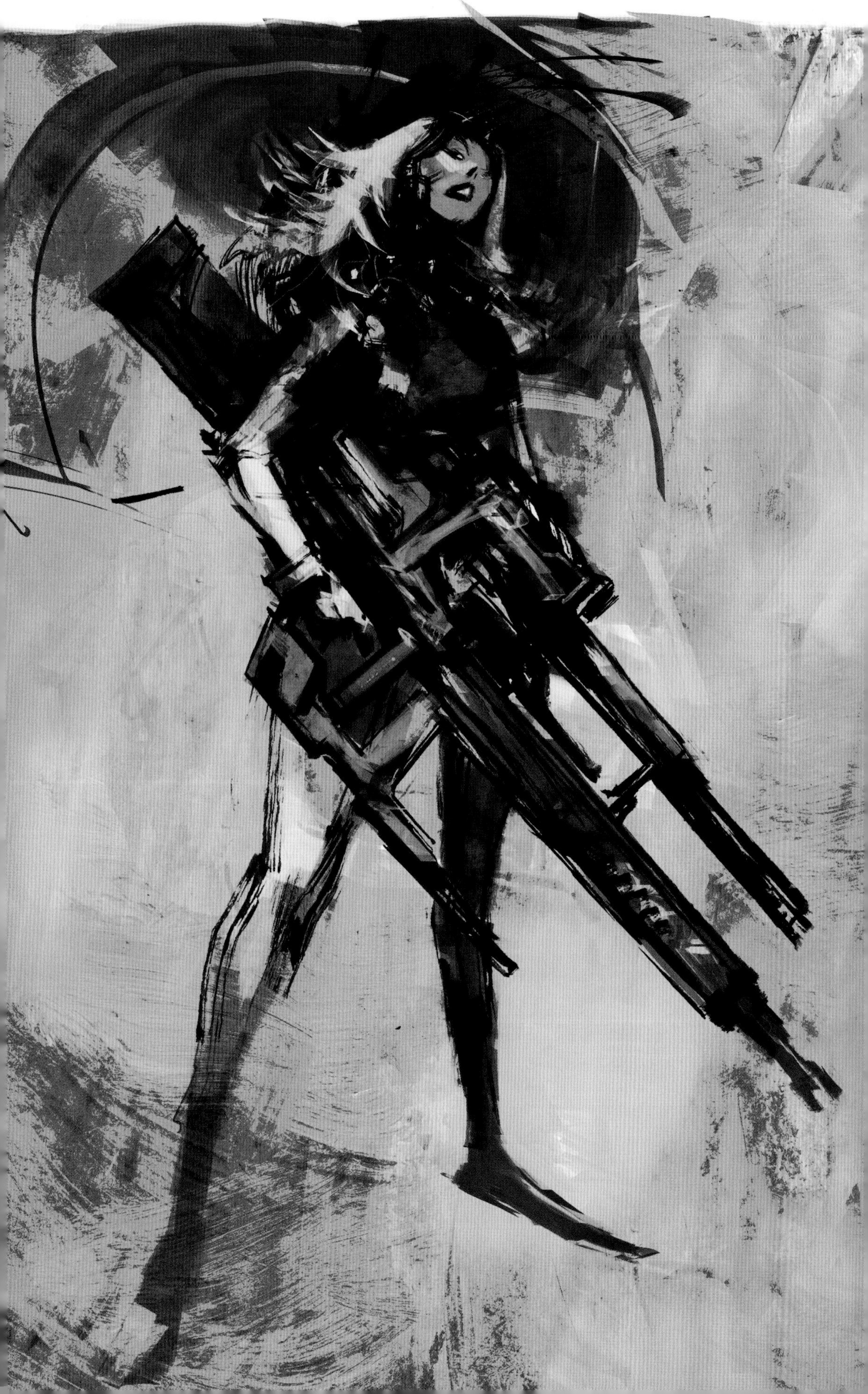

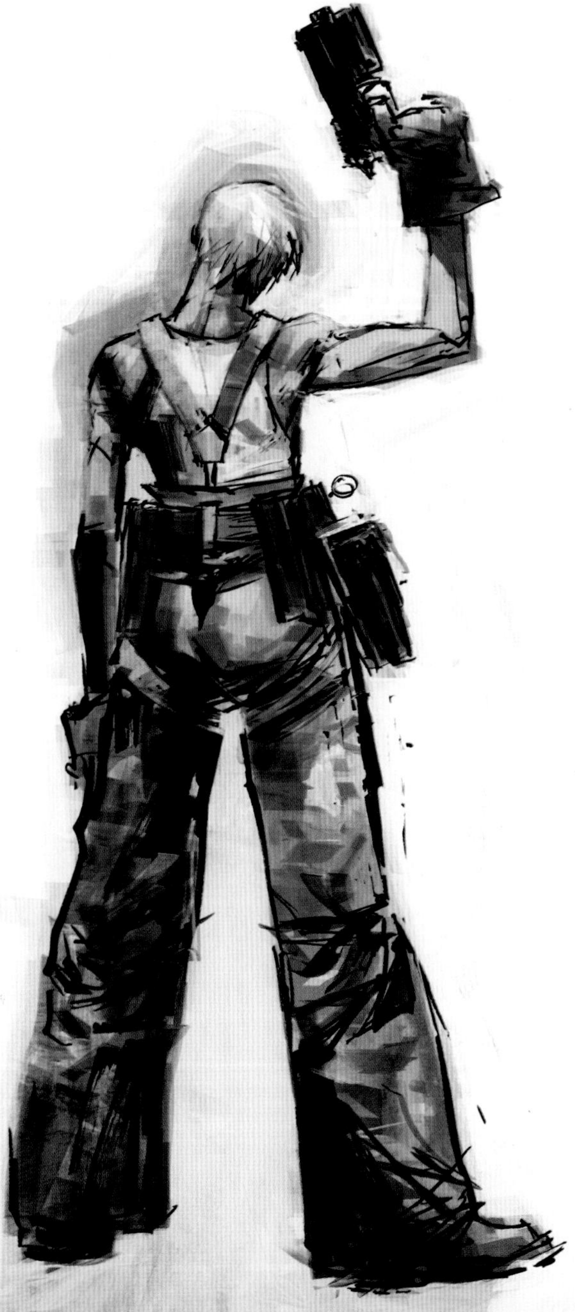

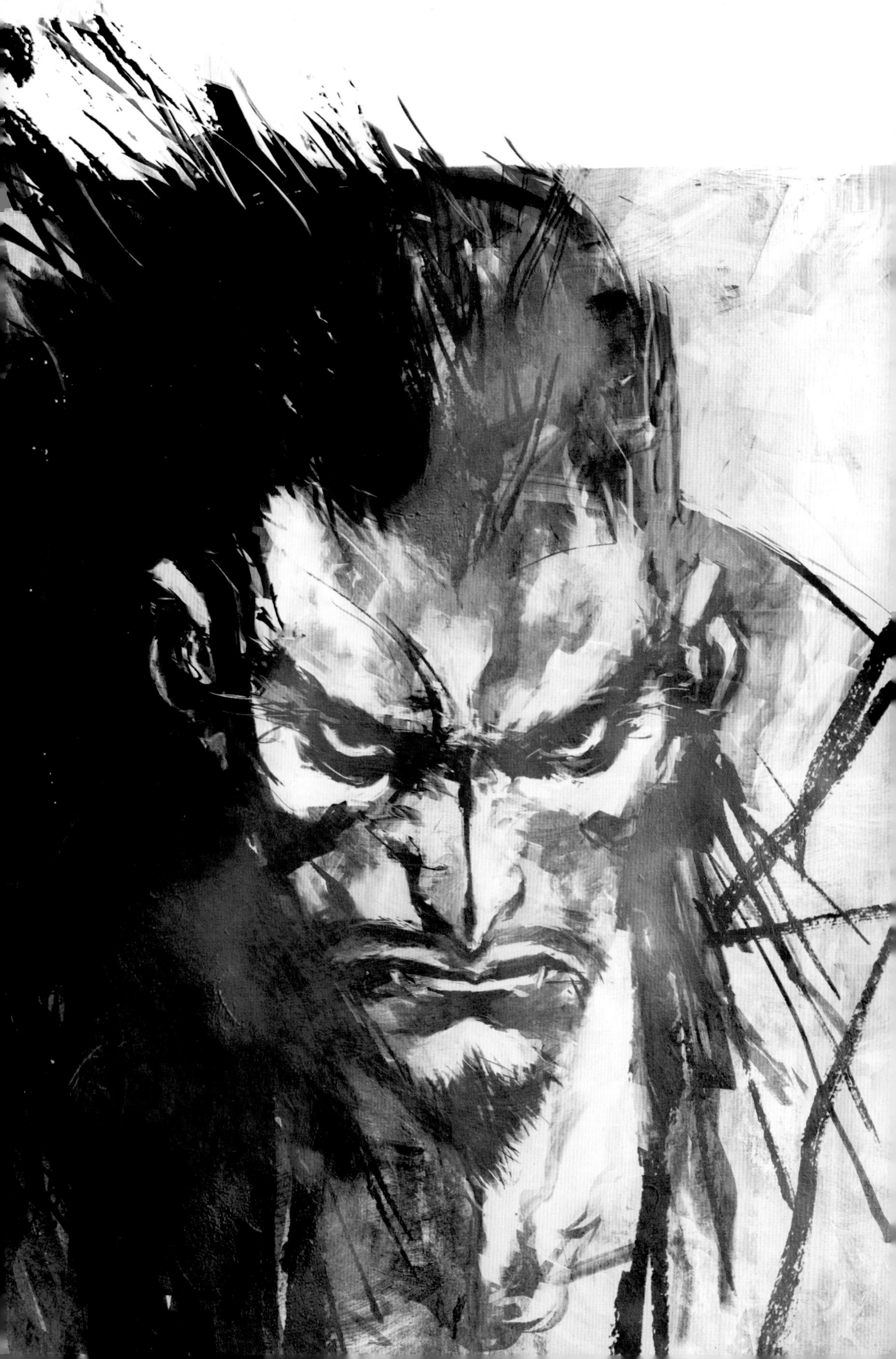

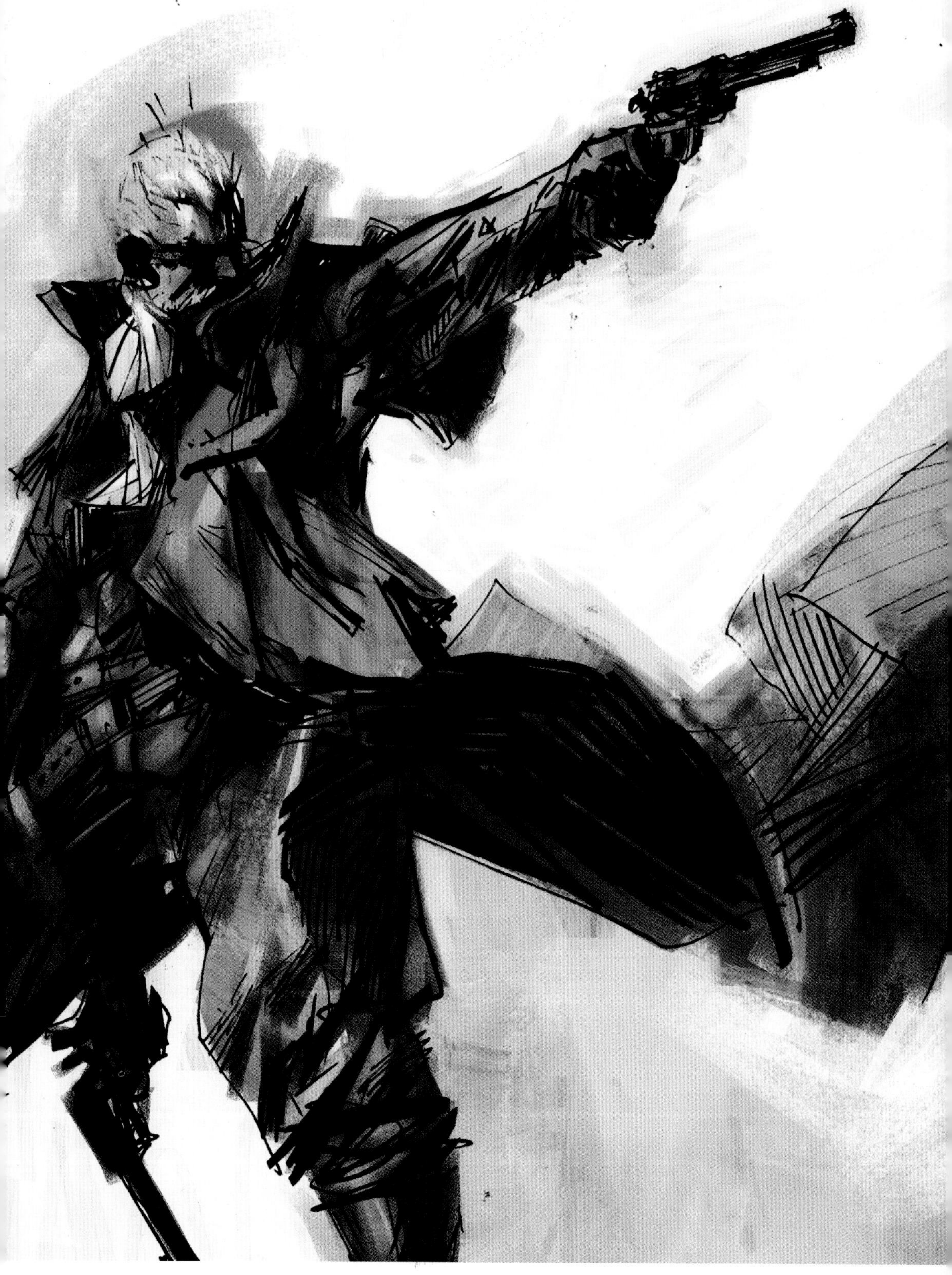

>This Page **: Number Four Cover A**

>Next Page **: Number Four Cover B**

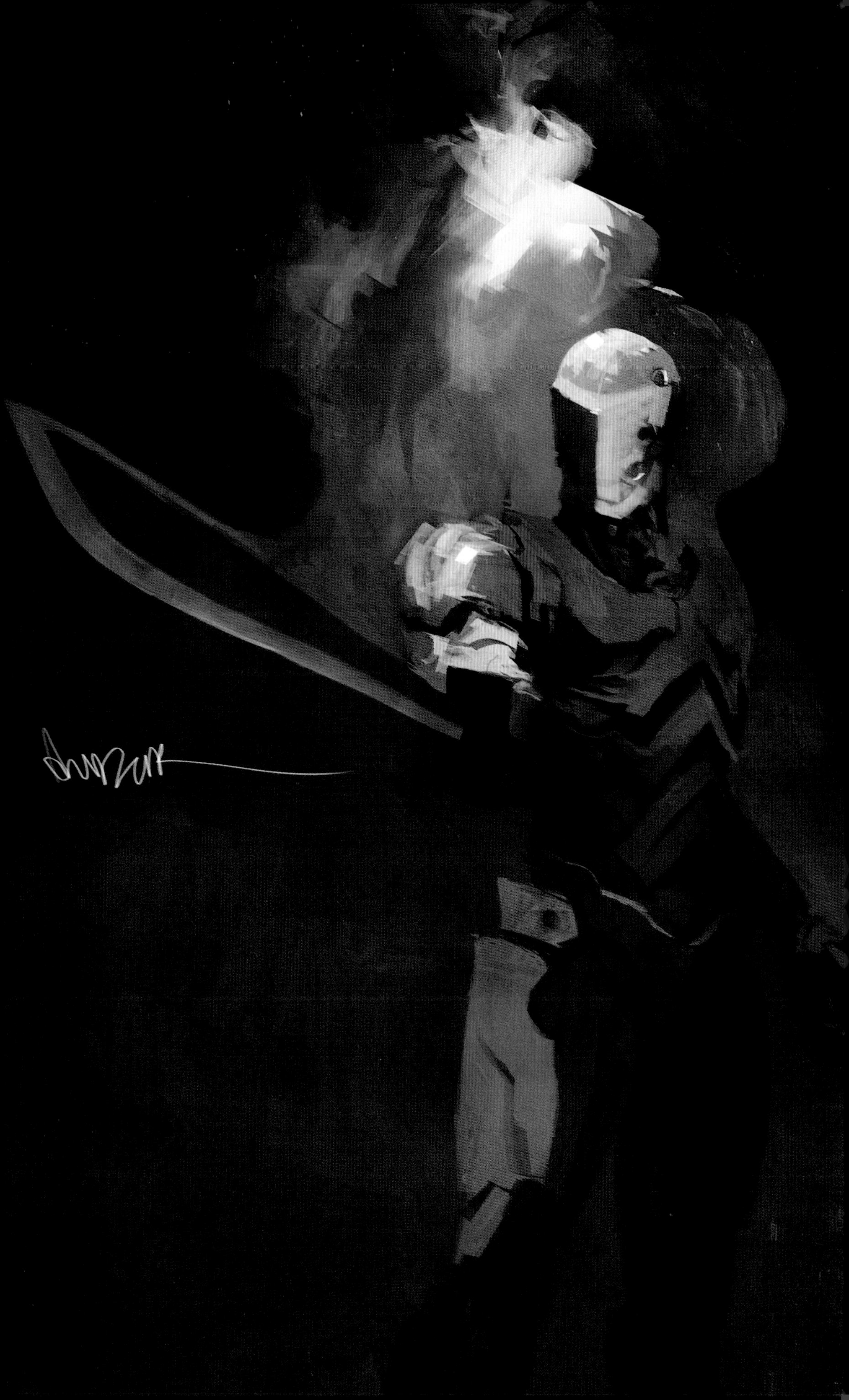

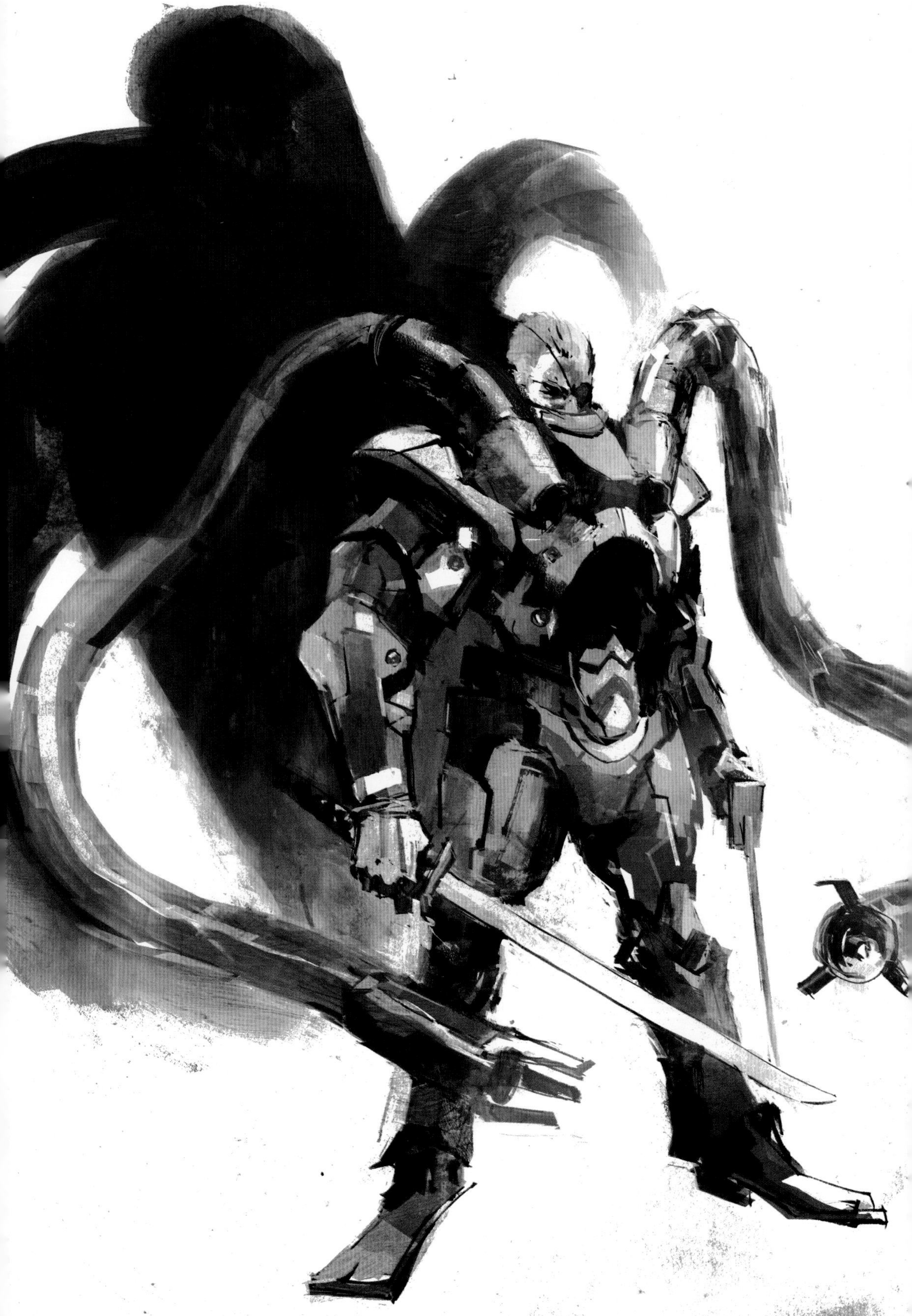

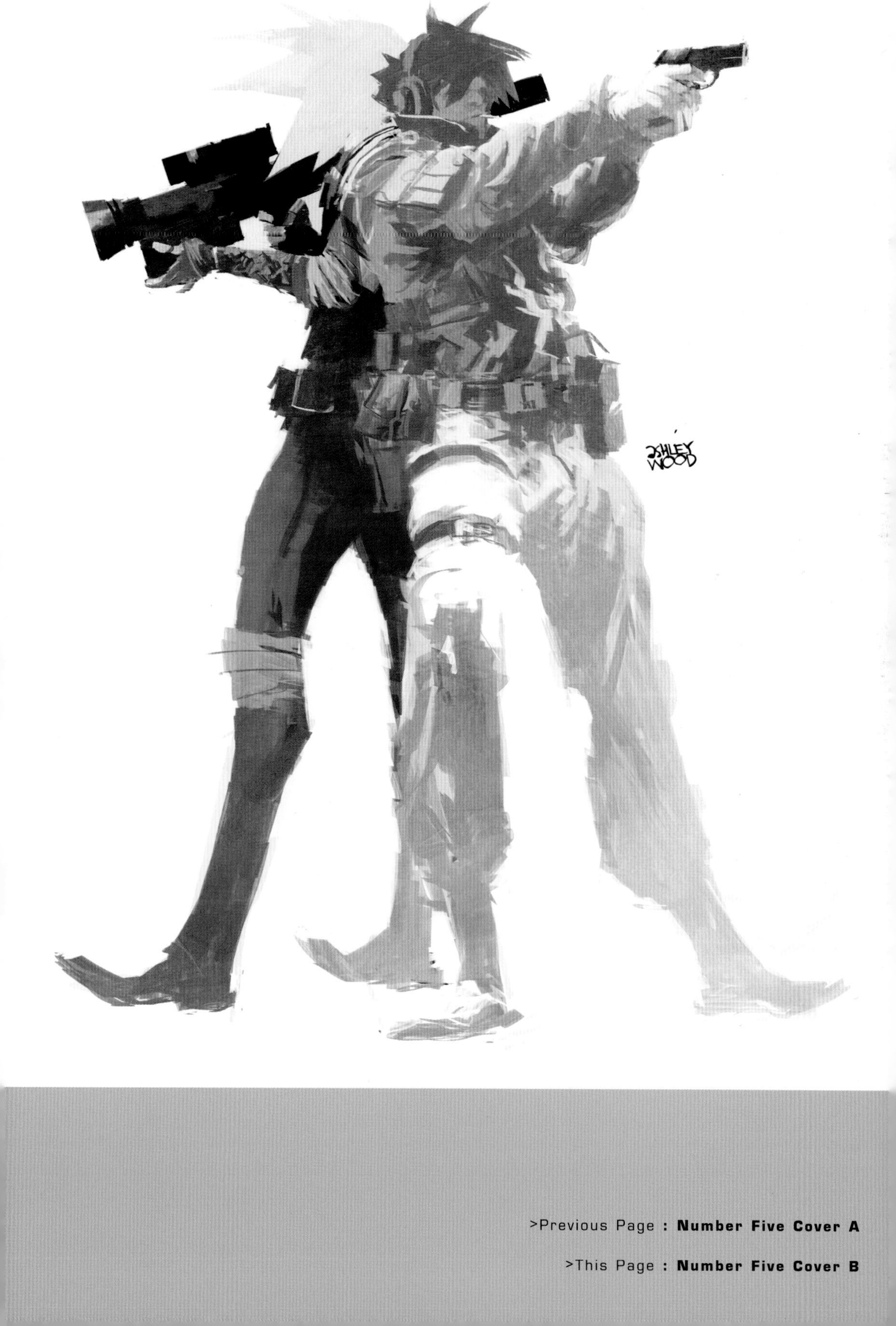
ASHLEY
WOOD

>Previous Page : **Number Five Cover A**

>This Page : **Number Five Cover B**

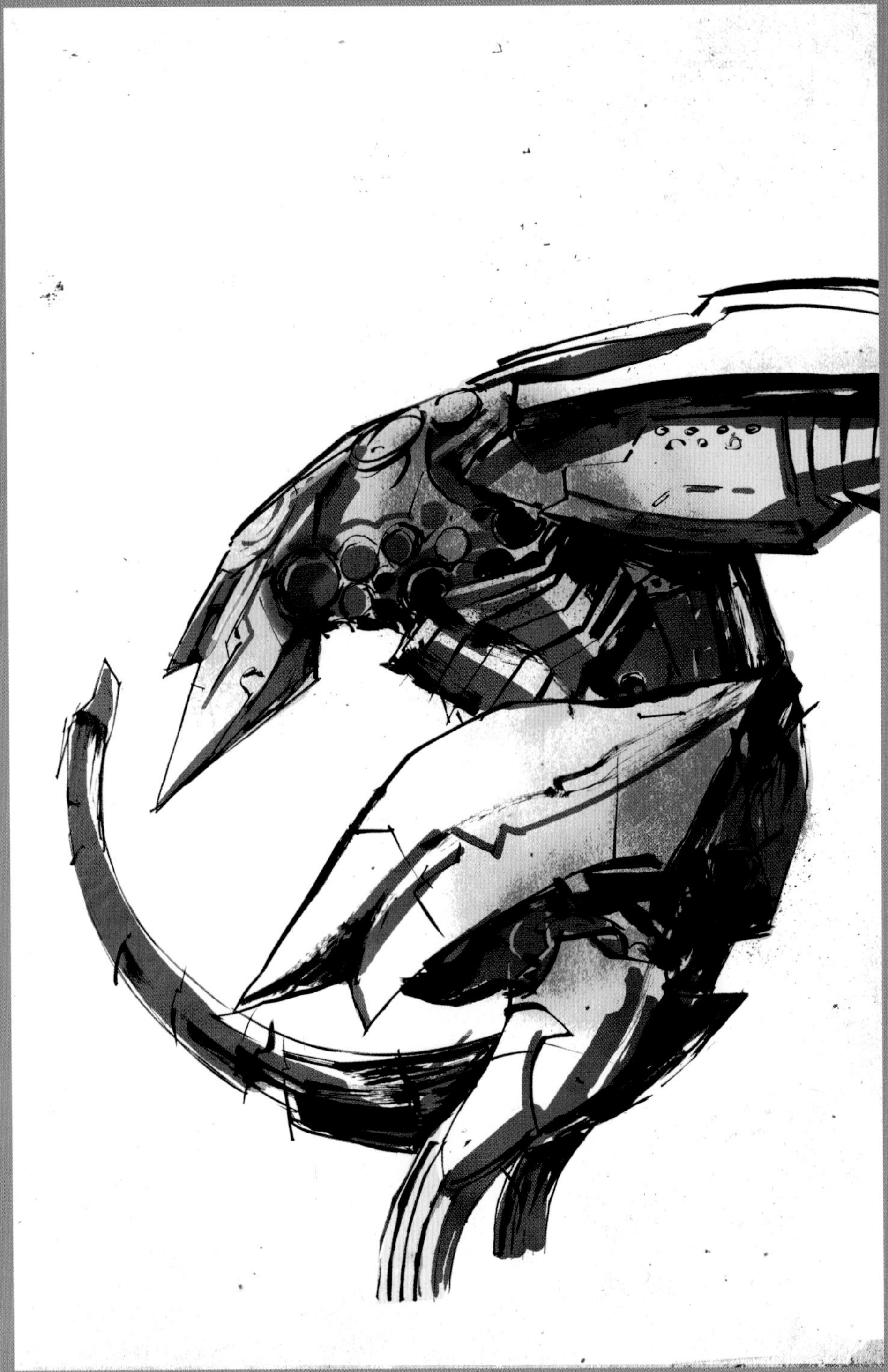

>This Page : **Number Six Cover A**

>Next Page : **Number Six Cover B**

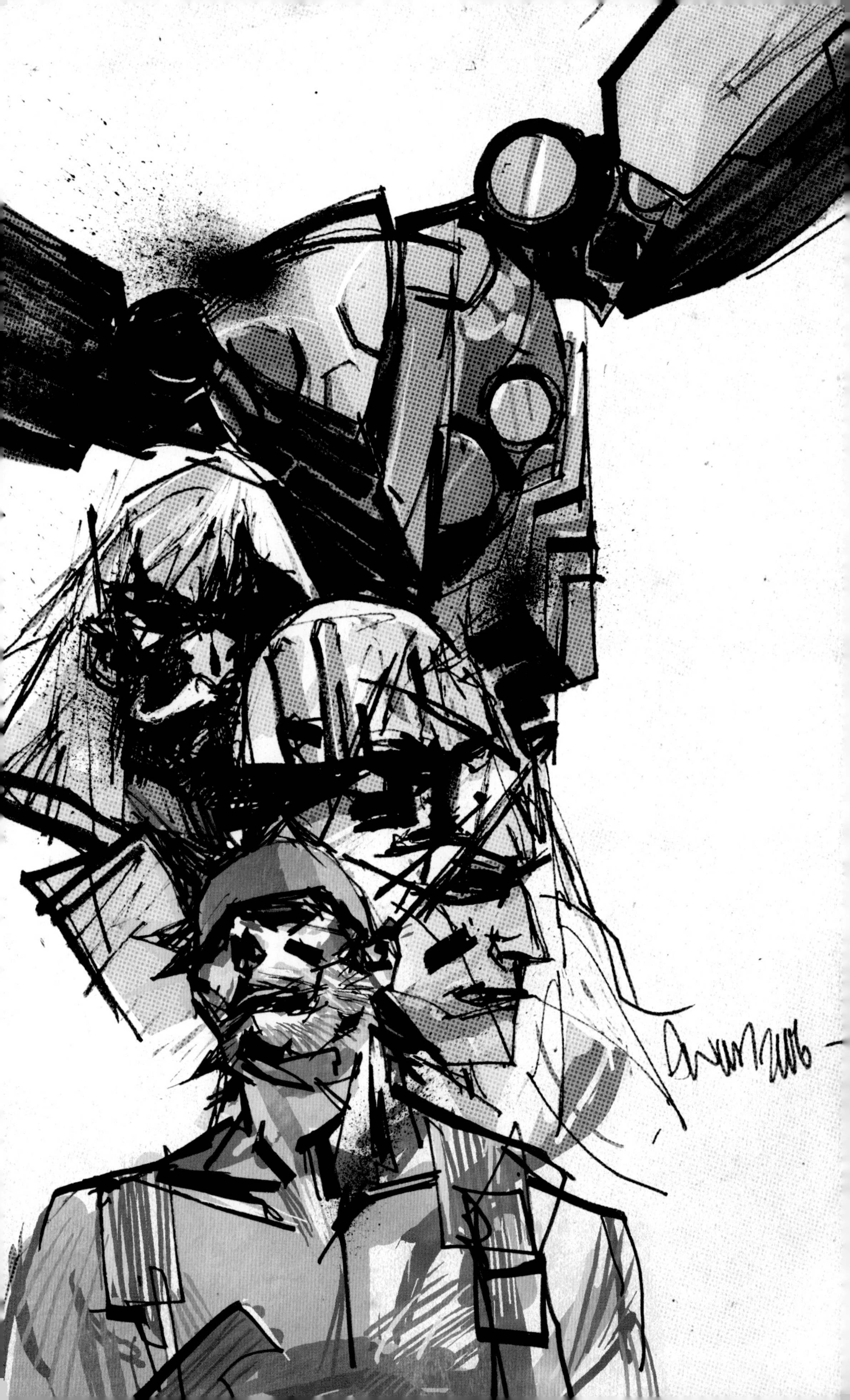

MORE METAL GEAR SOLID GRAPHIC NOVELS:

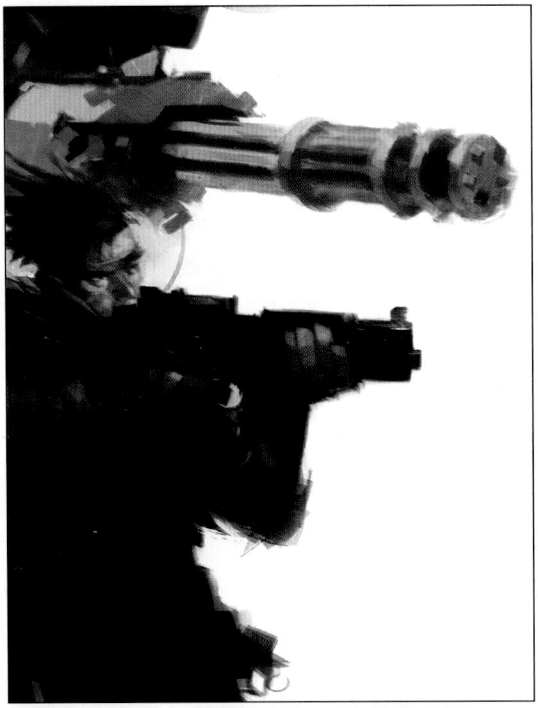

METAL GEAR SOLID VOL. 1

When genetically-enhanced terrorists threaten the United States with nuclear annihilation, Solid Snake, the world's foremost expert in infiltration and espionage, is sent in to preserve the peace. Written by **Kris Oprisko** with brilliant artwork by **Ashley Wood**, this special trade paperback collects issues 1-6 of the comic based on Konami's extremely popular videogame.

TPB • Full color • 152 pages • $19.99
ISBN: 1-932382-81-X

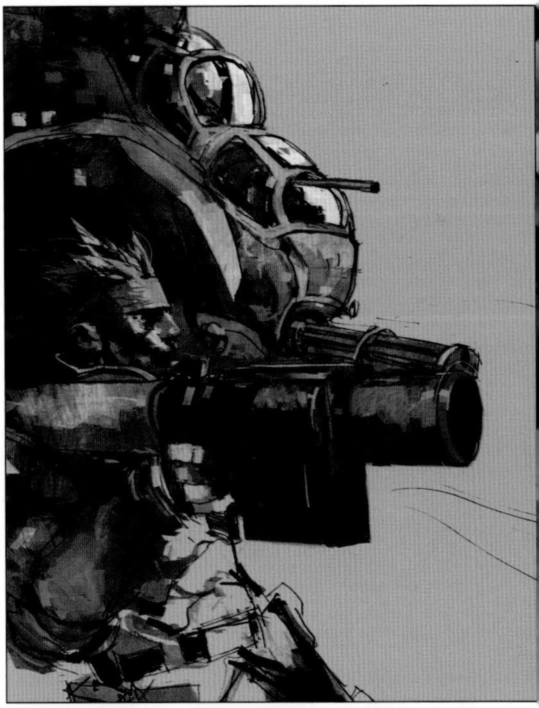

METAL GEAR SOLID VOL. 2

When a genetically-enhanced band of terrorists overrun a secret weapons facility in Alaska, the future of America–and the world–lies in the hands of infiltration expert Solid Snake, who must defeat the terrorists or die trying. Collecting issues 7 through 12 of IDW Publishing's exciting conclusion of the comic's first major story arc. Based on the smash hit Konami videogame and featuring artwork by **Ashley Wood** (*Popbot, Lore*).

TPB • Full color • 144 pages • $19.99
ISBN: 1-933239-30-1

SILENT HILL GRAPHIC NOVELS:

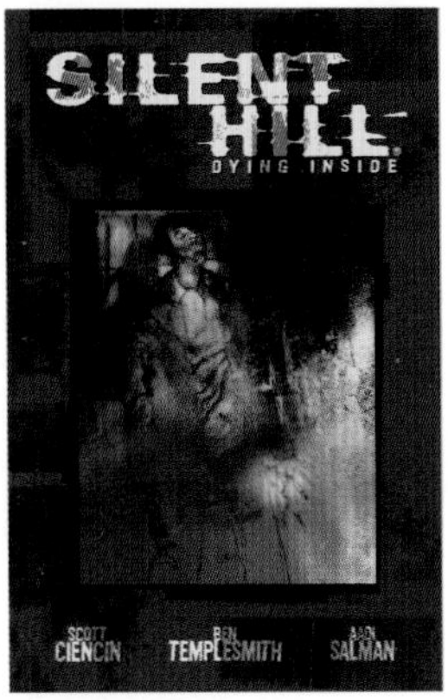
SILENT HILL
DYING INSIDE
SCOTT CIENCIN
BEN TEMPLESMITH
AADI SALMAN

Silent Hill: Dying Inside
Story by Scott Ciencin
Art by Ben Templesmith, Aadi Salman

ISBN: 1-932382-24-0
$19.99 • Full Color • 136 Pages

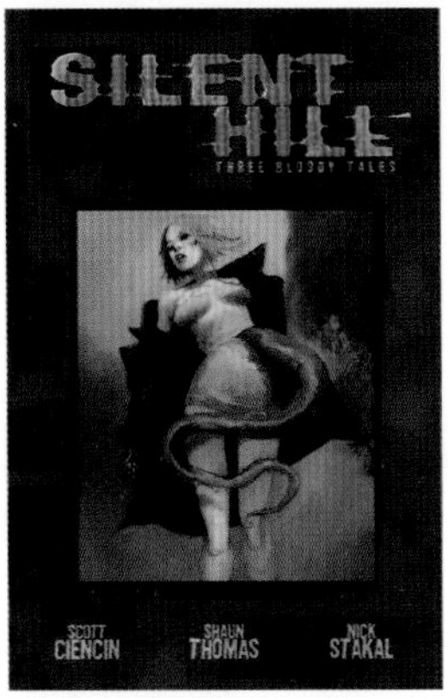
SILENT HILL
SCOTT CIENCIN
SHAUN THOMAS
NICK STAKAL

Silent Hill: 3 Bloody Tales
Story by Scott Ciencin
Art by Nick Stakal, Shaun Thomas

ISBN: 1-933239-16-6
$19.99 • Full Color • 152 Pages

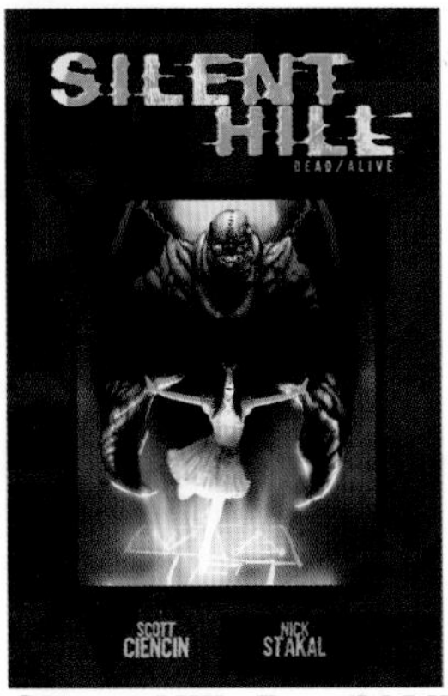
SILENT HILL
DEAD/ALIVE
SCOTT CIENCIN
NICK STAKAL

Silent Hill: Dead/Alive
Story by Scott Ciencin
Art by Nick Stakal

ISBN: 1-933239-94-8
$19.99 • Full Color • 144 Pages

888-COMIC-BOO
comicshoplocator.co

www.idwpublishing.c